D0706457

The **LOCUST** *and the* **BEE**

The LOCUST *and the* BEE

PREDATORS AND CREATORS IN CAPITALISM'S FUTURE

Geoff Mulgan

PRINCETON UNIVERSITY PRESS

PRINCETON AND OXFORD

Copyright © 2013 by Princeton University Press
Published by Princeton University Press, 41 William Street, Princeton, New Jersey 08540
In the United Kingdom: Princeton University Press, 6 Oxford Street, Woodstock, Oxfordshire OX20 1TW

press.princeton.edu

Jacket photographs: Desert locust: (*Schistocerca gregaria*), laboratories in Department of Zoology, University of
Cambridge, UK, 2009. Bee: © irin-k. Courtesy of Shutterstock.

Library of Congress Cataloging-in-Publication Data
Mulgan, Geoff.
The locust and the bee : predators and creators in capitalism's future / Geoff Mulgan.
p. cm.
Includes bibliographical references and index.
ISBN 978-0-691-14696-6 (hardcover : alk. paper) 1. Capitalism—History. 2. Economic history.
3. Economics—Philosophy. I. Title.
HB501.M837 2013
330.12'2—dc23   2012024145

British Library Cataloging-in-Publication Data is available

This book has been composed in Adobe Caslon Pro

Printed on acid-free paper. ∞

Printed in the United States of America

10 9 8 7 6 5 4 3 2 1

Contents

The **LOCUST** *and the* **BEE**

Chapter 1
· · · · · · · · ·
After Capitalism

ONLY A FEW YEARS AGO the question of what might come after capitalism appeared to have been permanently parked, deemed about as sensible as asking what would come after electricity or after science. Capitalism looked unchallenged. Global markets had pulled China and India into their orbit. The medievalist fringes of Islam and the ragged armies that surround global summits jostled to be capitalism's last, enfeebled, challenger. Multinational companies were said to command empires greater than most nation-states, and in some accounts had won the affiliation of the masses through brands, with Coke, Nike, and Google displacing the red flag and the raised fist. Religious institutions were being transformed into highly profitable enterprises, marketing a flood of multimedia products to the faithful. Communist leaders were mutating into investors and entrepreneurs in the booming cities of Shanghai and Shenzen. Nature was being privatized, whether the DNA of rare insects or the rain forests of South America, and mining was advancing from the land to the oceans, and then to space.

That China had doubled its GDP in ten years, a task that took the United States more than forty years to accomplish in the twentieth century, and Britain more than fifty years in the nineteenth, suggested a global economy undergoing dramatic acceleration, and a system so superior to its competitors that all argument was closed.

There remained no shortage of dissatisfied and skeptical opponents. But the serious dissidents and critics were marginalized. Fidel Castro,

embargoed on his island, was growing old, sick, and irrelevant, Aya-
tollahs in Qom in Iran had tried and failed to export their alternative
in the 1980s and were now losing the battle for the hearts and minds
of their young people, who were secretly partying in the suburbs of
Teheran. The counterculture that had challenged capitalism in the late
1960s, offering love, peace, and authenticity, had been largely co-opted
into a business ethic of open shirts and jeans, carefully allied with
ruthless attention to the bottom line. It seemed that the war was over,
and that capitalism had won.

Yet the lesson of capitalism itself is that nothing is permanent:
"all that is solid melts into air," as Karl Marx had put it. Within capitalism there are as many forces dynamically undermining it as there
are forces carrying it forward. Creative destruction is its nature, not
an unfortunate side effect. We cannot easily predict what capitalism
will become. But we cannot sensibly pretend that it will continue
forever.

For most of the 170 years that the term capitalism has been in use,
it has been accompanied by furious debate about what it might evolve
into. Utopians offered elaborate descriptions of what a future society might look like, without money or profit. Theorists showed how
capitalism was just a phase in humanity's evolution—like feudalism,
a necessary staging post but not one you would want to be stuck in.

That debate went largely silent after 1989. If part of the reason
was capitalism's apparent triumph, the other was a failure of theory.
The year 1989 marked a victory for economics over sociology and
for the claims of the market as a vehicle for human progress.[1] Yet
although the intellectual tools of economics are good at explaining
how non-market economies might become capitalist, and even better
at explaining how change happens within markets through the rise
and fall of businesses, sectors, and technologies, they offer little guidance as to how a capitalist market economy itself might evolve into
something different.

My aim in this book is to provide tools for thinking about capitalism as a system in motion, rather than one which, in its fundamentals,
has come to a stop. I began writing it at the high point of market

euphoria in 2007, and continued through the crisis that began the next year and still shows few signs of coming to an end.

My main message is simple. Capitalism at its best rewards creators, makers, and providers: the people and firms that create valuable things for others, like imaginative technologies and good food, cars and healthcare which, at their best, delight and satisfy. Its moral claim is to provide an alternative to the predatory, locust-like tendencies of states and feudal rulers. It rewards the people who work hard and innovate, the human equivalents of industrious bees, and by doing so makes everyone better off, more than any other economic system in human history.

But capitalism also rewards takers and predators, the people and firms who extract value from others without contributing much in return. Predation is part of the everyday life of capitalism, in sectors as mainstream as pharmaceuticals, software, and oil, where people's money, their data, their time, and their attention are routinely taken in fundamentally asymmetrical exchanges. It's commonplace in the behavior of slum landlords and loan sharks, in pornography, and prostitution. Beyond the boundaries of the law, organized-crime syndicates extort hard-earned money and fuel addiction to drugs. Within the law, a large proportion of financial activity exploits asymmetries to capture rather than create value, and over the last twenty years that proportion rose, as capitalism shifted the balance of returns away from production and innovation and toward speculation.

These problems aren't new. The historian George Unwin attributed the failure to turn the dynamic invention and entrepreneurship of sixteenth-and seventeenth-century England into an industrial revolution to "the feverish delusions of speculation and the selfish greed of monopoly" that overshadowed honest enterprise and sucked resources away from new technologies and manufacturing.[2] Adam Smith was acutely aware of capitalism's dual character, and wrote extensively about the temptations to collusion and exploitation that can be found in markets. Two centuries later, some of the sharpest thinking in modern economics has grappled with the complexities of "economic rent" and predatory behavior, and why these seem to be amplified in economies based much more on information and knowledge.³ Political scientists also have shown the ubiquity of predatory behavior, and have shown that the tension between productivity and predation explains much about the uneasy politics that has always surrounded capitalism, and why the liberal dream of markets left to govern themselves turned out to be a chimera.⁴

Yet much writing about the economy, and capitalism, is either ignorant or oblivious of these tensions. The critics of capitalism are blind to its creativity, while its complacent advocates resist any suggestion that the system might sometimes reward predation, or that the creation of value for some might destroy it for others.

All over the world, the dramatically widening asymmetries of power, wealth, and reward that have accompanied the shift to economies based on information and knowledge have left societies richer but also stretched and uncomfortable. Capitalism has never been as creative as it is now. But it has also never been as predatory. The result is a landscape in which politics and economics face radically different challenges to those they faced at the high point of the industrial era, challenges that they find hard to acknowledge, let alone to solve.

No one legislated capitalism. No one planned it. Even the word was invented by its critics and not by its advocates. The capitalism described by Adam Smith has only a tenuous connection to the capitalism of today. Yet capitalism is for all that a common property, part of the world's commons, like literature, science, or the great religions. It is a system with extraordinary power, and we should all be interested in where it is heading. As the English poet Matthew Arnold said of freedom: it is a very good horse to ride, but you have to ride it somewhere.

Modernity has spread many things around the world: the rationality of science; the predictable rule of law; and the messy, but generally robust, forms of democracy. Yet none of these is as controversial or as contested as capitalism, the other system that spread in tandem with them.⁵ Capitalism has run into repeated crises of profitability. But it has also run into periodic crises of meaning. Amidst every capitalist economy there are anti-capitalist movements, activists, and even political parties, in a way that there are no longer anti-democratic movements, activists, and parties. There are hundreds of millions of skeptics and cynics, who look with distaste on the bland reassurances of corporate advertising, dissidents in their heads even if not on the streets. For all its achievements in raising living standards, capitalism has, quite literally, failed to make enough sense, not just for the losers, but often for the winners too. For all its success in satisfying what some Africans call the "lesser hunger," the hunger for things, it has failed to satisfy the "greater hunger," the hunger for meaning.

The many crises of profitability that have punctuated capitalism's short history led to compromises and adaptations, mainly with governments, and the crises of meaning too have led capitalism to compromise with its critics to survive. Again and again capitalism has had to be remade, its energies channeled, tempered, and constrained in new ways, whether by the creation of welfare states and public health systems, or by laws that ban the sale of everything from drugs to body parts, unsafe foods to public offices. Sometimes it has tried to adopt its critics' ideas as its own, for example, presenting the corporation as a religion, or as a place where hierarchies are overturned and bureaucracy is rejected. It has presented itself as a force for equity, for saving the environment, and even for solving the world's social problems. Always the challenge has been to make it work, not just in a narrow economic sense, but also cognitively, as a system that has meaning for the people within it.

There are many possible futures for capitalism. Predation could become more aggressive with new monopolies around energy, natural resources, or intellectual property backed up by state power and helped by the shift of capitalism's center of gravity to the east. Capitalism could deepen, turning anything from genes and tunes to the ocean floor into property. With ubiquitous data and networks every fact, however private, could become a commodity in a world where the real and the virtual merge.

But my interest lies in exploring possibilities that align capitalism more closely with life, that help it to enhance, to enrich, and to enliven, and to overcome its deficiencies of meaning and sense. As I show, capitalism has thrived in part because of the radical ambiguity of its defining ideas that offer immense rewards to predators but also offer the chance for everyone to be a creator, a maker, and a provider. Latent within it, I suggest, are radically different ways of thinking about growth, value, and entrepreneurship, as well as love and friendship.

Through the course of the book I therefore set out some of the tools with which we can think and act to bring these to fruition. Methodologically that involves shifting between different scales—from the micro to the macro and back again. The method mirrors what I take to be the pattern of social and economic change, a constant iteration between the specific and the general, as well as between the bottom and the top of societies, the lived world of individuals, organizations, and the world of aggregates.

Crises speed up this to and fro. Institutions and nations respond to crises at first with urgent attention to the symptoms they see before their eyes: the businesses going bankrupt, the workers losing their jobs, or the homeowners being dispossessed. Some never get around to dealing with the causes, which, as I show, often have their roots in overreach by predators and free riders seeking to capture value that they don't create, whether in the form of rising technology stocks, land prices, or cheap debt. But some make the most of crises to heal themselves, dealing with otherwise ignored ailments. Indeed, one of the definitions of leadership is the ability to use the smallest crisis to the greatest effect, and our hope must be that new accommodations will grow out of the current crisis and address some of its fundamental causes.

Yet with much of the developed world facing the prospect of a long period of low growth and stagnant incomes for much of the population, few if any political parties can offer confident accounts of where prosperity, the good life, and good jobs will come from. This failure risks worsening an already toxic level of political mistrust and opening the way toward lurches to populist authoritarianism, and a search for scapegoats rather than answers. The need for political and economic creativity is as pressing as it has ever been.

No one can predict the precise forms new accommodations will take, whether at a global, national, or local scale. But it is possible to sketch the elements they might draw on, and I hope that any reader will by the end of the book have a sense of other possible worlds that are within reach, and of how much our views of what wealth is, how wealth is created, and how wealth should be used, may be transformed.

Chapter 2 sets the scene by describing the crisis that unfolded in the late 2000s, and how it changed the world's political economy. The crisis had its origins, like many others, on the edges of capitalism, in the household sector and land, and in the most dramatically unbalanced parts of the system, before spreading into every other part, freezing the flow of credit in the banks, and then precipitating a cascade of collapses. In retrospect we can now see that the late 1990s brought an historic shift of surpluses away from production and toward finance, which, like any excess of predation, inevitably harmed the vitality of the system being preyed on. Crises can be either barren or fertile. But the sheer scale of the public subsidies and guarantees needed to avert financial collapse, the contradictory results they achieved, and the gravity of the ensuing fiscal and political crises, make it more likely that attention will in time turn from tackling the symptoms to more fundamental reform.

Chapter 3 describes capitalism's origins, and how it has evolved. Capitalism has been defined in many ways, through its rules and laws, through the power it gives to investors and entrepreneurs, and through the flows of money, information, and goods that it supports. I define it as an idea—the relentless pursuit of exchangeable value—that became a form of life. In this sense it is starkly different from social systems that prioritize the conquest of territory, the saving of souls, or the brotherhood of man. But capitalism is a matter of degree. Societies can choose how capitalist they become, how much they extend the capitalist idea into fields such as health or art. All real capitalisms are impure hybrids, mongrels mixed with other strains.

These compromises arise at the intersection of what I call "lived value"—the value of food, homes, cars, or relationships that we experience, and that has a biological basis in our needs for survival and thriving—and the "represented value" of money, stocks, bonds, and credit cards. Value only becomes meaningful within life—in real places and times. But its representations transcend place and time. Capitalism exploded the world of represented value; its power lay in the abstract, universal nature of represented value, and the application of mathematics to so many fields of activity. But its many vulnerabilities also derive from the gap between lived value and its representations, including its patterns of widespread alienation and its vulnerability to crises (which arise when the connection between lived value and represented value is stretched too far).

Chapter 4 explains in more depth capitalism's dual character, its bees and its locusts. The first face of capitalism is productive, creating better products and services, from smarter looms for textiles to smarter ways of running a shop. This side of capitalism has transformed living conditions through millions of small improvements and thousands of big ones. It is exemplified by the innovations of the factory system, the car, the microprocessor, and the mobile phone. The ability systematically to create new value through production is the most striking feature of capitalism as an economic system, one that has made it a great engine of material wealth. More recently it has made capitalism a brilliant mobilizer of material desires, fantasies, and dreams. This is the capitalism of hope; the promise of turning base metals into gold, muck into brass, the poor into the rich, and mobilizing millions as inventors, entrepreneurs, and improvers. It is the capitalism that offers fair rewards in place of expropriation by oppressive states or feudal lords.

The other face of capitalism is that of a predator, taking value from people or nature and giving little or nothing back. Throughout history, people have stolen crops, cattle, and others' lives through the mechanisms of feudalism, slavery, and empire. Financial predators extracted value from naïve consumers. Mines extracted value from the land. Nor was predation limited to the economy. It is no coincidence that the leading capitalist nations have always also been leading military nations, willing to use force to open up markets. In the past, predation involved very tangible things—food, homes, or lives. But in a world dominated by representations of value, predation happens as much at one remove, without a visible connection between the loss by one person and the gain by another. Moreover, the forms of predation change—and are now as much about minds and hopes as about material things. But the presence of predation in capitalism hasn't changed, and explains its dubious legitimacy. In capitalist systems we see, alongside hope, some of our most primordial fears.

Chapter 5 explores the consistent criticisms that have been made of capitalism over two centuries and that continue to be made. They have damned capitalism as a conspiracy of the powerful; as the mindless enemy of mindful reflection; as the destroyer of true value, whether in nature or culture; as the enemy of community and social bonds; and as against life. This last point shows just how different capitalism is from the market. Where markets are full of life and social interaction, the places where capitalist power is most concentrated can be the opposite of life. Dull and soulless central business districts, automated factory production lines, or the grimly abstract headquarters of global banks embody an aesthetic that runs counter to the vibrant, variegated patterns of living things like forests or coral reefs.

Chapter 6 describes the radical alternatives that can be found in the traditions of utopian thinking that have offered fully formed alternatives to a flawed present, from Thomas More to Ursula LeGuin, William Morris to Ivan Efremov. Utopias are one of the ways societies imagine alternative futures, and many utopians put their ideas into practice too, creating islands of the future. Then as now they were healthy antidotes to the lazy pessimism which claims that all attempts at progress are futile. If utopias are worlds where predators have been eliminated, dystopias are ones where they rule. But utopias both promise too much and deliver too little, their greatest weakness now as in the past being that they lack an account of how change will happen, of how we get from here to there.

Chapter 7 takes up this challenge and provides a theoretical framework for understanding how capitalism might evolve. No one can easily design and then legislate an entirely new kind of economy (though some have tried). Nor can anyone simply assert different principles and hope that they will become real. Fundamental change occurs only when existing systems are seen to have failed, including by their own standards. Often that happens because of dynamics within the system.

Many have analyzed the ways in which capitalism might be its own gravedigger, some disproven by history, others vindicated by it. These include the pressures of productivity (which paradoxically shrinks the most successful sectors), changing patterns of demand (which have tended to shift from quantity to quality, from things to services), and what have been called the "cultural contradictions of capitalism" (the tensions between the need for puritanical hard work in production and the need for hedonistic excess in consumption).

Capitalism's very success creates the conditions for change: forecasters predict a trebling of the size of the world economy and a doubling even in the old economies of Europe and the United States by 2050. Past experience suggests that greater prosperity brings changed perspectives, and an adjusted view of the balance between work and life. I suggest a more comprehensive framework for thinking about changes of this kind, and how interlocking combinations of interests, relationships, and mentalities can both resist change and accelerate it, as new truths pass through the stages described by Schopenhauer: first being ignored, then violently opposed, and finally viewed as self-evident.

Chapter 8 addresses the widespread assumption that capitalism's future can best be understood as made up of more, and better, technology. The scale of scientific and technological activity today is wholly unprecedented, and guarantees a flood of new knowledge and things. Global R&D spending by the middle of this century can plausibly be predicted as five times higher than it is today. A succession of "long wave theories" have tried to make sense of the long cycles of economic change, and now hint at a new kind of economy emerging from low carbon technologies, broadband, genomics, and nanotechnology. But technologies have always been as much shaped by societies as shaping them, and we should expect struggles to shape technology and science—struggles that will often pit big governments and big business against the public. Mature innovation systems, I argue, will need to align better understanding of the most important challenges facing societies; better ways of directing the most creative brainpower to solving them; and more efficient channels for putting the ideas that result into practice. In this chapter I also look in greater depth at the cyclical character of both creativity and predation in the economy and how these cycles interact.

Chapter 9 argues that although most of us think of the economy as made up of stuff—new cars, tins of food, or mortgages—in many of the wealthier economies the dominant sectors will no longer be cars and steel, microchips and financial services, but rather health, education, care, and the loosely defined territory of green industries and jobs: all fields where relationships are critically important. Pre-capitalist economies were mainly concerned with maintenance; with the cycles of farming, craft, and manufacture; caring for children and caring for the home. The vast majority of work done was maintenance—weeding, cleaning, preparing, and cooking. Much of it was repetitive, and much of it was contained within a relationship. Capitalism by contrast introduced linearity into the economy, with the idea of cumulative growth, and an economy based around things that are simply used and then disposed, generalizing what was always true of parts of the luxury economy. I suggest that this may turn out to be an aberration in the long view, and that more of our economy will again become circular, concerned with maintenance and sustaining, albeit greatly enriched by knowledge and information. The household will again become an important site of production as well as consumption. In the material economy we increasingly aspire to homeostasis and equilibrium, just as we do in our physical bodies. But the world of knowledge, like the capacity of our own brains, has the potential for limitless growth. Put these together and it's possible to see how our ideas of growth may change from "more and bigger" to "again and better," which is already how we think about such things as food and sex, friendship and pleasure.

Chapter 10 turns to theory, showing how a cluster of generative ideas could give shape to a world after capitalism, and a world fit more for creators than predators. These I draw less from the utopian traditions, or from Marxism or liberalism, than from capitalism's own ideas, which contain within them the potential for radical transcendence. These include a broader notion of growth that is about quality of life rather than quantity of consumption: I ask the reader to imagine an economy where all growth was qualitative in this sense rather than quantitative, with fewer inputs of energy, materials, and time contributing to ever greater outputs, and often prioritizing reduction rather than expansion (for example of obesity or waste). I also look at the idea of exchange. Capitalism has made it possible to imagine widely dispersed populations engaged in exchange with each other for mutual benefit. In markets these exchanges are governed by money, the decision whether or not to buy and sell. They are systems with a very limited bandwidth, concerned with quantities rather than qualities. But they allow us to imagine more sophisticated systems in which exchange is richer and multidimensional, about qualities as well as quantities, and values as well as value. I call this the ideal of perfect community, of perfect communication and exchange within large complex systems, of which the limited capacity of market exchange is a special case. Seen through this prism we can be more rigorous about the moral limits of capitalist thinking. I also look at ideas of maximization, and how we might think of the maximization of relationships rather than monetary value, and at the potential for extending measurement. Markets have mobilized mathematics in often extraordinary ways; the rest of society can do the same. Other generative ideas include the idea of entrepreneurship that applies as much in politics, religion, society, and the arts, as it does in business.[6]

Chapter 11 applies the theories to practice, describing the threads that may lead to radically different social and economic arrangements in the future. I show how at decisive moments in history whole societies have remade themselves, not through violent revolutions but through rough agreements that allowed capitalism to evolve. New Zealand, Sweden, the United States, South Korea, and Germany are a few of the examples from the past, Iceland may be an important one from the present. Always these accommodations took ideas and organizations that already existed, albeit on the margins, and made them central; and always they had a strongly moral tone. Reformers, radicals, and what we now call social innovators provided the menus from which new deals could be cooked, and they helped capitalism to become more civilized by giving people a voice. Looking ahead I suggest the elements that may be drawn on in future accommodations, redefining the roles of capital, work, production, knowledge, welfare, and play. Each embodies a changed view of what wealth is; of how wealth is created; and of how wealth should be used. The answers may take different forms in different contexts—Marx was right to argue that we "make the circumstances dance by singing to them their own melody." But if history is any guide, there will also be strong tendencies to convergence, and here I set out elements that can be drawn on to shape political programs in the years ahead, amplifying economic creativity and reining in predation.

I end in chapter 12 with reflections on where we go from here. Capitalism has been both a maker and a taker; a mobilizer of creativity and labor and a despoiler; both productive and destructive. It has been a great accelerator of cooperation, inspired by competition; a great accelerator of efficiency, spurred by constant duplication and waste. Perhaps it is not surprising that it leaves behind paradoxical people, with more than enough to live on, but struggling to find enough to live for, and with more than enough means but not enough meaning. These paradoxes, I suggest, can be resolved in a different kind of capitalism that is better oriented to life, creativity, and cooperation, and reconnects its representations of value to the lived value that underpins them.

There are many competing stories of what might happen next. There is a familiar story of capitalism's ever deepening triumph, in which it is spread through every sinew of life, becoming common sense and fending off enemies from communism to Islam. We are told that this triumph is inevitable because capitalism is rooted in nature—people are designed to be acquisitive, selfish, materialist, slaves of their genes. We are told that other systems fail because they clash with nature. This view was epitomized by Margaret Thatcher's comment, "there is no alternative," and variants of this comment have been used again and again to batter dissent and skepticism, a modern version of Walter Benjamin's famous description of the painting, the *Angelus Novus*. In the painting a storm has blown up in paradise, and blows with such force that "the angel cannot close its wings and is driven inexorably into the future to which his back is turned, as a pile of debris before him grows skyward. This storm is what we call progress."[7] The storm appears resistant to reason or argument, and suggests either submission or disaster, leading just as naturally to stories of apocalyptic collapse, perhaps through financial crashes or ecological disasters.

Here I suggest a different story, influenced by what history tells us about other periods when it was assumed that what is, is also what must be. Two centuries ago the world was run by monarchies. There were occasional republics, like the great Italian cities, or the young United States. But the wave of revolution that had begun in Paris in 1789 had run its course, leading many to conclude that mass democracy was an aberration, an experiment that had been tried and failed. Monarchy was rooted in human nature: people were designed to be hierarchical, divided into the weak and the strong, with the strong in charge. Democracy meant mob rule and chaos, and was bound to be loud, crude, and cruel.

As we know, every element of this common sense turned out to be wrong. Monarchies appeared all-powerful but were beginning what would prove to be a slow, then accelerating decline, punctuated by revolutions and parliamentary revolts that would leave them the quaint exception rather than the rule by the second half of the following century. The successors of the all-powerful emperors, tsars, and kaisers became tourist draws, relegated to opening public buildings and filling the pages of gossip magazines, and rudely put in their place if they attempted to influence the governments that often still retained their names and insignia. In 1914, Europe had seventeen monarchies including empires in Germany, Austria Hungary, Russia, Britain, and Turkey. Within five years all but one of the empires had disappeared.

What lessons can we learn from this period? We can imagine something very similar happening to our apparently all-powerful rulers, as capitalism, after its period of triumphalism in the wake of 1989, is slowly marginalized by conscious choice, or to be more precise, by the accumulation of millions of conscious choices. The assumption that it is founded in immutable human nature is tempered, mainly by science, and the burgeoning awareness of the many sides of our

nature—cooperative and selfish, fearful and hopeful, anxious for recognition and resentful of slights. The assumption that capitalism is
an end point in history is tempered by growing appreciation of its
varieties, partly thanks to the rise of other capitalisms in China, India,
Brazil, and other nations around the world.[8] Europe accounted for
40 percent of world GDP in 1900, and 25 percent in 2000, and could
shrink to as little as 10 percent by mid-century.[9] These forecasts may
be exaggerated—just as past straight-line forecasts for the growth of
the USSR and Japan turned out to be misleading. But a more mul-
tipolar economy is probable, and none of the rising powers is likely
to mimic the capitalism of the earlier front-runners, any more than
Japanese capitalism is the same as English capitalism.

Karl Marx thought that capitalism, by concentrating workers in
factories, would create the very public that was destined to overthrow
it. My argument is that capitalism may indeed call into existence the
public that is necessary for it to be transcended, but in a very different
way from that imagined by Marx. The decisive force will be connectedness rather than concentration: ultimately connectedness alters interests and perceptions, and connectedness in one field, such as trade,
spills over into other fields. It spills over into personal relationships,
into cultural awareness and then into moral awareness, as investors and
consumers become interested in the consequences of their choices and
actions. This was, surprisingly perhaps, the prediction made by Adam
Smith and others at the dawn of modern capitalism. They assumed
that the market would bring with it civility and even empathy, and rein
in the scope for predators: growth and reciprocity were expected to be
twins. For them civilization meant both a growth in capacities to act
and a shrinking of opportunities to exploit.

Bernard Mandeville wrote one of the great founding works of modern capitalism called *The Fable of the Bees* in the early eighteenth century, a few decades before Adam Smith. Ever since, the bee has served
as a metaphor of the best side of capitalism. It is quietly productive,
providing benefits to many. It is also intensely cooperative, and blessed,
like the best markets, with a collective intelligence that far outstrips
the sum of its individual intelligences.

The predatory side of capitalism is symbolized by the locust: locusts are parasites and well-designed to harm the innocent. They strip everything away in a mindless frenzy. We fear and dislike them for good reason, and for thousands of years they have stood for a power that can destroy both environments and human life, appearing in both the Bible and the Koran. Rampaging armies and greedy states have been experienced as locusts all too often, and from African warlords to North Korean bureaucrats, locust-like behavior remains common. Capitalism should be an alternative. But too often its own predatory behaviors have let rip. So what can be done to empower the bees and restrain the locusts? That's the question this book tries to answer.

Chapter 2
· · · · · · · · ·
Barren and Pregnant Crises

EVERY CRISIS is different. But all crises share the same messy mix of numbness, and adrenalin, the sudden energizing of a few individuals, while others are left baffled and incapacitated.

The financial crisis that began in 2008 didn't have a neat beginning, middle, and end. Instead it unfolded in a series of seismic shocks. Its first phase was purely financial. In 2009, the IMF estimated that the American banking system faced losses in excess of $3 trillion.[1] Japan fell into depression. China's pulsating economy stumbled, at least momentarily. Greece headed for bankruptcy; tiny Iceland, once a paragon of both good government and economic management, faced debts ten times the size of its GDP; Ireland, for a time seen as the low-tax, deregulating model for developing countries around the world, crashed dramatically. Martin Wolf, a sober enthusiast for global capitalism, described one of the more turbulent moments as "the day the dream of global free market capitalism died." Then, in its later phases, the financial crisis spawned other crises: a fiscal crisis that forced states to sharply cut spending; a social crisis of persistent unemployment and destitution; and a political crisis as leaders, and in some countries whole political classes, lost not just the people's trust but also any remaining shreds of self-belief.

So how should we understand the causes of these overlapping crises, and what might come next? Were they a crisis within the system or a crisis of the system? Were they, as Winston Churchill said of the

17

crisis in 1930, so profound, and so unprecedented, that no maps could provide any guidance, and in any case the compasses were broken? Or were they just a turning of the tide?[2]

The easiest place to start is with the people in charge. Joseph Schumpeter defined capitalism as a system that "entrusts its economic process to the guidance of private businessmen."[3] Their prestige comes from past success. If those businessmen act in error, incompetently, or without moral compass, then the system falters, just as monarchies falter if the monarchs are seen to be foolish and venal rather than wise and just. Jeff Immelt, the chairman and chief executive of General Electric, perhaps the most consistently successful capitalist enterprise of modern times, stated his views without equivocation. The crisis of 2008–9, he said, resulted in part from "the meanness and greed" of business leaders. "The richest people made the most mistakes with the least accountability."[4] Bankers in particular were widely reviled for their greed and their folly, and when they excused themselves by blaming regulators who should have reined them in, this only confirmed their loss of compass. Charles Perrow, who won fame for his careful analyses that showed why airline crashes and accidents like the nuclear disaster at Three Mile Island were caused by systems and not caused by human error, was certain that this crisis wasn't an example of systems going awry, but of irresponsible individuals and "knowing malfeasance." Yet one of the remarkable features of the crisis was that almost no one was punished (the hapless Prime Minister of Iceland, Geir Haarde, was a rare exception): in general, the villains endured a period of public humiliation, but retained their power, their salaries, their bonuses, and their self-respect. No snowflake ever feels responsible for the avalanche.

Another set of explanations focused on imbalances. The crisis was attributed to the distortions of the sub-prime market, or the imbalances between the United States and China. The vast expansion of credit to people with low incomes had seemed like a great democratization of the tools of finance that had once been monopolized by the rich, but it had gone far too far (or to be more precise, some countries had managed to do it in prudent ways, while some had ignored the laws of economic gravity).[5] Others saw the crisis as a by-product of an unduly complex financial system that had created products and risks that no one understood. It was attributed to asymmetries—investors were rewarded when markets went up but not punished when they went down—and to the huge growth in private sector debt. Greater financial liquidity has usually been good for capitalism, putting money to work harder. But now it seemed to have mutated into a fantasy world of numbers chasing numbers without regard to the activity they represented.[6] The value of foreign exchange trading had mushroomed from eleven times the value of global trade in 1980 to seventy-three times by 2009. Interest rate trading derivatives had grown from nothing to $390 trillion. Oil futures trading had grown to ten times the value of physical consumption and production.[7] Yet another view attributed the crisis to pathologies of the real economy. The financial crisis echoed looming crises over water, energy, and food (food consumption has more than doubled since 1990 in China, and the Food and Agriculture Organization expects food demand worldwide to double by 2050, potentially prompting much more vicious competition for resources).[8] The housing booms and busts in many countries (in 2006 a quarter of Ireland's GDP was accounted for by construction) looked like cruel parodies of the physical challenges faced by a world coping with fast-rising population and rapid urbanization (Shanghai at one point in the 2000s claimed to be using 17 percent of the world's cranes, and sustained intensive building activity while the West crashed).

Another view simply reminded us that crisis is endemic, and not a strange aberration. Schumpeter described "stabilized capitalism" as a "contradiction in terms";[9] and at the beginning of the 2000s, the World Bank calculated there had been 112 systemic banking crises in ninety-three countries between the late 1970s and the end of the twentieth century. Almost half led to losses of output of 10 percent or more. Some of the common patterns could be ascribed to the very nature of markets that encourage people to pile in as prices rise and hope that they will be among the few wise enough to bail out in time. The severity of the crises could be ascribed to more connected economies with fewer buffers, in which contagion is likely to spread further and faster. A frictionless world was bound to be a more dangerous one. Computer hackers talk of the "attack surface" of a system as a measure of its vulnerability, and the modern global economy had greatly expanded its attack surface. Various studies have suggested that the number of links and nodes in the world economy has multiplied by as much as a factor of ten, and that crises have become twice as prevalent as in the years before World War I. Indeed, since the early 1970s, countries have had a nearly one in eight chance of suffering a currency crisis, banking crisis, or twin crisis in a given year, nearly double the rate before the 1970s.[10]

But there was also a deeper reason for the vulnerability of the system. Finance had evolved ever further away from the real economy. The justification for capital markets is that they move capital to its most productive uses. Yet this was no longer their main work. Financial markets do little to finance either production or innovation. In the United States, for example, the vast majority of technological innovation is financed either through internal funds or from public sources. Stock markets join in once firms like Facebook or Google are ready for an initial public offering (IPO)—but they play no role in financing the innovation itself. Instead, their activities have become ever more removed from everyday value. The numbers tell of a vast imbalance. The world economy is worth some $75 trillion. But financial trading was an order of magnitude more. Derivatives markets had grown to some $1,200–1,300 trillion.[11] Trades were being made on trades, gambles on gambles. Risks were being securitized but made less, not more, secure.

Capitalism's leading financial interests tend to want to minimize the buffers in the system, like bank or energy reserves, because they come with a cost. Resources tied up in reserves can't be used to make profits. They also tend to want to multiply feedback loops, the flows of data, analysis, and adjustment, partly because each of these comes with fees attached. But the result of the first tendency is to make periodic crises worse, and the result of the second tendency is to make systems over-responsive and jittery. A basic problem amplifying both of these flaws was that the growing distance between the real economy and its representations involved a degradation of knowledge. Markets might be rich in data and information. But with each degree of separation between the people making decisions and the factories, shops, and warehouses affected by their decisions, the decision maker was likely to know less about the true prospects or dangers associated with any financial product, or any piece of data. Firms relied on algorithms; but these used data from relatively benign times and therefore gave spurious scientific confidence where none was justified. They assumed normal distributions of risks when in fact markets are characterized by what the statisticians call "fat tails"—more events at the edges, the extremes, than one would expect.[12] The sheer complexity of the system meant that the people whose money was being invested, such as pensioners, and the institutions they charged with managing their money, such as pension funds, simply lacked the knowledge and rigor to keep their agents—the investment banks and others—under control. So the latter tended to take unnecessary risks; tended to rake off a far higher share of profits than they should have; and tended to have an interest in making the system more opaque.

The practical distance between the real economy and its representations was matched by a moral distance. As the gap between the investor and the real economy widened, any sense of responsibility for the effects of decisions diminished even further. So the system became not only practically blind, in the sense that its decision makers were unable to see the factors that should have been critical to making good decisions, but also morally blind. However clever the people, the system they were part of drifted into stupidity (an inversion of what is so often found in nature, where stupid creatures like ants and bees live in clever systems that are able to find food, adapt, and evolve). As one Merrill Lynch trader put it, describing the cumulative errors made around mortgages, "we fell for our own scam."[13] Even if the individuals had moral values, they were required to leave their morals at the door each morning when they arrived at work. This distance became even more marked among the very rich, who literally detached themselves from the economies that made them rich: according to one authoritative report by Merrill Lynch and Gemini Consulting, a third of the wealth of the world's richest individuals—some $6 trillion—was held offshore by the 2000s.[14]

How crises are interpreted shapes whether they play any useful role. Seen in the long view crises can either be barren or fertile. When the barren ones come, the most that can be hoped for is a return to what was there before. But with the fertile crises, once the first shock is over, people look at what lies beneath, and reject the option of return. This sometimes happens in wartime, when weary soldiers demand that new rights be there for them when they return home. And it sometimes happens with economic crises. As the great depression of the 1930s rumbled on, with false dawn after false dawn, and repeated doses of the wrong medicine, or cures that were worse than the disease, a groundswell of opinion called for a very different way of organizing things which led in time to the radical settlements of the 1940s, so that societies should never again have to live with mass unemployment. With barren crises, imagination doesn't reach beyond addressing the immediate causes of the crisis. With fertile ones, people dig deeper, and try to cure the underlying malaise of their society. In chapter 11 I describe some of the most fertile crises of the past and the new societal accommodations they led to, from the New Deal in the United States, to the creation of welfare states in New Zealand and Sweden. Past crises also prompted creative intellectual responses, such as the rise of ideas of modern management in the Long Depression of the late nineteenth century,[15] and the rise of human resources and marketing theories, and the political ideas of Christian and social democracy during the Great Depression.

It is too soon to say whether the crises of the late 2000s and 2010s will turn out to be barren or fertile. They certainly were a dramatic shock to the people most immersed in the system. While many noticed the widening imbalances, and the unsustainable debts, others were oblivious. Ben Bernanke, chair of the Federal Reserve, lectured regularly in the middle of the 2000s under the slogan "The Great Moderation": better monetary and fiscal policy had allowed economies to achieve the magical combination of stability, low inflation, and growth. Mervyn King, governor of the Bank of England, agreed:

thanks to innovation, risks were "no longer so concentrated in a small number of regulated institutions but are spread across the financial systems . . . a positive development."[16] Cycles of boom and bust were a thing of the past.

It's not hard to understand why they talked up hope. Capitalism depends on hope: hope in growth, hope in future profit, hope that every indicator will always in the long run go upward, and hope in the possibility of rational control. It is hope that persuades people to put their hard-earned money at risk. Modernity is optimistic by design and not just by chance; its very premise is the possibility of continuous improvement in science, in the economy, and in standards of living. But hope periodically overreaches, and the physical legacies of that hope could be seen in the thousands of empty offices in Dubai (half stood empty in 2012) and across Ireland (where 300,000 new homes stood empty in the same year), all financed in the hope that the sheer act of building would conjure up customers. It is hope that also fuels demand. At one point, U.S. financial services companies promoted home ownership as the foundation for ever more borrowing with the slogan: "let your home take you on vacation." In moderation, optimism is good for your health and good for success in life; in excess, it leads to ruin. So too does hope unleavened by experience. One of the odd features of modern economies is that their very success in achieving stability sows the seeds of instability as people come to systematically underestimate dangers and overestimate opportunities for profit.[17]

The result was a crisis that didn't fit the prevailing mental models. The head of the European Central Bank, Jean-Claude Trichet, said that "when the crisis came . . . we felt abandoned by conventional tools," and the investor and philanthropist George Soros funded an ambitious program to create nothing less than a new kind of economics. But in the short run, governments had no option but to act, however uncertain they were that their actions would work, and they did, indeed, act, bailing out banks, guaranteeing deposits, and pouring liquidity into economies that had started to freeze. The scale of bailouts and fiscal stimulus was extraordinary. In the United States and in China these approached $1 trillion. The European Central Bank pumped €95 billion into credit markets to improve liquidity. Even the Swiss government had to invest CHF 6 billion into UBS, and relieve it of $60 billion of bad assets. The fear of meltdown, fear that the very lifeblood of advanced economies would freeze, justified actions that in normal times would be scarcely contemplated. Socialism arrived—but as some wits put it, only for bankers. Banks that had been gloriously international in life, turned out to be prosaically national in death. Credit cards were the first widespread tool for representing value in history[18] without any sovereign or symbol of a state, and signaled a financial system that believed itself to have broken free from the constraints of government or national borders. Yet in crisis, the banks ran back to mother to bail them out.

Many feared that recession would lead to depression, the best definition of which is "a recession where the policies don't work." But the actions worked in the short term, with the odd mix of cut sales taxes, and dramatic public works (from schools in Australia to electric cars in San Francisco and cathedrals in France) all helping to stave off collapse.[19]

Yet the most striking feature of the responses was that they combined radical tactics and conservative strategy. The speed and scale of the immediate responses were breathtaking. But as the months and years passed the big countries appeared to have little strategy, and where there were hints of strategy these were as timid as the tactics had been bold. Many of the underlying causes of the crisis were not touched. Overconsumption in the United States, and overproduction in China, were if anything exacerbated by the emergency measures that were put in place. Easy credit was a cause of the crisis and then became a desired part of the answer to it: for example, 40 percent of the U.S. stimulus was used on household tax cuts to boost consumption. A system skewed toward easy profits in banking became desperately concerned to build up banks' profits once again.[20] This may not have been surprising given the makeup of the decision makers. President Obama, unlike Franklin Roosevelt, surrounded himself with Wall Street insiders and largely deferred to them. His top executives were imbued with the values and assumptions of the global banks and steered clear of remedies that might challenge their wealth and power.[21]

Some of the remedies threatened worse crises in the future. One particularly creative central banker coined the term "doom loop," to warn that governments' implicit guarantees for banks would encourage ever riskier behavior, and thus a likelihood of even more massive financial failure in due course which could ultimately threaten the very stability of the state.[22] What had happened to Iceland could happen elsewhere. Rather than making the system safer, the bailouts worsened the risk of moral hazard by offering greater incentives for banks to take imprudent risks, safe in the knowledge that governments would pick up the bill if they turned sour. Others warned that even if growth did return, it would not result in new jobs.

If bankers and regulators agreed on one thing it was that risk needed to be curtailed. Stricter rules requiring larger reserves certainly made sense given the excesses of the 2000s. But the diagnosis was too blunt. The problem wasn't just that finance had taken too many risks; it was more that it had taken the wrong kinds of risks. The longer-run demands of growth require not less risk but rather different kinds of risk. Growth depends on investors being willing to invest in highly risky innovations, new technologies, and services. It depends on investors being pushed toward productive risks rather than the essentially unproductive risks of financial engineering. New regulations that simply reduced risk overall threatened both good risk-taking and bad risk-taking alike.

A measure of the problem that needed to be solved was the retreat from production and innovation of many of the firms that should have been pioneering the new economy. Fifty companies spent $1.59 trillion on share buybacks during the 2000s. It might not be surprising to learn that eight of the biggest bailed-out banks spent $182 billion in the decade before the crash of 2008. But why did Intel spend $48.3 billion on buybacks, more than four times the total budget of the National Nanotechnology Initiative for 2001–2010? Why did Cisco spend 126 percent of its profits, and big pharmaceutical companies like Merck, more than half the sums they spent on R&D, buying their own shares?[23] Even companies heavily involved in new technology were prioritizing financial re-engineering over productive investment. Having lost faith in their ability to create value, they were instead putting money back into the financial system, where as we know it was highly unlikely to be reinvested in innovations.[24] More recently these companies have simply sat on vast piles of cash.

The many countries that are sharply cutting back on public spending face a parallel problem. It's not just that spending cuts threaten to slow down any economic recovery; the problem is more that cuts will do as much damage to productive investment in the health, science, or education that's essential to growth, as they do to revenue spending. Here we come up against a deficiency both of governmental technique—the lack of accounting tools to distinguish different categories of spending—and of political debate, which so often treats debt and deficit reduction as meaningful categories. Healthy businesses distinguish between investment on the one hand, and spending on such things as wages and dividends on the other. Governments don't.

These many failures to deal with the fundamentals mean that slow growth, faltering recoveries, and periodic relapses could be the pattern in some parts of the world for many years to come. Worse, the financial crisis has spawned a slower moving fiscal and political crisis. The International Monetary Fund (IMF) estimated the direct costs of the bailouts at less than 3 percent of GDP. But the indirect cost has been more like 50 percent of GDP, much of which has been added to public debts, forcing country after country into programs of swinging cuts, that now layer over the deeper fiscal imbalances associated with aging populations. In Ireland, for example, a typical family of four will be saddled with public debts of around €200,000 by 2015, primarily to cover the costs of bailing out the various industries, from real estate to banks, that had prospered most in the boom and had most lost sight of economic reality. Across Europe, technocrats were installed in power to cut spending, grimly accepted by fatalistic citizens who were fearful that the alternatives were even worse. But everywhere there was the sense that a political time bomb was ticking, as grievance and resentment were added to shock.

No one can predict which remedies will work. But we can be sure that, as with so many other crises, predation lies at the heart of the current one. Representations come unstuck from reality most often when a predatory mind-set is in the ascendant: when people seek value out of nothing, whether in rising prices for land and housing, or in the euphoria that surrounds some new technologies. This is as true of governments piling up debt—and acting as predators on future generations—as it is of banks leeching value from the providers of goods and services. Since ultimately value is real, and experienced in finite time and space, there never can be something for nothing, and crises can only come to an end when systems adjust, and turn their attention once more to real value, and to the necessarily hard work of meeting wants and needs.

We understand other systems through crisis: the human body through illness, the brain through brain damage, ecosystems through their responses to drought or flood. We understand the strengths and weaknesses of political systems through their ability to deal with stress and conflict, and so it is too with economic systems. But crises also accelerate solutions—they force attention to new possibilities and new accommodations, and the best ones leave behind systems that are more resilient.[25] Nietzsche's comment that "what doesn't kill you makes you stronger" may not be wholly accurate (and wasn't for him: he spent the last years of his life suffering from syphilis that neither killed him nor made him stronger). But even the most painful crises sometimes pave the way for progress.

Chapter 3

. . . .

The Essence of Capitalism

It was made up of irregularity, change, forward spurts, failures to keep step,
collisions of objects and interests, punctuated by unfathomable silences; made
up of pathways and untrodden ways, of one great rhythmic beat as well as all
the chronic discord and mutual displacement of all its contending rhythms.
All in all it was like a boiling bubble inside a pot.

ROBERT MUSIL, *THE MAN WITHOUT QUALITIES* (1930–1942)

TO UNDERSTAND what capitalism might become, we first have to understand what it is. This is not so simple. Capitalism includes a market economy, but many traditional market economies are not capitalistic. It revolves around capital—but Egyptian pharaohs and fascist dictators commanded capital and surpluses too. It includes the systematic pursuit of technological improvement—but quite a few noncapitalistic societies have done the same, and much of the investment that drives industries like computing and aerospace came from states, not private investors. It includes trade, but trade, too, long precedes capitalism.[1]

Capitalism's etymology is not much help, either. It derives ultimately from the root "kaput," meaning head, and referring to cattle, chattels, or any kind of moveable wealth. In the early Middle Ages it came to mean money or the assets of a trader, and by the eighteenth century a capitalist was simply someone who was rich. But capitalism isn't the same as plutocracy, rule by the rich, though it sometimes comes close.

The French historian Fernand Braudel offered a more helpful description of capitalism when he wrote of it as a series of layers built on top of the everyday market economy of onions and wood, plumbing and cooking. These layers, local, regional, national, and global, are characterized by ever greater abstraction, until at the top sits disembodied finance, housed in gleaming glass towers in cities like London and New York, seeking returns anywhere, uncommitted to any particular place or industry, and commodifying anything and everything.

Each layer derives its energy from the simple fact that resources are distributed unevenly, and in ways that are unlikely to correspond to demand or need. At the lower layers, markets distribute everyday commodities like oil, wheat, and wine, and skills. At the highest layers, they distribute money, or rights to property and knowledge, and from its uncertain start capitalism was associated with a hierarchy of abstraction. The embryonic capitalism that emerged in Bruges, Antwerp, and Amsterdam was mainly concerned with international trade, with little interest in manufacturing and even less in agriculture, and its characteristic device was the trade in contracts rather than goods themselves. A similar hierarchy is visible today, reaching from the tangible facts of daily life up to the wholly abstract representations of global markets. The lower layers can be found most easily in the yellow pages or equivalent in any major city. There you see the living market economy of restaurants, plumbers, accountants, and builders, working in what are usually highly competitive fields with many players and slim profit margins. This market economy long predates capitalism and is distinct from it. Indeed, you could almost take it as a definition of the power of a firm in the capitalist economy that it doesn't appear in the yellow pages, but rather lies one step behind, providing the credit, the big brands, and the big distribution systems. You won't find Goldman Sachs there, or JP Morgan. Toyota will appear, but only through its dealers. In developing economies the lower layers are even more removed: roughly 50 percent of economic activity is informal.

If those are the lower layers, what of the higher ones, the disembodied commanding heights of Braudel's account? A good vantage point to see these is the World Economic Forum which meets in the

Swiss ski resort of Davos each January. Several thousand participants attend the meeting, along with several thousand hangers-on around its periphery. At first glance it looks like any other conference, with plenary sessions, smaller side sessions, dinners, and receptions. Upon closer examination, however, it turns out that some are more equal than others. There are layers of exclusivity; closed meetings; areas you can only enter with special passes. An elaborate hierarchy has been constructed. At the top are the global corporations, the banks, and the most powerful or prestigious political leaders. The top circle also includes a handful of multibillionaires surrounded by courtiers. Newcomers from Ukraine or China may sponsor events to claim attention, buying their way into respectability. In the succeeding circles come big IT firms and oil; then further out the consultancies and accountants; and then in the outer circle, the invited academics, journalists, and civil servants.

This is a food chain, a hierarchy, if ever there was one. Yet it's one that feels the need to hide its gradations, to sustain the idea that anyone can talk as an equal to anyone. Its dominant ideas are those that chime with the interests of the people who are there: favoring free and open markets, less rather than more regulation, less rather than more tax. It instinctively stands against particularism or tradition, let alone socialism. Some dissenting voices are allowed in, perhaps according to the principle that you should know your enemy. But this is where capitalism speaks to itself, takes the pulse of the political and economic mood, and tries out new positions, like the idea of corporate social responsibility or open innovation, to see if they can be made to fit.

Similar shifting hierarchies were there in earlier phases of capitalism when merchants and bankers met together in Genoa and Venice, London, and Bruges. They could be found in a recognizable form when the great Arab empires straddled the Mediterranean and when China's internal trade went through periodic booms. Indeed, each great empire mastered some of the same tasks as the prominent heroes of Davos: the control of economic connections, the links between separate markets, the arbitrage that turns a piece of news or knowledge into a profit. Even Islam, sometimes portrayed as anti-capitalist and reactionary, grew out of trade, with Mohammed married to the daughter of a trader, and encouraged by merchants to make his decisive move to Medina.

What has changed is a matter of degree. The hierarchies now stretch far more widely and across far more intermediaries, suppliers, financers, and traders than ever before, as capitalism has evolved beyond trade and small-scale manufacture to vast combines, enjoying the economies of scale reaped by mass manufacturing and marketing, and equally vast markets. A $75 trillion global economy includes around $12 trillion in exports, a far higher ratio than ever before. The result is a stretched and disaggregated capitalism—so that an iPad shaped by a British designer in California is manufactured by some of the 300,000 workers in the vast complex in Shenzen in China owned by a Taiwanese company (Foxconn), to run apps from Finland for a consumer in Brazil.[2]

No one could have predicted that Sheffield would be a city of steel, Pakistan a great exporter of footballs, Taiwan a world leader in microprocessors as well as bicycles, Denmark a leader in wind power, south India a titan in software, Bangladesh in hats, and northern Italy in ceramics. But the bigger story of which they are all a part is a deepening interdependence. From the three billion people paid less than $2 a day to the thousand dollar billionaires, this new interdependence has at least some of the characteristics of a system rather than a series of connected markets, and it is this system, whose higher reaches at least are truly global in nature, that now faces us, and forces us to ask which parts of it are good and which are bad.

Historical data confirm its novelty. The precapitalist economy was dominated by war and food; war was what taxes were raised for, agriculture was the work that the great majority did. Yet today military spending accounts for barely 2 percent of GDP, agriculture for barely 4 percent, and much less in the most advanced economies. The precapitalist economy was domestic, the capitalist economy is not. In 1790, for example, 80 percent of all clothing in the United States was made in the home; a century later, 90 percent was made outside the home. The precapitalist economy had few intermediary organizations: most transactions were direct. The capitalist economy is full of intermediaries, dealing at one remove with value and money. In the 1790s there were only three banks in the United States; a century later, 12,000.

DEFINING CAPITALISM

If these are some of the facts of capitalism, how should we define it? You might expect such a central part of modern civilisation to have a commonly agreed definition. Instead, radically different views compete. In some accounts, what defines capitalism most are the people at its heart, with the power to make things happen. Sometimes these are the entrepreneurs, people described in previous eras with names such as "undertakers" ("*unternehmer*" in German) and "projectors" (in sixteenth-century England), and first theorized by Jean-Baptiste Say. Joseph Schumpeter gave them a starring role in the life of capitalism, showing that their hunt for value provided the animating energy for the system as a whole. They might be motivated by money or by what Schumpeter called "social distance."[3] What they do is not wholly rational. In Schumpeter's words, "the success of everything depends on intuition, the capacity of seeing things in a way which afterwards proves to be true, even though it cannot be established at the moment, and of grasping the essential fact, discarding the unessential, even though one can give no account of the principles by which this is done."[4] Not all of the intuitions turn out to be right—just think of Alexander Graham Bell's comment that "someday every town in America will have a telephone." And the most successful entrepreneurs are rarely the most creative innovators: much more often, the pioneers see others reap the rewards (it was Bill Gates, for example, not DARPA or Xerox, who made the most from personal computers). But the restless competition of entrepreneurs could be counted on to aggregate into a much more dynamic and productive economy.

In other accounts it is not the entrepreneur, but rather the investor, the capitalist, who dominates. The great sociologist and historian

Charles Tilly defined capitalism as "the system of production in which holders of capital, backed by law and state power, make the crucial decisions concerning the character and allocation of work."[5] In this view it is the investor more than the entrepreneur who defines the character of the system and usually takes the largest share of the rewards. In some societies, the holders of accumulated capital really do rule, dominating politicians (or sometimes simply mutating into ones themselves, like Silvio Berlusconi in Italy or Michael Bloomberg in New York). Then again, fifty years ago it was common to see organizations as far more important than individuals. Finance was relatively invisible, the meek servant of great industrial combines, and capitalism meant rule by the corporate bureaucracies of IBM and General Motors, DuPont, Coca-Cola, and General Electric.[6]

Another vantage point, popular perhaps in the age of software and programs, is to understand capitalism through its generative rules, the codes and principles that govern who can do what and how. The genetic code of modern capitalism can be found in a cluster of concepts and laws: the joint stock company, the market for goods, intellectual property laws, and the various other property rights that were introduced alongside industrialization, and which subordinated the older customary rights, whether of lords or the common people. Karl Polanyi's influential book *The Great Transformation* on the emergence of capitalism describes the many ways in which the laws changed, strengthening money as the universal medium of exchange, and turning labor into a commodity to be bought and sold. The laws were reformed both to free things up and then to tie them down with new restrictions. It is no coincidence that the global centers of capitalism in Wall Street or the City of London are packed with lawyers: capitalism is heavily dependent on laws, courts, and shifting judgments. Free markets are anything but free. The cost of lawyers represents some 2 percent of U.S. GDP.[7] Indeed global markets work only because legal and other codes are widely adopted, and anyone who tries to export a crate of apples, or a shipload of cars, soon discovers this. Here we find that the free market depends upon the rules: standardization has been the motor of growth, with a succession of agreed common languages to make trade possible. They began with the rules governing post, telegraph, and telephones in the nineteenth century; then spread to accounting; then to barcodes, now part of a hugely sophisticated system for tracking over 40 million products overseen by a nonprofit organization, GS1. Just as important are the protocols that underlie the Internet (HTML, URL, and others, loosely governed by another nonprofit, ICANN) and the standards for mobile phones. The lesson is clear: exchange rests on rules; private wealth on public goods; competition on cooperation.

Another way of seeing capitalism—is through its circulation, rather as a body can be understood by examining the role of the heart and the blood, and the networks of synapses and signals. Manuel Castells has been perhaps the most articulate documenter of societies now constructed around "flows of capital, flows of information, flows of technology, flows of organisational interaction, flows of images sounds and symbols."[8] Justifying this approach are the four billion mobile phones and two billion people in cyberspace, and the 50–60 percent annual growth of Internet traffic.[9]

The flows consist of bits and pixels as well as gadgets and clothes. Alongside the licit flows there are also hidden flows, the four million people smuggled across international borders each year, and the $500 billion in illegal world trade. There are the flows of energy, still predominantly fossil fuels and likely to remain so for years to come, that keep the wheels turning,[10] and the flows of waste in a world where the average person now produces 45–85 tons each year, vastly more than in the past.[11]

Even more powerful, perhaps, are the financial flows shaped by algorithms: the "black box" and "algo" trading which pit one group of brilliant minds against another to create invisible patterns of trades, and then countermeasures, a mathematical arms race whose battles take place at astonishing speed, and well beyond human comprehension.

Free flow is both a means and an end: a means to more optimal allocations of capital or people, and an end in that it breaks down attachments of culture and tradition that are seen to block the full realization of human productivity. OECD projections indicate that the proportion of foreign-born people will grow much higher than it is at present—to between 15 and 32 percent of the total population in most European countries by 2050.[12] In the United States, minorities which now make up about one third of the population, are expected to become the majority of children by the 2020s, and of the population by the 2040s, unless draconian restrictions on migration are introduced.[13] In one vision of the future, everywhere, and certainly every major city, becomes a fractal microcosm of a diverse and cosmopolitan world, and capitalism becomes, even more, a vast system of pumping and pushing, of things in perpetual motion. Henri Lefebvre argued that cities cannot be understood through still pictures, or data, but only through watching the patterns and rhythms of movement as people move, and things move, during the course of days and weeks.[14] Seeing things in motion reveals the true character of the city. The same is true of capitalism: every snapshot deceives, because even something as banal as today's price of wheat is the product of a circuit of supply and demand, weather conditions, and production technologies.

CAPITALISM AS AN IDEA ABOUT VALUE

Here I suggest a different answer to the question of what capitalism is at heart. I don't discount the importance of looking at who has power, or at the rules, or the culture, or the flows. All of these are dimensions of what we call capitalism, and all shape its character. But capitalism is better understood as something altogether simpler, that lies behind these manifestations. It is at root an idea, an imaginary, a way of seeing the world. This idea is the single-minded pursuit of growth in value, or more specifically of growth in representations of value that can be exchanged with others.

Braudel's description of a hierarchy of markets captures this well: each move up the hierarchy brings with it a purer embodiment of the idea, and ever greater distance from everyday life. From this idea many other ideas derive, including the myriad of rules, techniques, organizational forms, and measurement tools that make up capitalism. From it derive the values and ideals that make capitalism a culture, a form of civilization as well as an economy. And from it, too, derives a logic of power, in which power gravitates to those who can accumulate the most representations of value.

If value really is so important, it then becomes vital to understand exactly what it is. Value appears to be a solid concept, especially when embodied in a strong currency, or the gold held in the central bank's vaults. Yet we know that value can prove ephemeral and volatile—and the ways in which currencies and stock markets crash, or company accounts turn out to be fictions, reveal a great deal about value's true nature.

The roots of value can be found in our nature as biological creatures: we value what helps us live and flourish. We know how to distinguish happy from unhappy; safe from unsafe; comfortable from uncomfortable. We value things that contribute to our survival, and enhance our experience, and our ancestors, like us, could distinguish the relative value of different things such as an axe or a carcass, in terms of their contribution to survival or flourishing. This is "lived value"—value that is real and experienced in space and time as part of life.

A very different kind of value exists in representations, which are abstracted from daily life: money, gold, and more recently a proliferation of devices from the stock and bond to the credit card. Their appeal is that they promise lived value in the future, and they provide a store as well as a measure and medium of exchange, and perhaps a sense of security and pride. But the representations are radically different in nature from the value they represent. The representations only come alive, paradoxically, at their moment of death, when they are disposed of, and turned into real things. And value is ultimately only meaningful in real places and times: we may sit on a bulging bank account or a vault full of gold, but it's only when we spend it on a meal, a home, or a journey that its potential is realized.

These distinctions are obvious, or at least they used to be. Many past societies distinguished between the production of value, which is seen as good, and money making, which is of doubtful virtue (Aristotle used the term "oekonomia" for the first and "chremmatistica" for the second). For Thomas Aquinas just exchange meant each side received exactly his due, and he opposed lending money for interest as a breach of this principle. A later fourteenth-century writer, Nicolas Oresme, summed up the prevailing view when he wrote that "it is monstrous and unnatural that a . . . thing specifically sterile such as money should bear fruit and multiply of itself."[15] These ideas can seem quaintly anachronistic amidst an economy so dependent on money in all its forms. But we have lost an important insight as modern economics (unlike classical economics) has become uncomfortable with value that isn't at least notionally monetized. This may be because capitalism has done so much to amplify the means of representing value, and orchestrating these representations, through everything from double entry bookkeeping to management accounts, futures markets to actuarial tables. In all of these cases, value has been made abstract, manipulable, and thus amenable to the creativity of mathematics. The promise, all along, has been that new ways of manipulating represented value will lead to the expansion of lived value, and that has indeed happened. Turning future value into a number makes it easier to justify investment; turning knowledge into an asset makes it easier to justify devoting resources to research.

But most of the vulnerabilities of capitalism also derive from the less than solid relationship between lived value and its representations. These include the high incentives for predation and free-riding and the tendency of crises to spin out of control when representations stretch too far from the reality they represent. They include capitalism's crises of meaning, which derive from the perception that it knows the price of everything and the value of nothing, and the corrupting moral ambivalence that comes from the distance between decisions and their effects.

What I'm describing here as lived value isn't exclusively material. From the earliest times some things became representations of value despite having no direct use: symbols of status, or continuity, or magic, had a cognitive value even if they had no obvious material one. Today, too, meanings and values are hard to distinguish: we genuinely enjoy a bottle of wine more if we think it's expensive, or a work of art if we think it's not a fake. We appreciate cars or clothes more if they are se-miotically rich—and not just fast or comfortable. And, as Adam Smith was keen to point out, we admire systems and institutions as much for the beauty of their design as for the utility they provide.[16]

I also don't want to imply that representations of value float freely. They may appear to be abstract, but all monies, and all other represen-tations of value, are grounded in institutions and social relationships. The orbit of money expands when there are strong states and strong institutions—like banks, monastic orders, or corporations—and it contracts during times of social and political crisis. But the crucial point to emphasize is that capitalism's uniqueness lies in its handling of representations of value, even though its usefulness derives from its ability to create genuine, lived value. Capitalism institutionalizes a way of seeing that's very different from that of any other system. What is seen is the potential for exchangeable value in anything, and then the infinite ways in which value can be measured, traded, or stored. Possibility can be seen in otherwise inert places and things. All things can be measured by their degree of use and waste, and judged not by what they are or what they mean, but by the value latent in them, whether it's a field waiting to be turned into an orchard, a seam of metals waiting to be mined, or a tune or a talent waiting to find a market.

What isn't seen is everything else: meaning, context, belief. Market capitalism is in this sense precisely analogous to the information the-ory developed by Claude Shannon and others which sees all informa-tion as equivalent, and amenable to being manipulated, transmitted, or stored, but only so long as everything else is ignored: all meaning, context, or culture.[17] Information theory made possible an explosion of new tools for communication, from the computer to the fiber-optic cable, just as the pure idea of the market made possible an explosion of innovations around money and value, such as the application of sophisticated probability theories to the management of risk.

What follows is much more than a tool, an economic system that serves practical goals. Instead the tool also shapes us. Everything that we know about cognition shows that we do not experience reality directly. Instead we create representations of reality through which we engage with an external environment. Much of our mental energy goes into sustaining its coherence. Capitalism works by becoming a way of seeing and thinking. Like so many other parts of human civilization, it thrives by becoming part of us, not just a tool, so that we see things only through their representations, through their potential to be bought and sold, like the singer of the "Trader's Song" in Bertolt Brecht's opera, *Die Massnahme* ("The Measure Taken"):

> How should I know what rice is?
> How should I know who knows what it is?
> I've no idea what rice is, I only know its price

THE VIRTUE OF PRODUCTIVITY AND CAPITALISM'S COMMITMENTS

If capitalism suggested a way of seeing the world that was often detached from the morality of everyday life, it nevertheless also made claims to a moral purpose: making things productive was a moral mission, a rejection of indolence, excess, and indulgence. At its harsher end it was bound up with the suppression of the unproductive habits of dance and carnival, the banishing of the lords of misrule that distracted people from the daily grind, and the end of an era when even churches were full of light, laughter, and dance. Value meant work, order, self-control, and godly discipline. Where Catholic theology often presented work as punishment for Adam's sins, Protestantism presented it as a good in itself. Realizing value was our duty, our greatest service to god. Productivity was a moral purpose in itself, and brought with it strict responsibilities as well. Markets were places of conscious moral restraint, with prudence and discipline repeatedly extolled as vital virtues. Individuals were expected to take responsibility for their actions.

This principle was reflected in institutions. When London banks were being regulated in the early nineteenth century all, other than the Bank of England, had to be partnerships in which the partners, of whom there could be no more than six, were legally responsible for the bank's obligations (it's intriguing to speculate how different recent financial history would have been if these rules had survived). Two centuries later mutual guarantees underpinned the finance flowing into Italy's most globally competitive firms. Germany's were overseen by supervisory boards responsible for guardianship of values as well as relationships. These were at least attempts to construct a capitalism relatively free of venality or hysterical greed, and grounded in morals. Sobriety; productivity; responsibility went together to make a new order, and the path they offered was a virtuous one, of creation not predation. Max Weber captured well this idea of divine providence intervening in the economy:

> If God shows you a way in which you may lawfully get more than in another way (without wrong to your soul or to any other), if you refuse this, and choose the less gainful way, you cross one of the ends of your calling, and you refuse to be God's steward, and to accept His gifts and use them for him when He requires it: you may labour to be rich for God, though not for the flesh and sin.[18]

This enthusiasm for productivity fitted happily with other ideals of virtue and art. Here is a description of the appointment of Sir John Swinnerton as Lord Mayor of London in 1612, an early example of this synthesis: the celebration had at its center an installation that included a chariot in which stood virtue, and around it figures representing the seven liberal arts, and showing a love of the arts, commerce, science, and knowledge as "the stairs and ascensions of the Throne of Virtue and the only glory and upholding of cities."[19] Now there was to be no shame in the counting house, "only honour."

This moral dimension was not just a desirable add-on, or a fig leaf. It mattered because capitalism, like all human institutions, does not rest only on interests; it also rests on agreements and commitments that together form a dense web that supports the system's ability to represent value. They include the commitment to recognize money itself; the commitment to pay back if you borrow; the commitment to honour contracts; the commitment to share profits; the commitment to recognize private property; and many others. Each of these commitments has its own moral logic, but at their heart is fair reward for productive creation.

These commitments are examples of what the philosopher John Searle calls declarations. Declarations are neither factually true nor false. But by acting as if they are true we reinforce them, and build social institutions that can then make claims on us. So capitalism depends not just on very visible rules with the force of law such as those governing advertising or trading standards, prohibiting child labor or regulating health and safety. It also rests on self-imposed restraints: the ways in which people choose to rein themselves in because of the promise of greater rewards.[20] The saver saves rather than spending for the sake of future reward; the investor takes risks in the hope of greater future wealth; the worker sacrifices leisure, and freedom, for the sake of income and the chance to buy a house or a car. The lure of acquisition and greed is tempered by self-discipline and patience, and much of that happens within organizations, held together by commitments that provide a shape, and a meaning, to the events that make up our lives.[21]

No market and no enterprise can survive for long without declarations, and the moral voice that underpins declarations and commitments of this kind has always been present in capitalism's history. It's not enough to proclaim the power of self-interest or that greed is good. A higher purpose has always had to be invoked as well.

Yet it's the very ambiguity of that higher purpose that has made capitalism's agreements more controversial, and more uncomfortable, than many of the other agreements that crystallized in tandem with capitalism, such as the agreement to abide by the results of democratic votes or the agreement to accept the decisions of independent courts. The pursuit of value has always rubbed up against values,[22] and bred a fear that capitalism would crowd out the very trust, commitment, and cooperation on which it depends. In a later chapter I describe how capitalism fought back against the threat from rebellious younger generations with an allergy to work, or managers with an allergy to hierarchy. The absence of a consistent moral foundation for capitalism means that its moral shifts are constant and unpredictable, so that today the fashion is for recycling (which was once a mark of poverty), and for the wealthy not the poor to have big families, to be thin not fat, and to work hard rather than living a life of leisure. Soon, perhaps the rich will define themselves by their ability to go off-grid, where only a few years before the ever-present Blackberry was a symbol of status.

If all other purposes and morals are unstable, then money, represented value, at least appears to be a more honest and reliable foundation on which to build a working economy. Credit derives from the Latin "credere," meaning to believe, to entrust, and it is faith in money that drives us to act as if pieces of paper, or numbers on a screen, represent something real. But such faith is both unnatural and recent. The advance of money was slow and fitful until the twentieth century in most developed countries, as many people living in rural areas used money only to buy the handful of things they couldn't make for themselves. Ancient Egypt, like most ancient civilizations functioned largely without money. The Roman Denarius rose to become tender over thousands of miles, but then fell. China's Ming dynasty invented paper money but found it hard to sustain. Spanish pieces of eight were perhaps first global currency, but didn't turn Spain into a market pioneer, and didn't have much impact on the vast majority. Fernand Braudel described the arrival of money into the lives of peasants as a mixed blessing: "What did it actually bring? Sharp variations in prices of essential foodstuffs; incomprehensible relationships in which man no longer recognized either himself, his customs or his ancient values. His work became a commodity, himself a 'thing.'"[23]

But the shapers of money did nevertheless prevail, as advantage went to those who innovated the cleverest ways to make money circulate and fructify while retaining its links to genuine production. Britain's greatest edge over its eighteenth-century competitors came from the existence of banks that could take savings and mobilize them to finance manufacture, trade, and commerce. That the city of London, contained "a place like Lombard Street where, in all but the rarest times, money can be obtained on good security or upon decent proposals of probable gain [was] a luxury which no other country has ever enjoyed before."[24] Credit fed both business and government, which pioneered the multiplication of debt (in defiance of common sense, and domestic logic, which said that debt was the way to ruin). Gilts, for example, were invented to fund the expansion of the navy. The more that money could be made to circulate, the faster new businesses would be created and grow.[25]

Money continues to hold the system together, but it does so in ever more tenuous ways. Until roughly the end of the Bretton Woods system in the early 1970s, currencies were backed by assets, mainly gold, that provided a literal guarantee of value. Anchoring money in something real was thought to be the necessary assurance that it could be trusted, and that the representations represented something real. Now most currencies are pure fiat—blunt assertions of confidence by the state, and sustained only because of ultimate confidence that states can, in extremis, pay their debts. Governments still hold gold, and the U.S. government still keeps some $300 billion in gold reserves, at great expense; but none could cope with a true collapse of confidence. So all of the players in the system have a shared interest in sustaining belief. As the Chinese Prime Minister Wen Jiabao put it: "confidence is more important than gold." But many are aware just how fragile monetary systems would be if confidence waned, and in particular confidence in the ultimate capacity of the state to raise funds.[26] For a few days in 2008, it looked as if the financial system would grind to a halt: banks stopped lending to each other in the interbank market because they lost trust in each other's capacity to pay their bills. All transactions, all cash payments from ATMs, all salary transfers, and all trade could have stopped abruptly if central banks hadn't stepped in with drastic measures to restore confidence and liquidity. Iceland served as a warning: a small nation once considered a model of productivity, whose government ranked second in the World Bank's listings of the world's most competent, and whose society ranked top in the UN's Human Development Index. In 2008, after a period of aggressive expansion and acquisition, all of its major banks went bankrupt, and the nation's debts rose to between five and ten times GDP.[27] The "Hrun," or downfall, left the people stunned; nearly half were technically insolvent. But one moral of the story was that capitalism still remained ultimately dependent on trust in the state's ability to guarantee money.

If money is pure representation, a useful, socially constructed fiction (yet one that has no odor, to recall the Latin saying *"pecunia non olet"*), it follows that we need to understand it as such. Charles Peirce, the founder of semiotics, wrote that "the sign is not a sign unless it can be translated into another sign in which it is more fully developed," and the same is true of money, at least in its more complex expressions as assets and investments. Like other signs, each individual one exists only in relation to others. Every price is influenced by every other price, every monetary promise or claim by every other promise or claim. It is also influenced by the systems of communication that surround it: business newspapers, TV programs, websites, and commentary, as much as by the twists and turns of the real economy. Rumors, fashions and hysterias are as powerful factors as technologies and underlying costs, which is why the prices even of basic commodities such as oil fluctuate so violently. This dependence of the economy on networks of meaning is largely absent from economics,[28] but it becomes visible in times of crisis when confidence shudders, and central bankers try to allay panic with calming speeches for the cameras and frenzied measures behind the scenes to pump money and liquidity into the system.

Yet it takes a leap of imagination to see the fragility. Because the greatest achievement of capitalism, as of any social system, is to appear natural: we, the people born in it, struggle to imagine a world without billboards, credit cards, and corporate brands. Language makes people more than people language, and the same is true for capitalism as a form of life: by becoming a language, a prism for seeing and thinking, it naturalizes itself. By shaping human nature, it becomes human nature. By becoming natural, its unnaturalness is hidden, as is the fragility of a system that is ultimately founded not on things but on confidence and collective belief. But there is no objective reason why an old master, or a New York house, or a hundred thousand tons of carbon, should be worth $10 million or half as much or even a tenth as much. Each is only worth as much as it is because others are willing to believe, because of a shared fiction rather than a grounded fact. Nor are we wise to trust too much in money: banks have a capacity to create credit which is regularly abused, just as governments are often tempted to expand the money supply, leaving to their successors the problems of inflation, devaluation, and a stretched gap between real value and its representations.

CAPITALISM AND THE STATE

So how is this vulnerability kept at bay? One answer is that capitalism is protected by what isn't capitalist. No society or economy has ever become capitalist in any complete sense, and the non-capitalist parts provide buffers. When markets collapse, governments step in. When money disappears, people turn more to their families and communities. And vulnerability is reduced because instead of a pure capitalism, what exist are messy hybrids, partial not whole, capitalist in niches and slices of life, but not in everything. The capitalist spirit is most apparent in finance, investment, and accounting, and we can recognize the most capitalist economies because they confer the highest paid and highest status roles to people associated with concentrations of financial capital, not to the most creative, the cleverest, or the most productive. But everywhere, even in the most capitalistic societies, the underlying principles of capitalism have been largely kept out of family, religion, health, and art. A world of truly capitalistic families is an interesting thought experiment, but one that soon reminds us why it hasn't happened. Imagine parents charging their children for time and accommodation, or renting them out for profit (admittedly the parent-managers of some child stars do exactly that but usually forfeit their child's love along the way). Imagine too if employers had to pay the full cost of the upbringing and socialization of their employees. A truly capitalist society would be an impossible dystopia. Friedrich Hayek advocated a "catallaxy" of markets everywhere, and some decision-support systems (providing price comparisons and recommendations) appear to achieve it. Yet attempts to create these on any more comprehensive scale regularly stumble. Deductive purity is at odds with the grain of human nature and human life. The most durable systems combine multiple, often contradictory elements. They are hybrids, mongrels, rough concoctions adapted and improved by experience. Their extensive networks, made up of links and connections, work only because they combine with spheres, self-contained and often opaque units like the family, or the firm.

The most striking proof of the partiality and impurity of capitalism is the extent to which capitalism has depended on states' roles as investors, producers, and regulators. Ronald Reagan loved to describe governments' view of markets: "if it moves tax it; if it keeps moving regulate it. And if it stops moving subsidize it." But, however much business people understandably resent paying their hard-earned money over to bureaucrats, any observer is soon struck by the interdependence of commercial power and sovereign power, including close alliances with the state as a source of finance for technology (40 percent of the research investment in Silicon Valley for example) or housing (Fannie Mae), great industrial combines (as in Korea), and the strange hybrids of mercantilist communist capitalism in China and tycoon-led capitalism in southeast Asia.[29] One measure of the state's importance is that in the United States, seventy-seven out of the most important eight-eight innovations (rated by *R&D Magazine*'s annual awards) were dependent on federal government support, which covered the risks associated with new ideas, mainly but not only in the early stages.[30]

This interdependence is not new. Modern banking grew up as a response to the state, from the first Italian banks of the thirteenth century to the Bank of England, set up in the late seventeenth century to finance the war debts of the king. Default by governments has been the single most important cause of banks' collapse[31] (the Bank of England charged the government 8 percent for its first loan, twice the rate at which it discounted trade bills). Yet over time the tables were turned, transforming the state into "the last-resort financier of the banks," and leaving "one big difference between the situation today and that in the Middle Ages. Then the biggest risk to the banks was from the sovereign. Today, perhaps the biggest risk to the sovereign comes from the banks."[32] No wonder Thomas Jefferson described banking institutions as "more dangerous to our liberties than standing armies."

But banks are just one example of an extent of interpenetration of state and market that would have appalled Jefferson. From Switzerland to Taiwan and the United States, capitalism has evolved as a plurality of hybrids, like China[33] allowing farmers to sell their produce on the open market once they had delivered their quotas to the state, and allowing municipalities to hold property rights in local town and village enterprises as an alternative to ownership either by the central state or private capital.[34] Many countries have kept public ownership of capital as a good source of revenue: Chile, for example, has long retained its largest export industry—copper—in state ownership. Today, nine of the world's thirty largest enterprises are based in emerging market economies and have substantial government shareholdings. The heavy investments in satellites and rocket launchers, not just by China and India, but also by Brazil and Iran, are classic examples of governments working in tandem with commercial interests, combining the push for prestige with the push for profit.

These hybrids are reminders that there has never been a capitalist society—only societies with limited realms of capitalism. England and the United States were exceptions, not the rule, the sole examples of what could be called the organic development of capitalism, where capitalist life emerged spontaneously from the primordial social soup, and even they retained strong public and civic institutions alongside those of the market,[35] and then gave the state a decisive role in developing new technologies, from the jet and the Internet to GPS and multitouch displays.[36] Everywhere else the new economy had to be genetically engineered, developed artificially as a survival response by states and aristocracies keen to preserve their power. In this respect, the ideas of Friedrich List have had as much long-term influence as those of Adam Smith. List advocated, and then helped establish, the extraordinary network of training and research institutions that took

Germany to economic greatness (though he thought it impossible that Germany would ever overtake Britain). He took it for granted that competitiveness had to be organized, and that capitalism had to be supported by non-capitalist institutions, insulated from pressures for profit.[37]

CAPITALISM AS FREEDOM AND DEMOCRACY

Such views are absent from capitalism's more recent theorists, such as Friedrich Hayek and Milton Friedman, who didn't write much about the state, except as a problem to be overcome . For them capitalism meant unfettered freedom, and they were right that capitalism's culture favors escape from constraint. Wage labor meant escape from a feudal landlord. Self-employment and starting a business meant getting away from a boss (and this is still the single most common motivation for entrepreneurship). Getting rich meant getting away with things, not having to say sorry, and not being called to account. For everyone else there was at least the possibility of desire democratized: that any wish could find expression without permission or authority. Alexis de Tocqueville's summary of American democracy serves well as a summary of this spirit of capitalism: "what the few have today, the many will demand tomorrow."

The promise of freedom was a promise to transfer power, down from the state and the big corporation to the breadwinner and the housewife, whose "power to choose" would drive everything. This was the ideology that underpinned modern economics, with all decisions in the economy ultimately deriving from the "revealed preferences" of individual consumers. And it provided a mission for other fields, like the generations of designers who worked to make luxuries accessible. Bauhaus modernism, for example, promised to use mass manufacture to improve the lives of the people (once it had overcome its initial commitment to arts and crafts). The German architect Peter Behrens overhauled AEG's marketing, factories, and products and almost single-handedly created the modern field of design. The designers made good products available to everyone and then, a few generations later, their successors melded mass production, digital technologies, and craft production to make a vastly wider variety of distinctive objects available at affordable prices, a move that effectively repelled the critics of numbing conformity in mass production and standardization.

Freedom to buy doesn't deliver everything. It has never been easy to buy, or to sell, security, love, or friendship. But markets have attempted to turn these, too, into commodities, and they can be bought indirectly through an insurance policy, a dating agency, or a club, and there have always been industries selling pleasure, from prostitution and drugs to nightclubs. Much ancient trade was about luxuries, including gold, jewels, incense, and wine. In Neolithic times polished jadeite axes, made in Switzerland, were taken over thousands of miles to be treasured as icons of luxury. But capitalism has made luxury and glamour available to everyone. The technologies of pleasure now include immersive technologies and business sells not only sex and drugs but also risk and adventure, from whitewater rafting down a remote river to jumping out of planes. In one account of capitalism's future, this trading in psychological states becomes ever more intensive, ever more sophisticated, and ever more able to match the particular experience to a particular desire, through the combination of pharmacology and virtual worlds. In this story we detach from the dull lived world of material things and explore the outer reaches of our minds. Korea, for example, already has twenty television channels broadcasting live from computer gaming tournaments, and many people became multimillionaires through their success at computer games such as Counterstrike and Warcraft.

This democratic ethos, which has encompassed everything from family cars and mortgages, to computer games and foreign holidays, has kept capitalism's critics at bay. If capitalism really could ensure that "what the few have today, the many will receive tomorrow," then what room would be left for the alternatives? The vast expansion of credit to people on low incomes that took place in countries like the United States and the UK around the millennium certainly headed off anger about rising inequality (as well as playing its part in the financial crisis). Many critics of capitalism too easily painted themselves into a corner, becoming puritans against pleasure, denying the poor their modest comforts, and scorning the newly prosperous when they choose glamour over art, luxury over beauty. In their more extreme stances the critics became enemies of the everyday. Theodor Adorno, guiding intellect of the Frankfurt School, argued that art should make us unhappy. It should be critical of a flawed capitalist world and make us ready to change it. Otherwise we were always at risk of being charmed by dictators, and lulled into infantilism by Hollywood or Tin Pan Alley, an intellectually coherent position, but one whose anti-democratic whiff limited its appeal.

Some of capitalism's most active participants profess to be winners in a Darwinian contest to find the fittest, the smartest, and the most cunning. But others claim to live a more democratic ideal. Markets are brutal but honest. They are the ultimate level playing field. They reward the efficient, the innovative, and the effective, and they punish the lazy. They are open—anyone can become an entrepreneur; anyone can make it. They are equal—in the market people meet as equals, trading where there is a common advantage, avoiding trade when there isn't. The market takes notice of anyone's needs so long as they have money: it doesn't ask who your parents were, where you went to school, or which church you pray at. In this vision the market is quite unlike the world of hierarchies and bureaucracies. It is open and willing to discover. Albert Camus said that democracy exists because we don't know everything, and this is also not a bad argument for markets.

This vision of rough equality is also at the core of modern economics, a discipline that grew in tandem with capitalism. Its theories today describe a world of equilibrium in which buyers and sellers come to agree on fair prices and fierce competition ensures that no one is unfairly exploited. Indeed, ultimately prices are fair in a profound way—they reflect the state of demand and the state of nature. If someone fails, it's because what they provided wasn't wanted, or was too costly. This is the world of the trader—a world of contracts, deals, always seeking out mutual advantage, the space for arbitrage. In the more

extreme versions the market comes to be seen as ineffably wise, a genius at taking disparate human wishes and coming up with creative
ways of meeting them. Eugene Fama, author of the "efficient market"
theory of asset pricing, provided an elaborate account of why all prices
reflect all available information. As a result the market came to be seen
as something that not only can't be bucked, but shouldn't be. The fact
that stock markets become promiscuous, switching and churning their
investments far more often than in the past, is not something to be
lamented but rather celebrated. Nor is it a problem if businesses have
to put all of their efforts into appearing beautiful to the casual investment window-shopper, with eye-catching quarterly rates of return,
rather than concerning themselves with the well-informed investor
who might understand what they do. The market is wise enough to get
the optimum result regardless.

Yet if we return to our definition of capitalism as the search for
exchangeable value, it soon becomes clear that these accounts are radically incomplete. The ways in which they are incomplete explains a
great deal both about the true nature of capitalism and about the reactions it has elicited, and why, two centuries after its birth it still fuels
such mixed emotions. One of the Achilles' heels of a system founded on
the discovery of value in all things is its failure to see value in so many
people and places. Mass unemployment has in the past prompted support for radical alternatives to capitalism, and today it is not hard to see
the link between youth unemployment rates over 40 percent in Sudan,
Somalia, and Yemen and support for terrorism.[38] Places bypassed or
forgotten by markets drift easily into fatalism and anger.

But the other Achilles' heel is the tendency of capitalism to take
rather than to make. In the next chapter I turn to this double nature.

Chapter 4

· · · · · · · · ·

To Take or to Make

The Roles of Creators and Predators

IF YOU WANT to make money, you can choose between two fundamentally different strategies. One is to create genuinely new value
by bringing resources together in ways that serve people's wants and
needs. The other is to seize value through predation, taking resources,
money, or time from others, whether they like it or not. Your choice, in
short, is whether to be a bee or a locust.

Capitalism's advocates see only its productive potential, its brilliance as an "innovation machine," a formidable generator of wealth
and multiplier of human productivity, while the critics see only its tendencies to predation. These mirror views have persisted for two centuries. As explained by Andrew Bernstein in his *Capitalist Manifesto*:

> Regarding the enormity of capitalism's success, both morally and prac-
> tically, in different centuries, on far-flung continents, involving a hun-
> dred issues, the explanatory principle that will emerge is: capitalism is
> par excellence the system of liberated human brain power.[1]

At the opposite extreme is François-Noël Babeuf, the leader of the left
in the French revolution who was much admired by Marx:

> a man only succeeds in becoming rich through damaging others . . . all
> our civic institutions, our social relationships, are nothing else but the

expression of legalised barbarism and piracy in which every man cheats and robs his neighbour.[2]

Either quote could have been matched by dozens of others, a century before or after.

Yet the advocates and the critics are wrong. Both characters—creative productivity and predation—are inherent to a system devoted to the discovery and realization of value. And both are inherent to every aspect of a capitalist economy, from entrepreneurship and innovation to finance and consumption.

CAPITALIST PRODUCTIVITY

The primary claim of capitalism is that it improves well-being and welfare. As the economist William Nordhaus has shown, improvements in health contributed as much to economic welfare as growth in consumption during the twentieth century.[3] But there is no doubting the extraordinary transformation of living standards that capitalism has helped to achieve in country after country.

This, the productive character of capitalism, has been extensively theorized. Indeed, understanding it has been the primary concern of modern economics which tells a story that goes roughly like this: the incentive to become rich motivates inventors to invent, entrepreneurs to assemble, investors to invest. Consumers then pay more for better products. And so long as capital is easily available to finance creative ideas, the market automatically drives constant improvement, and ever better ways of meeting our wants and needs.

Yet one of the fascinating aspects of the history of capitalism is that understanding of its productive power has been so partial, and often so belated. Economics has succeeded much better at explaining dynamics within markets than explaining the dynamics of the economy as a whole. A succession of theories have attempted to explain growth, but all have faced so many exceptions as to be suspect.

It was once thought that quantities of capital should explain higher growth: more inputs leading to outputs. But the many growth models that attempted to show how capital and labor would drive GDP all left a huge unexplained residual (the economist Thomas Balogh ironically called this third factor the "co-efficient of ignorance"). Investment is a necessary but not sufficient condition for growth, and can be grotesquely inefficient (economies as varied as 1990s Japan and 1960s Soviet Union proved that it's possible to pump vast sums of money into investment without generating real growth).

At other times, it was assumed that good education must feed through into economic growth. The OECD claims that better exam results for fifteen-year-olds are followed a few years later by modest but measurable improvements in economic growth. But though partially true, this thesis too has many counterexamples, again, most glaringly the former USSR or 1980s Ireland, and it remains the case that there is no clear correlation between education spending and economic results. Another set of arguments ascribe growth to geography—temperate climates without too many vicious diseases are where capitalism triumphs.[4] There can be no doubt that climate, and shifts in climate, can dramatically change economic fortunes: there are good reasons for expecting new areas to boom as a result of climate change, from northern Canada to Siberia and Scandinavia, which combine the benefits of strong educational institutions, extensive global links, and a rapidly improving climate.[5] But the argument that climate is a primary cause of growth is threadbare, unable to explain why for so much of human history the temperate zones were relatively backward, or why such tropical places as Malaysia or Guangdong are prospering now.

Then again culture has sometimes been given the leading role. For Max Weber it was Calvinism, and the need to demonstrate God's goodwill that explained the birth of capitalism. Fifty years ago a famous book by the Swedish social scientist Gunnar Myrdal explained why east Asia was condemned to slow growth because of its Confucian culture, which would militate against risk and innovation, smothering progress in excessive deference to tradition and hierarchy. Barely two decades later many other books argued that the same Confucian culture's dedication to education and hard work explained why east Asia was booming.

Similar arguments attribute growth to cultures of entrepreneurship: some countries are just better suited to taking risks. Each year more people in the United States start a business than get married or have children, and we're told that it's easier there to pick yourself up after an initial failure or bankruptcy. A culture in which it is acceptable to take risks is likely to be more conducive to innovation and new ideas. But here, too, the facts are reluctant to fit the stereotypes. The most entrepreneurial countries are not the ones usually seen as entrepreneurial. According to the most thorough recent analysis of the available data, the United States is "in the bottom third when measured by the number of young businesses per capita . . . and in the middle of the countries when it comes to new business formation per capita."[6] As economies grow, levels of entrepreneurship tend to fall (mainly because of the rising opportunity costs associated with giving up a paid job), and many economies would probably grow more slowly if more people left their jobs and tried to start new businesses. Many people say that they start businesses to avoid working for others, and the majority of entrepreneurs are not technology whiz kids but middle-aged people in typical towns and cities starting new services. Whatever the motivations, a high proportion fail, and governments' support for start-ups has rarely made much economic sense, even if a small minority of entrepreneurs grows very rich. Entrepreneurship clearly matters for economic growth; but it is quality more than quantity that counts.

Another set of recent explanations—vigorously promoted by Douglass North—emphasizes institutions: get the institutions right, with the rule of law and well-functioning markets, and growth will follow. To some extent this is true, but advocates of this point of view have struggled to explain China, which has substantially ignored the prescriptions of Western theorists and grown all the same (although China's institutions have changed markedly, they still fall far short of the conventional prescription). China and India also challenge the widespread view that worsening corruption is incompatible with rapid and sustainable growth. We'd much rather believe that vice is punished by history: but the evidence suggests that it isn't.

Then there are the many theories ascribing growth to technology, and incentives for invention. A century and a half ago Karl Marx predicted that what he called "general intellect" would become a productive force. He imagined it as embodied in machines, yet it is as much embodied in people, highly skilled scientists, managers, or lawyers. At roughly the same time Friedrich List wrote that "the accumulation of all discoveries, inventions, improvements, perfections and exertions of all generations . . . form the intellectual capital of the present human race,"[7] and he persuaded Prussia to invest not only in railways but also in technical training institutes and business subsidies to grow that capital, a strategy that succeeded beyond his wildest dreams.

Knowledge is clearly a decisive contributor to growth: new products and greater variety of products and services have a direct effect on human welfare.[8] A recent study suggested that a one standard deviation rise in the economic complexity of a nation's economy increases its growth rate by 1.6 percent a year.[9] Recognition of the importance of general intellect has justified a great expansion of public subsidy for basic research, and a battery of legal protections for inventors. China is boosting spending on research and development to 1.5 percent of GDP, and 2.5 percent by 2025; India aims to build 800–1,000 new universities, and already produces three million graduates each year.[10] All assume that greater state spending on knowledge will boost the economy. But despite rapid growth in spending; despite the publication of some 3,000 academic papers every day; despite the daily filing of almost 2,000 patents in the U.S. Patent Office; and despite the world's creation of as much data every two days as it did in all its history up to 2003, there is no evidence that innovation is speeding up. R&D has a modest but not strong correlation with GDP per capita (though the direction of causation is unclear), and there is no clear correlation between growth of R&D spending and per capita GDP.[11] The same applies to firms in the late 2000s, when, before its near-terminal collapse, General Motors had the largest research budget of any company in the United States (and globally three of the top four R&D spenders are car companies).[12]

Nor is there much link between the ever more sophisticated worlds of private finance and the worlds of innovation. Venture capital has provided significant flows of finance for risky and imaginative ideas but now funds only a tiny fraction of technology start-ups, even in the United States. Within business as a whole, the largest source of finance for innovation is the retained earnings of big firms. Silicon Valley is typical in its continued dependence on public funding, and in other countries that have established strong competitive positions in technology, such as Taiwan, Israel, or Finland, public funding has played decisive roles as well. When examined globally, the surprise is how small a role capital markets play in financing innovation, not how large.

Most governments accept that they have to finance risky and unproven ideas. But it's less clear whether they should fund basic research or technologies that are closer to market. When a nation's scientists achieve extraordinary breakthroughs in genetics or polymers, they're undoubtedly benefitting the world; but it's not guaranteed that they'll benefit their fellow citizens more than anyone else. To the extent that R&D does influence growth, it's as much through people as through codified knowledge: for example, gifted PhD students going to work for high-technology companies. Yet on all of these issues weak measurements make definitive conclusions difficult.[13]

The role of intellectual property in explaining productivity and growth is even more uncertain. Intellectual property is neither very intellectual (it's hard to think of any important intellectual advance that was protected in law) nor is it exactly property. The theory of relativity, the invention of computing, and the discovery of DNA were certainly not incentivized or rewarded by property rights. Penicillin was discovered by accident, and ultimately commercialized mainly thanks to funding by the Rockefeller Foundation. The Internet and the World Wide Web were invented by employees in public laboratories. Some countries with relatively weak legal protection for intellectual property—such as Japan—have proven very innovative, and much of the most important current research—such as the human genome and the cancer genomes—are in the public domain. The economist John Kay comments that "the returns from intellectual property rights went not to those who had the great capacity for innovation, but to those who had the greatest capacity to pursue legal processes in order to claim intellectual property rights, deserved or otherwise."[14] What is protected is too narrow, and then too fiercely protected.

Other economists, notably William Nordhaus, while supporting the principle that ideas and inventions should benefit from legal protection, have shown that much of the benefit of new ideas and technology comes from their "spillovers" to the many people who don't pay for them directly. Any rules that constrain these spillovers too tightly work against public welfare. Similarly, protecting some kinds of knowledge is likely to impede innovation rather than help it: the extension of U.S. patent law to cover not only inventions but also discoveries—like the breast cancer gene BRCA1—turns a tool for rewarding imagination into a predatory tool for blocking off the imagination of others. Property rights clearly do play an important role in incentivizing investment and effort. But at least some of recent economic history can be understood as more like literature, where "the secret of all imagination is theft" as the novelist Richard Powers wrote. All businesses and cultures evolve through adaptation, and all adaptations skirt the borders of plagiarism,[15] a point made magnificently clear when Bill Gates observed to Steve Jobs that both had stolen ideas to make their fortune ("We both had this rich neighbor called Xerox and I broke into his house to steal the TV set and found out that you had already stolen it").[16]

The idea that commercialization of university research will fuel growth has also been more hype than reality: a "cargo cult" as one prominent academic put it.[17] In the mid-2000s, IBM registered nearly ten times as many patents as the whole University of California and twenty times as many as MIT, and only 197 patents out of 27,322 held by U.S. universities made more than $1 million in earnings. Again and again second movers have done better than first movers; dull sectors have grown more than glamorous ones (wholesale and retail contributed more to U.S. productivity growth in the 1990s than telecoms); and the adapters of ideas have grown richer than the inventors.[18] China may now be a good demonstration of this; through companies like

Baidu, its equivalent of Google, it aims to run "as fast as possible . . . to remain at the cusp of the global technology frontier without actually advancing the frontier itself."[19]

The ambiguous effects of property rights have led some to emphasize a very different view of how knowledge helps growth. The French socioeconomist Yann Moulier Boutang writes about growth-promoting "cognitive externalities,"[20] and societies in which the presence of general knowledge makes it easier to cross-pollinate ideas, thus generating more profitable opportunities. This is partly why innovation is still so shaped by clusters. Intensive networks in particular places, or horizontal clusters linking similar firms, and vertical clusters linking supply chains—grow up mainly because of the flow of knowledge that isn't protected by the law.

British shipbuilding in the mid-nineteenth century is a good example: founded on learned societies and clubs where thousands of engineers shared their ideas, there was a strong culture of sharing and openness, and a principled hostility to intellectual property rights. Indeed, every feature of what came to be called "open innovation" could be found there, and the result was an industry that utterly dominated the global shipbuilding market.[21] So innovation, and growth, thrive primarily where the elements of new ideas already exist—in the form of technologies or practices—alongside skilled intermediaries, brokers, and connectors to combine them in new ways. Knowledge and collective intelligence in this view are public goods that can be shared at very low cost; one person's consumption doesn't reduce what's available to anyone else. It is certainly true that innovations breed other innovations, with combinations of existing things leading to dramatically new things. The iPod, for example, combines ideas from the digital music devices put on the market by others a decade earlier and the MP3 compression software developed in Germany by the Fraunhofer Institute, while the iTunes it plays directly adopted the music listing techniques pioneered by Napster. The more elements there are lying around, the more new ideas are likely to emerge. The deeper the craft skills available to design to shape them, the more likely it is that the economy will grow.

New industries and businesses have risen up around this insight, no longer selling a service, or even knowledge, but rather providing the platforms on which others can create knowledge or services. eBay, Google, and Skype are businesses of this kind: much of what they provide is given away free to users, and yet their value comes less from their own inventiveness[22] than from the value that is then produced by users in collaboration with each other, and for each other. That value also depends in turn on the cognitive abilities of their users, much more than was the case for earlier infrastructures like roads or railways: indeed, all of these newer industries thrive from a kind of co-creation that is very different from the classic economic idea of consumption. Together they constitute a digital base for the economic superstructure, a base that allows for constant feedback for an economy and society that are becoming ever more self-aware. Google is in this sense halfway to being a public service, closer in spirit to utilities or universities, even though it can also be seen as just a much more efficient vehicle for organizing advertising (and over 96 percent of its profits still come from just one, brilliantly executed, idea—targeted advertising linked to search).[23] Either way it's troubling that a more reflexive, intelligent economy may do so little to create jobs: General Electric, with a comparable capitalization to Google, employs ten times as many people.[24]

What conclusions can we draw? We know that technology plays a disproportionately important role in growth;[25] more broadly we know that knowledge in a wider sense is also decisive, and probably becoming more so. But we don't know quite how; we can't meaningfully measure either the inputs to knowledge or its outputs; and the actions that follow are uncertain, as much a craft as a science.

Other issues that are equally fundamental to the nature of capitalism's productivity also remain unresolved. It was once assumed that poor countries would grow faster than rich ones as they caught up, taking advantage of superior technologies developed in the rich west. Yet between 1960 and 2000, rich countries grew faster than poor ones. Then there was the assumption that inequality is part of what gives capitalism its energy: it creates a stronger incentive to succeed, and not to fail. But some of the strongest performers have been relatively equal, sometimes benefitting from radical redistributions of wealth and land (as in South Korea). So perhaps equality helps growth: the rich may be more prone to unproductive investment than the poor (think of conspicuous consumption); boosting human capital for the poor rather than the rich may deliver better returns because their talents are more likely to have gone unrecognized, and the patterns of demand from poor people are more likely to be for local goods and services.[26] Here again, though, there is no definitive pattern, and certainly no clear correlation between either equality or inequality and levels of innovation.

The former U.S. Treasury secretary Larry Summers once said that the laws of economics are universal. Yet there are no absolute laws that remain true across time and space. Higher prices should mean less demand—but luxury goods prove the opposite, and there are many examples of firms raising prices and then finding more consumers. Lower interest rates should mean less savings—but repeatedly lower interest rates have had the opposite effect, either because savers were targeting a future rate of return, or because they had become more fearful of the future. Economics has been brilliant at spotting patterns and regularities, and providing a disciplined way of thinking about human behavior and counterintuitive causal relationships. But where economics does find regularities these seem to be contingent, limited to particular eras and places rather than being as universal as the laws of physics.

Nor have the theorists of capitalism been successful in their forecasts. To take just one example, who anticipated the extraordinary growth of intermediaries that has accompanied economic growth? Between 1870 and 1970 the transaction sector of the U.S. economy grew from 25 percent to 45 percent of GNP as the economy learned to deal not only with the uncertainties of the physical environment but also with those of the human environment. Intermediate roles grew because their impact on productivity outweighed the costs, in a remarkable rebuff to many forecasts that capitalism would see the radical "disintermediation" of intermediaries. Schumpeter described bureaucracy as the unavoidable handmaiden of democracy. But it's also turned out to be the unavoidable handmaiden of capitalism, which probably outdoes even communism in the sheer scale of its paperwork, its records, bookkeeping, and now its vast data warehouses, all overseen by a prosperous army of overseers—the information managers, accountants, auditors, lawyers, inspectors, and assurers.

If the conventional explanations for capitalism's productivity all turn out to be at best partial, there is always the fallback of basing your explanation on divine will. John D. Rockefeller saw the growth of big business as "merely the working out of a law of nature and a law of God." When a century later Goldman Sachs's chairman Lloyd Blankfein said that his company did "God's work" he won few friends, but this explanation at least has the virtue of being hard to disprove.[27]

It would be going too far to say that capitalism is a mystery to capitalism. But it is opaque. Capitalism is seen by itself through a glass darkly, prone to surprise its own experts.

CAPITALIST PREDATION

If capitalist productivity and creativity are less obvious than they appear, what of its other side, its predatory character? Predation has been rather less extensively theorized, yet it has always been part of the human condition. In the natural world predators kill their prey: ambushing, poisoning, or wearing them down. This is a binary world where one lives and another dies, and where even the predators face intense competition. A cheetah has a 50 percent chance of losing its kill to other predators, and up to 90 percent of cheetah cubs are killed in their first weeks of life by leopards, lions, and hyenas.

Throughout our history and prehistory we too have been beset by predators. Once they were saber-toothed tigers, the beasts that lurked in the dark as people huddled around the fire. When people turned to farming, plagues of locusts became an even worse threat. But from the earliest times the predators also included other people. Society meant dog eating dog, man eating man. As Plautus and later Thomas Hobbes put it, "*homo homini lupus*": man is a wolf to man. The record is full of villages and communities utterly laid waste, with mass graves of butchered and decapitated men, women and children. And so our history evolved by fits and starts to contain predation: to protect us from each other. We learned to extend the principles of the small group and the family where we share and take turns, and where the strongest don't automatically bully the weakest. History can be read as the continuing struggle for a society free from predation, free from neighbors taking advantage of neighbors, firms exploiting workers or politicians lining their own pockets.

As I've shown, the advocates of capitalism claimed to offer an alternative to the predatory instincts of feudalism and strong states alike, while the critics castigated it for legitimating the greed of the speculator and the rapaciousness of the factory owner. In this view it is always about imbalances of power, and those imbalances are invariably exploited by the winners to crush the losers. The more concentrated the power, the more opportunities for predation; the more invisible the relationships of power, the more chances there are to take advantage of others.[28]

The view of orthodox economic theory is the precise opposite of this. It has tended to describe all exchanges as happening between equals. We go out into the market to sell our labor in competition with others, but with choice. We go out into the market as consumers to freely spend our money as we wish.

Predation certainly has a place in economic theory, but it is a strictly limited place, defined as the exceptional result of monopoly rather than as the rule. If one firm has a monopoly in a market it will exploit it—driving up profits, raising prices, and possibly lowering quality (which then justifies competition authorities to move in to break firms up or ban anti-competitive practices). Not all monopolies are bad: they may just result for a time from entrepreneurial brilliance—being ahead of the game. But at least there is a recognition that excessive power will usually lead to abuses.[29]

The other lens through which economics has made sense of predation is through the study of how firms and others extract economic rent: "directly unproductive profit seeking activities" in the definition of Jagdish Bhagwati.[30] This use of the word "rent" to describe predatory behavior goes back to Adam Smith, who distinguished between three types of income: profit, wages, and rent. His starting point was that profits, like wages, result from mutually beneficial trade, whereas rents result from asymmetries and the exploitation of assets that aren't in themselves productive (landowners for example benefit from rent, even though it is only the labor done to their land that makes it useful). In this view profits are good, while rents are bad.

Although land plays a much smaller part in economic life today, rents of all kinds are arguably much more important, and since the 1970s the phrase "rent-seeking" has come to be used to describe any type of strategy to derive income through means other than the creation of value: lobbying, manipulating standards or regulations, or blocking new entrants.[31] As the world's leading contemporary expert on public finance commented on the 70,000 pages of the U.S. federal tax code,

> strange and previously unnoticed special tax preferences, worth billions of dollars to some industry or even a specific company, find their way into these laws and occasionally surface, surprising everyone except those who had inserted them or lobbied for them.[32]

Mancur Olson claimed that rent-seeking of this kind explained much about why some nations stagnate: the vested interests of big firms, trade unions, and other incumbents use their power to suck value out of the genuinely productive economy.[33] Much the same could be said to happen within politics: in the public choice theory that applied economic concepts to the state, predation is also presented as common. Bureaucrats and politicians who gain monopoly power over such things as the award of licenses, or public procurement, will tend to grant themselves greater rewards, or to collude with well-entrenched vested interests. States will tend to overtax; agencies will tend to overcharge; and in all cases the default will be to prevent competition or the free flow of information.

Rent-seeking and predation are much more common in some industries than others: oil and mining, for example, are organized around monopoly licenses for prospecting, drilling, and digging, close relationships with governments, and highly cartelized systems for distribution. Pharmaceuticals is built around the temporary monopolies of patent law, but also close relationships with public bodies that fund much basic research and buy many of the drugs that then result from the R&D.[34] Even the apparently dynamic field of biotechnology generates its own forms of predation: recent researchers have shown, for example, how often biopharma companies have delivered large returns to investors, and executives with stock-based pay, even when the firms themselves have remained unprofitable.[35]

Retailing and retail banking are other sectors that often drift toward oligopoly and rent, in part because they create local monopolies, while information technology has tended to throw up monopolies too, partly because of the massive economies of scale associated with software (Microsoft), microprocessors (Intel), or search engines (Google). Some governments have drawn on economic theory to block predation, with aggressive anti-trust and competition policies, which have usually left behind more efficient firms. But the huge sums spent by many industries on lobbying attest to the fact that they often gain greater returns from proximity to power than from better serving their customers.

Indeed, without strict rules to prevent them, the richest industries will literally buy up politicians and their parties: it's no coincidence that Wall Street and the City of London have played such leading roles in financing the major political parties, and former leaders often find lucrative positions in and around investment banks.[36]

The economist William Baumol has argued persuasively that how a society's institutions are organized determines whether entrepreneurial energies go into creating genuine value, or into rent-seeking, whether legal or illegal. In some contexts lobbying pays off; so does aggressive litigation. Many past societies rewarded those who were most adept at gaining the favor of the king or nobles over those who were most adept at creating useful technologies or services, and ended up paying a price in the form of less prosperity.[37] The scale of the lobbying and legal industries in advanced capitalist societies is one symptom of the continued prevalence of predation; but so too is the ability of some firms to position themselves with privileged access to key markets, or to sources of capital, in ways that help them take the lion's share of the rewards from innovative activity undertaken by others.

The theoretical understanding of predation has advanced a good deal over the last forty years. But it still remains largely absent from the everyday account of market economies, and the assumption that the greatest possible freedom serves markets best. Yet these ideas of economics help us to give more precise definition to predation, which intriguingly converges with fundamental ideas from ethics. One of the foundations of most moral systems, including Judaism, Buddhism, Christianity, and Islam, is the golden rule—the principle that you should do unto others as you would have them do unto you. In a perfect market people act according to the golden rule, and this is also the moral basis of the free market: that it is founded in freedom and reciprocity. In Adam Smith's formulation profit abides by the golden rule; rent breaks it.

The golden rule is not a requirement for equality; indeed, it can lead to very unequal results; we may be willing to pay much more for another's time than we can earn if we see it as a fair recognition of the time they spent training to be a doctor, the intellect that made them a lawyer, or the sheer talent that made them a brilliant musician. A predatory trade or transaction by contrast is one that breaches this principle, one that is not reciprocal.

This principle is simple and immediately graspable. Yet predation as defined in this way is not always easy to pin down. It's not surprising that economics has struggled to distinguish between profit (the result of free exchange) and rent (the result of unequal power), since so few real markets involve equality of power and information. Often predation is easier to see in retrospect than in advance (and this is certainly true of technologies, an issue I address in chapter 8). When, for example, is it predatory for a supermarket to drive out small retailers thanks to its lower costs and aggressive marketing? When is it predatory for a group of teachers to demand that all teachers should have a teaching qualification? In all of these cases values intersect with measurable value.

That's far from being the only problem. Given that all resources are distributed unequally, there can be no precise definition of what counts as exploitation and what is merely the protection of self-interest. To make the most of your endowments isn't by its nature predatory or exploitative. Instead, there are shades of grey between the two extremes of giving all of your resources away like a saint, and using them in ways that harm, humiliate, and disempower others who need them more than you do. Doing unto others as you would have them do unto you leaves plenty of room for discussion, and we generally accept that someone who is endowed with talent, or an oil well, should enjoy some disproportionate benefit even if it's a matter of luck that they are so endowed: predation and exploitation refer to the more extreme uses of advantage that most obviously breach the golden rule.

There's also another ambiguity around predation, which I return to later but is important to mention here. At least some of the spirit of entrepreneurs is predator-like, even if it creates genuine value for others. The best entrepreneurs hunt out opportunities, and love the thrill of the chase. Their hunger and appetite help to drive change and creativity, and mirror the hunger of artists and scientists following their own hunches and curiosity.

A parallel to predation is the related phenomenon of free-riding. It's often possible to benefit like a predator without acting like one. A free rider gains without contributing. They may be part of a team, or a family, where others do the hard work. Clearly their action, or lack of it, breaches the golden rule. Given how much of our history has been spent living in small groups and families, it's not surprising that we are acutely sensitive to free-riding, and quick to resent or punish it. But in complex capitalist societies free-riding may be harder to spot. The nineteenth-century rentiers who lived a life of leisure funded by their shares were a very visible example of free-riding, which breached every capitalist virtue of productivity and hard work. The middle-income home owner who benefits from rising house prices, or the stock owner who simply tracks the market, are, strictly speaking, free riders too, but it's harder to see who is losing when they gain. Parallel questions surround the problem of inheritance: a system whose moral basis stems from its productivity creates groups of people with no need to work at all, free-riding both on their parents' hard work in the past, and, effectively, on the hard work of all the other people who serve their needs in the present.

Although economics has a crisp definition of predation in monopoly and rent-seeking,[38] few economists have wrestled with the subtleties of the predatory side of capitalism. One exception was Thorstein Veblen, who saw economics in evolutionary terms, shaped by the human instincts of emulation, curiosity and parental commitment, as well as predation. *The Theory of Business Enterprise*, published in 1904, portrayed the unstoppable dynamic toward trusts and combinations, driven by the economies of scale inherent in the new industrial processes. In Veblen's view, businessmen were the predators in the new industrial capitalism, while engineers were the true creators. Naturally, the two groups were often locked in conflict. Looking to the future, Veblen feared the predatory attitude might spread beyond businessmen. In time it might "become the habitual and accredited spiritual attitude" and the fight might "become the dominant note in the current theory of life."

Contemporary capitalism is certainly full of predation as well as extraordinary productivity, and much of the predation is not adequately captured by economic theory. Financial regulators have struggled to contain what they see as the many forms of rent-seeking achieved by investment banks, hedge funds, and derivatives providers taking advantage of asymmetries of knowledge in ever more complex financial products. They have also struggled to contain the temptations to predation that are so common in relation to land and property, which appear to promise profit without much work or even risk, and then, repeatedly, become the source of systemic crises when prices collapse.

Predation can also be seen, scarcely veiled, in the relationship between finance and the rest of the economy. Faced with pressure from shareholders for visible profits, it is rational for financers to act in predatory ways, extracting as much as quickly as possible. In 1947, the financial sector represented only 2.5 percent of U.S. gross domestic product. In 2006 it had risen to 8 percent, roughly the moment when $2 of every $5 of corporate profits in the United States were accounted for by finance. It is hard to imagine any plausible explanation of how finance could contribute such a high proportion of genuine value: systematic, if complex, predation is the only way to make sense of such strange distortions. Of course, predation made some people very rich: two-thirds of all income gains during the boom years (2002 to 2007) went to the top 1 percent of the population, with the top fifty hedge and private equity fund managers averaging $588 million in annual compensation, more than 19,000 times as much as the average U.S. worker.[39] To cap it all, they paid lower tax rates on income—15 percent—than their cleaners and secretaries. These were not rewards for creating value for others. Instead, they reflect complex patterns in which a few were able to exploit asymmetries of power and information.

In much of the world the investment needs of productive activity have to be met from cash flow, while financial markets simply circulate money, detached from real uses. No wonder Paul Volcker (the former Federal Reserve Chairman) commented: "I wish somebody would give me some shred of evidence linking financial innovation with a benefit to the economy" (the one exception he could think of was the Automated Teller Machine).

Predation is also to be found in the relationship between the employer and employee. In the Marxist critique of capitalism, what appeared on the surface as a fair and free exchange allowed the capitalist to extract surplus from the worker. To guarantee the conditions for exploitation, the capitalist had to construct a system in which the mass of the people would have no choice but to take exploitative jobs. This is Karl Polanyi on the ideologies of the nineteenth-century liberals who helped to design the social systems that allowed industry to thrive:

> while the pauper, for the sake of humanity, should be relieved, the unemployed, for the sake of industry, should not be relieved. That the unemployed worker was innocent of his fate did not matter. The point was

not whether he might or might not have found work, but that unless he was in danger of famishing with only the abhorred workhouse for an alternative, the wage system would break down, thus throwing society into misery and chaos.[40]

The sociologist Pierre Bourdieu argued that "*precarité*," precariousness, is a mode of domination: this is why politicians and business leaders so often deliberately talk up insecurity and the inevitability of change. Their aim is to encourage fear. So too does the "reserve army" of the unemployed keep discipline among the employed. It may appear wasteful, lacking any function. Yet one of its roles is to prevent the freedom of exit, the right to choose, the right to escape from the day-to-day iniquities of exploitation, the predation of the boss on the worker.

These accounts don't tell the whole story, and they don't easily explain rising levels of pay, improving work conditions, and the long periods when modern economies have sustained close to full employment. But they do contain important truths, and any employer knows that they are playing both a positive sum game with their employees (where greater productivity benefits both) and a zero sum game (where more pay for the workers means less for the investors and the bosses).

Perhaps an even starker area of predation is the home. The capitalist economy was built on the rock of the family (and the roots of the word "economy" originally referred to the household). But the women who worked at home to raise their children and to feed their men received no pay and remained invisible both to the employers and to successive generations of male economists. In societies where wives forfeited their property to husbands, they were doubly disempowered and alienated, their time and their freedom no longer their own. Coverture— the legal position that subordinated wives to husbands—ruled in both Britain and the United States throughout the period of industrialization, and according to some historians it was this provision of unpaid and unrecognized work that did as much to fuel the Industrial Revolution as Spanish gold or English inventions.[41]

Alongside predation in the home, and probably more dangerous, is predation of the mind: the capture of attention and thoughts. The threat of mental predation was much debated in the middle of the twentieth century, as advertising boomed and businesses experimented with new ways to make people want their products. Half a century after Vance Packard's *Hidden Persuaders* warned of subliminal advertising, whole industries have grown up that feed off mental vulnerabilities and addictions. In economies where information is almost free, attention has become far more valuable, and far more contested. The inhabitant of a typical city may see well over a thousand commercial images every day, fighting for their attention, seeding ideas or dissatisfactions—and colonizing mental space that might otherwise have been devoted to friends or family or God. These are sometimes sought out—but most breach the golden rule, and the more we understand them the less we want to be exposed and manipulated. The deliberate imposition of messages often also entails the deliberate exclusion of competing messages. The privately run public piazzas, malls, and arcades that have proliferated in modern cities usually ban any kind of civic action or communication, such as petitions, banners, and stalls. The "brand exclusion zone" in the London Olympics, which extended a kilometer beyond the Olympic Park, went even further, a particularly bizarre assertion of property rights: it banned advertising for brands competing with the official Olympic sponsors as well as preventing spectators from wearing clothes showing competing brands.

In these cases, as in the workplace and the home, predation is made possible by imbalances of power, and then reinforces them. But it can also lead to a perverse dependence, locking the prey into an intimate relationship with the predator. The Stockholm Syndrome is an extreme variant of this, when kidnap victims come to identify with their kidnappers; domestic violence is a more commonplace one. Usually it's the fear of change or of the unknown that locks the victim in. Sometimes it's just the "voluntary servitude" of habit that happens when the prey are less able to organize themselves than the predators. But all of us are vulnerable to predation simply because so much human work involves capturing the love, commitment, and time of others to a purpose that they didn't invent. The very qualities that make humans connect also make them possible to exploit—our desire to belong, to be recognized, or to be part of something larger, renders us vulnerable, and we can only fully escape predation by living in a cave.

Sometimes the victims even adopt predator ideologies. These are the ideologies that praise the hunters, the winners, and the masters. Nietzsche captured their worldview. So did Nazism, and the harsher strands of neoliberalism, or the neoconservatism of Leo Strauss. Ayn Rand translated similar ideas into a language more easily digested by business people, with the same contempt for the weak, the failures, the incapable, and an associated contempt for the philosophies of compassion that come from Christianity and the other great faiths. In this view the meek are anything but blessed. The meek are only weak.

It's obvious why these ideologies might appeal to the winners. Max Weber wrote of the "theodicy of good fortune"—how people who are successful want to feel they deserve it, even if they are in truth more free riders than creators of their own wealth. He also suggested a mirror "theodicy of suffering" that explains to the losers, the unlucky and the poor, why they are suffering and why they should accept the cruelty of the world. Marx called it "false consciousness": we certainly all have a great need to believe in the sense of the world, that it has meaning, and this pulls those on the receiving end of domination to want to accept it as natural, even if another part of our nature rails against the unfairness.

THE MEANS OF DESTRUCTION

No account of progress in the means of production is complete that doesn't account for its intimate connection to progress in the means of destruction. When Samuel Johnson complained in the eighteenth century that "the age is running mad after innovation," he cited as an example that the execution ground of "Tyburn itself is not safe from the fury of innovation."[42] A few decades later, France took great pride in the guillotine (and a century after that, one of the entrants for the competition that led to the Eiffel Tower was a vast model guillotine). In the United States the electric chair became a symbol of progress. Much of the logic of modern manufacturing was drawn from the military. Maurice of Orange designed detailed moves for soldiers, with thirty-two specified moves for firing and reloading, and obsessive practice, an approach justified both by its remarkable success on the battlefield and as a Calvinist solution to the problems of idleness in military life. Just as the mechanization of industry was preceded in warfare, so too was automation. Computing grew from the military tasks of anti-aircraft guns and codebreaking. More recently, military spending gave rise, through the Defense Advanced Research Projects Agency (DARPA) to the Internet.

It is no coincidence that every dominant economic power has also been a dominant military power. The Venetians, the Dutch, the English, and the Americans matched trading prowess with prowess at sea and on land. Traders need protection, whether from capricious governments, or from pirates. But the military role went far beyond protection. Conquest opened up markets, and military might governed the terms of trade. Capitalism spread in tandem with historically unusual superpowers, the United Provinces (of the Netherlands), the United Kingdom (of Britain), and the United States (of America), whose names signaled how different they were from the traditional empires built around a single center of power. In each case wealth was not only earned but also taken, on vast scales. Earlier, theorists of capitalism were perhaps more honest about this than later ones. Thomas More's Utopia justified colonization as a means to make the land more fruitful, while John Locke argued for the virtue of taking over underused land even against the wishes of its inhabitants. John Davies, the foremost advocate of the colonization of Ireland (whose ideas encouraged the displacement of my ancestors from their lands in Donegal) believed in a god-given right, or even duty, to make land as productive as possible. Productivity and the search for exchangeable value were presented by all of them as a moral imperative: rough, harsh even, but part of the higher purpose of humanity.

Empire and colonization was also a primary concern for Adam Smith. His books are packed with detailed analysis of long-distance trade in such things as sealskins and wool, and with the movements of a banking system that he called "a highway through the air." Writing at a time of perpetual war with France, he was as acutely conscious of the connections between military force and wealth as he was oblivious to the industrial revolution taking place around him.

Military power isn't always used very intelligently for economic ends—the extreme military dominance of the United States has only bluntly served commercial and other strategic goals. Empires tend to be drawn to overstretch, victims of their own lust for glory. But it is now, as in the past, hard to see how one nation could be supreme economically and another supreme militarily. Imagine, for example, that China dramatically overtook the United States in terms of GDP while the United States retained military superiority. How would each use its power? Would China invest its wealth in military technology? Would the United States use its might to block China from markets, or access to raw materials?[43]

If military power and predation are hard to separate from the dynamics of markets, another kind of predation may matter even more. This is the subtler, sometimes invisible, predation of the whole economy on the systems on which economic life depends. Economies appear to be self-sufficient, and are presented in economic theory as closed systems of circulation. Indeed, the radical break achieved by modern economics lay in the idea that there is a realm of production and consumption that is essentially detached from other social realities and can be understood as if it is self-contained. But real economies are not self-contained, especially if seen in any long view. They depend on flows from other systems. One of the most important is scientific knowledge, which can be organized either as a commons or as private property, but which has mushroomed over the last few centuries largely as an open commons guided by the pursuit of truth rather than ownership. Another vital input for any economy is the family, which produces children ready for work, socializing them, inculcating them with morality, and nurturing the ability to work in teams.

Slavery disappeared in part because the production of people is poor business, even with minimal pay and maximum power in the hands of the employer.

Perhaps even more important than these are the natural systems from which derives much of the value that appears in the economy. If businesses had to pay the full cost of clean air, water, natural waste management, and agricultural production, their business models would soon evaporate. The idea that the economy depends on natural capital as well as financial and human capital was first floated in the 1950s and has steadily become more widely accepted.[44] Kenneth Arrow and Partha Dasgupta are among the leading economists who have attempted to measure these patterns, with studies of "comprehensive wealth" that take account of education levels on the one hand, and natural capital on the other.[45] Seen in this light, the position of many developing countries deteriorated in the last quarter of the twentieth century. Businesses and governments had taken more than they had made, and a recent assessment put the deterioration of natural value at some \$2–4 trillion each year, a similar order of cost to the financial crisis.[46]

Ecological capacities are inherently limited, whereas human demands are not. So where consumption runs up against "planetary boundaries"[47] our behaviors may have predatory effects, however benign their intentions. This unbalanced relationship between economies and nature can be seen in the accelerating use of finite resources of coal, oil, and gas, with world energy demand forecast to rise some 50 percent over the next twenty-five years as economic growth and growth in energy use continue to be tightly coupled.[48] The ecologist Murray Bookchin ascribed both human and natural predation to hierarchy and domination; people who believe that they have the right to exploit others will also see the planet and ecosphere as resources to be exploited. "The plundering of the human spirit by the market place is paralleled by the plundering of the earth by capital," an idea more familiar in popular culture than in academic analysis. The 2009 film *Avatar*, for example, portrayed an indigenous people whose land is under attack from a technologically advanced, cold and cruel corporation, which aims not only to plunder its natural resources but also to destroy a society. This is a common trope in culture: clearly millions of people find it easy to identify with the creatures who literally become prey to the predatory corporation.

The predation that takes place in each of these fields is not irrational; often, as in the case of *Avatar*, it's hyperrational. If the goal of an enterprise is to maximize its profits, it should seek to extract as much as possible from these other systems and pay as little as possible back. Marshall McLuhan, the infamous theorist of the mass media, defined art as "whatever you can get away with." Predatory capitalism could be defined in the same way.

This is an ugly aspect of market economies, and often ignored by economists with the euphemistic language of "externalities" and "rent." Yet these different kinds of predation have long dominated politics. Governments and legislators, under pressure from the public, try to rein in such evils as the exploitation of child labor and the degradation of the biosphere. Governments are no slouches when it comes to being predators themselves: but much of their legitimacy derives from their ability to protect people against other predators, whether warlords and gangs or exploitative owners.

Looking to the future there will be new opportunities for predation. Some of these will come where economic power and military power reinforce each other: in the actions of a newly confident Russia and China improving the terms on which they secure the most valued raw materials and forcing open markets for their goods. Predation also happens through networks that range from organized-crime syndicates to currency trading. Some of the most malign new examples of predation are cyber attacks, like Stuxnet[49] in 2010, often unclear in their origins and potentially devastating in their effects. But within the rule of law there are also new opportunities for using intellectual property in predatory ways, like the dubious, and vigorously contested, claims being made for ownership of the human genome. Huge profits are being made by web aggregators, making available content that they do nothing to produce, a good example of classic monopolistic power in a new form.

All of these pose a theoretical challenge, particularly for economics. The great triumph of economics in the 1930s was its success in achieving a systemic view of how economies work. GDP was invented as a tool for measuring the economy in a comprehensive way. In the 1920s, governments simply had no way of knowing whether their economy was growing or shrinking: they could look at share prices, or freight volumes on the railways, but overall they were flying blind. GDP provided a framework for measuring output as well as income. In parallel, a group of economists, inspired by Keynes, developed theoretical models to illustrate the often counterintuitive dynamics of the macroeconomy. In time these became part of the armory of modern government, the indispensable tools for keeping economies growing.

We still need economics to better master the dynamic interactions of savings and investment, consumption and trade, demand and supply (and GDP needs constant improvement, for example to capture the productivity of public services that are currently measured according to what they cost, not what they produce). But perhaps we need, even more, an economics that can think systemically in a broad sense, and bring a comparable rigor to the interactions between the economy and the systems on which it depends: for example understanding the interactions between the resilience of economies and the resilience of natural systems, or understanding what happens when families are squeezed too hard. Here the energetic work under way on new indicators (such as measures of ecological capital or well-being) to adapt or complement GDP, intersects with new thinking about the dynamics to be found on the boundaries of systems, such as studies of time accounts. The research being done to analyze natural systems as producers of value, providing services such as clean water or removing waste, offers another part of the picture: the United Nations Millennium Ecosystem Assessment (MA) project involved more than 1,300 scientists worldwide in an attempt to estimate the value of such things as the production of food and water and†crop pollination.[50] Other estimates have shown radically new ways of thinking about the value of ecosystems: showing for example that global fisheries underperform by $50 billion compared to their potential if managed more sustainably.

The value of bees has been estimated at five times the direct value of their products, while measurements of what economics calls "existence values," our willingness to pay just to know that something exists, suggest that European households would be willing to pay $46 per hectare per year to preserve Brazilian rain forests.[51]

These remain sketches rather than precise estimates that can guide policy. But they provide a radically different way of seeing the world and thinking about the relationships between systems.

Chapter 5

· · · · · · · · ·

Capitalism's Critics

What happens to a dream deferred?
Maybe it just sags
Like a heavy load
Or does it explode?

LANGSTON HUGHES, "A DREAM DEFERRED," 1926

THERE WERE MANY CAPITALISTS in the eighteenth century, when the word meant people with money, but there were surprisingly few exuberant advocates of a capitalist world. Adam Smith evangelized the virtues of free markets and laissez-faire public policies—but there was no place in his picture for large firms or concentrations of accumulated capital. The idea of a capitalist system came much later, and is generally attributed to the French socialist Louis Blanc.[1] For Blanc the word capitalism described a particularly unpleasant species of evil. All the ills that afflict society could be attributed to the pressure of competition, whereby the weaker are driven to the wall by the stronger. Capitalism was the latest but most dangerous example. It stood against nature, and certainly against the best of human nature. And it deserved to be confronted, with politics providing the best way to do so. So Blanc demanded the equalization of wages, and the merging of personal interests in the common good—"*à chacun selon ses besoins, de chacun selon ses facultés*" (from each according to his means to each according to his needs)—and he devised schemes and plans that would take power from the rich and give it to the poor.

Catapulted into government by the revolution of 1848, Blanc had a sudden opportunity to put his ideas into practice. So he introduced a right to work, and lobbied for funding for a network of cooperative workshops that would pioneer the future economy, with the money coming from the new railways, then seen as the cash cows for the emerging industrial economy. His plans never materialized, as the hopes of 1848 were crushed in the successfully coordinated revenge of the emperors and monarchs. Yet Blanc's view of capitalism was a common one in the nineteenth century. It was captured perfectly in a famous cartoon from the later years of the century, titled "Pyramid of Capitalist System," which portrays a system of rigid hierarchy, at the top of which there is great wealth, and at the bottom, the miserable poor. The monarchs sit on the top tier ("we rule you"). Next come the priests ("we fool you"), then the army ("we shoot you"), and on the widest layer the bourgeoisie ("we eat for you"). At the bottom are the workers. For those on the receiving end of capitalist power in the age of industrialization, it is striking how little appeal the system evidently had, even if the prospect of a wage, or of life in the city, was often better than the miserable alternatives. Few capitalists then felt comfortable with the idea of universal suffrage—giving the workers the right to decide what system they should live under. The system that benefited them so richly was hardly likely to be freely chosen by the majority who benefited so much less. Instead, factory owners and merchants looked to enlightened despots, or parliaments based on property rights, to secure their interests.

For the rest, capitalism meant predation. Strikingly consistent arguments against capitalism have survived to this day, reenergized by successive generations of activists and intellectuals. The critics have changed, as Christians, luddites, shakers, socialists and anarchists, as well as conservative monarchists and churchmen have been joined by ecologists, new agers, and anti-globalizers. But the criticisms have hardly changed as capitalism has evolved from workshops and textile mills to cyberspace and supersonic aircraft. The criticisms made of science, democracy, or law two centuries ago now sound anachronistic. Those made of capitalism by contrast are very similar in content, if not in language, and unlike the critiques of science and democracy they've often succeeded. The famous comment made about socialists, that they are good at struggle but best at struggling with each other rather than capitalists, may apply more widely. Yet the critics won their fair share of battles in tempering capitalism's excesses. Here I describe five consistent families of criticism whose persistence makes them not just inherently interesting, but also suggestive of where capitalism will evolve in the future.

1. Capitalism Empowers the Strong over the Weak

The first, by now familiar, attacks capitalism as a conspiracy of the powerful against the powerless. All of its claims to equality and openness are cant, there to confuse and mislead, and to lend legitimacy to the successes of the predators. The images of capitalism usually play on this story: they portray fat cats and overweight pigs feeding on the poor, emblems of greed, gluttony, and excess. In cinema and fiction, powerful, faceless corporations are portrayed as conspiracies to destroy the lives of ordinary people living in harmony with nature, and representing death against life, ugliness against beauty, and force against love.

In these accounts the economy is a zero sum game. More for some means less for others. Higher profits mean lower wages. Bigger mansions for the businessman mean smaller hovels for the workers. Worsening inequality is endemic, not just an unfortunate by-product of a market system.[2]

In more subtle variants of these accounts the focus turns to how the conspiracy is conducted rather than its effects: the hidden networks of power that lie behind the corporate facades (as in the recent study of some 43,000 transnational firms by systems theorists at the Swiss Federal Institute of Technology in Zurich, which showed that less than 1 percent of companies, the great majority in finance, effectively controlled another 40 percent).[3] Others study the overlapping board memberships, the exchanges of favors and insider information, the headhunters who orchestrate and respond to who is in and who is out. And attention turns to the alliances forged between the revolutionary forces of capitalism and the reactionary forces of hierarchy, such as established religion, armies, and the state (all neatly in place in the cartoon of the pyramid of the capitalist system, described earlier), since these are usually the necessary allies who make it possible for capitalist forms of life to spread.

Most, but not all, of the leading theorists of capitalism were instinctively conservative. Adam Smith, for example, wrote that societies need people to respect visible status, hierarchy, and formal offices, because it makes the social order more durable than if it depends on recognition of such invisible virtues as wisdom or judgment. It's hard to find any examples of social movements of the poor and dispossessed clamoring for more capitalism. Even in stagnant communist societies the most eager enthusiasts for a rapid transition to capitalism were insiders who saw in markets and privatization a faster route to wealth and status than communism could offer (and the deals designed by bankers to lend Boris Yeltsin's government money in exchange for shares in Russia's raw materials industries represent one of the great moments of predation in modern history). It's true that the farmers and workers welcomed more open markets for food and greater freedoms. But they, and the groups or parties that represented them, remained deeply skeptical that any concentrations of capital would serve their interests.

Seen as systems for organized predation, it's no surprise that advanced capitalist societies have taken the shape they have. You might expect a market economy to generate returns in a roughly normal distribution, with a few rich at the top, the mass of the population in the middle, and a few poor at the bottom. This is the rough distribution of talents, or of capacities to do hard work. But few market economies look like this. Instead the distribution has stretched the top, leaving capitalist societies like an extended teardrop, with a tiny minority achieving almost magical rewards, the bulk of the population some way below the average, and a large clump of the very poor at the bottom. During periods of economic exuberance the distributions have become even more stretched. In the United States between 1979 and 2005, after-tax income for the top 1 percent increased by 176 percent, compared to an increase of 69 percent for the top quintile overall and 6 percent for the bottom quintile.[4]

It's sometimes suggested that this is the product of information technology and communications. In a highly connected world the very best singer or engineer can amplify their earnings. It's an appealing argument, which implies a strong meritocracy at work. But the pattern of rewards doesn't fit the thesis. It doesn't explain why some very globalized firms have much smaller income differentials than others (usually because their main country base is somewhere like Germany, Japan, or Sweden with a cultural aversion to wide discrepancies). And it doesn't explain why so many of the top 1 percent or 0.1 percent have inherited their wealth.

A century ago, Vilfredo Pareto suggested that unequal distributions reflected nature, and more specifically that income distributions followed power laws of income distribution. A power law exists when the frequency of an event or attribute varies as a power of some attribute. So the number of cities of a particular population size turns out to vary as a power of the size of the population. Such power laws are common in nature, from the size of oil reserves to the size of files transferred on the Internet. Pareto observed that wealth distributions also followed power laws (the Pareto principle is taken to be that 20 percent of a population will hold 80 percent of the wealth), and suggested that this was a fact of nature. Yet any detailed analysis of particular societies dispels the idea that distributions occur automatically. Statisticians show that Gini coefficients—the standard measure of income inequality—vary greatly, while historians show that the arrangements needed to sustain unequal distributions over long periods of time are complex and difficult. Like any serious conspiracies they require hard work clear, coordination, and calibrated compromise, and many ruling classes have failed at all of these tasks and lost their preeminence, whether because of divisions, overreach, or overexploitation.

Even generosity could be seen as part of the conspiracy, a cover for predation. Oscar Wilde wrote provocatively in *The Soul of Man Under Socialism*[5] that

> just as the worst slave-owners were those who were kind to their slaves, and so prevented the horror of the system being realised by those who suffered from it . . . so in the present state of things in England the people who do most harm are the people who try to do most good . . . charity creates a multitude of sins. . . . It is immoral to use private property in order to alleviate the horrible evils that result from the institution of private property.

His cynicism is undoubtedly excessive. But charitable giving in most advanced economies rarely rises much above 1–2 percent of GDP, an order of magnitude less than tax-funded welfare or alms in more traditional societies.

2. Capitalism Destroys What Is Truly Valuable

The second set of arguments against capitalism that have been used and reused since Louis Blanc's time, attack capitalism for what it values, elevating the material and money over people. A system that pursues exchangeable value must devalue everything else, and that means ignoring or even destroying much of what is truly valuable, from beauty to truth. The result is that capitalism's road to heaven is paved with approximations of hell, from the mid-nineteenth-century Manchester graphically depicted by Friedrich Engels, hastily thrown together with little care for anything other than profit, to the crime- and disease-ridden neighborhoods of the east end of London or Paris. Even when they function well, the cities where people come together for exchange typically breed vice and degrade values: in London in the early mercantile era, for example, a popular play warned that "there is no abiding in the city for Conscience and Love,"[6] and always there is the trope that the things that matter most are the very things that can't be bought in the city.

The angry and consistent criticisms of capitalism's tendency to destroy what is truly valuable draw on deep currents of anti-materialism in all of the world's religions. The Bible is full of injunctions against wealth, from the comment that it is harder for a rich man to enter heaven than for a camel to pass through the eye of a needle, to the warnings that money is the root of all evil. Repeatedly the Bible and Koran tell of temptation leading people astray, and it became a tradition in the Islamic world for invaders from the desert to cleanse the sins of the cities. The restrictions on lending for interest in Islam and Christianity were meant to rein in the temptation to destroy and exploit. The Koran describes usurers as "like men who Satan has demented by his touch." Most of the prohibitions were muted in practice, as religious leaders found common interests with merchants and bankers. Yet from time to time religion has reasserted itself, offering its own ideas about how the economy should be run (usually to the annoyance of those who lived their lives in manufacture or trade). The founder of Liberation theology, Gustavo Gutierrez, for example, believed that economic development and theological regeneration were linked. "We are passing" he wrote "from a theology that concentrated excessively on a God located outside this world to a theology of a God who is present in this world."[7] History meant "the progressive revelation of the human face of God." What that meant was liberation from the injustice and poverty of capitalism and the creation of a new economy based on very different principles, freed from subordination and dependence. Liberation in other words was a far preferable goal to mere development and economic growth.

Buddhism was never as hostile to trade as Christianity and Islam, perhaps because so many of its early adherents came from the merchant class. But its teachings advised that the only way to avoid suffering was to eliminate desire. Greed, along with hatred and delusion, was one of the three evils that had to be resisted to live a good life, and in recent years Buddhist writings have offered not just personal alternatives to capitalism but also public ones—most famously in E. F. Schumacher's book *Small is Beautiful*,[8] which argued that "since consumption is merely a means to human well-being, the aim should be to obtain the maximum of well-being with the minimum of consumption. . . . The less toil there is, the more time and strength is left for artistic creativity. Modern economics, on the other hand, considers consumption to be the sole end and purpose of all economic activity." And so Buddhism became another source for denouncing the delusions of capitalism, and its tendency to destroy not just nature but that part of humanity that connects us most intimately to nature.

Then there is the waste of wealth—the profligacy of the very rich, owning ten houses, twenty sports cars, or two thousand pairs of shoes. It's an oddity of a system that prides itself so much on its efficiency that its greatest successes are associated with such extraordinary levels of waste. A system that grew out of Protestant distaste for the squandered surpluses of feudalism, the indulgence of great feasts and luxuries, has ended up with the equally grandiose excesses of the twenty-first-century super-rich, thinking nothing of spending millions on a party or wedding, or taking a private jet to attend a conference on the future of the environment.

If nature is one of the victims of capitalism's distorted view of value, the other is community. The rise of industry brought with it the dislocation of rural communities in favor of the atomized misery of the city, leaving everyone pitted against everyone else in a war of all against all. Competition is valued over cooperation. Relationships have no value because they cannot be bought and sold (or rather only a shadow of relationships can be bought and sold in the burgeoning markets for counselors or escorts). If we act toward others only with a view to maximizing our monetary advantage, we will soon lose our friends, since friendship, like love, depends to a degree not on what it provides, but on the promise of what it might provide in different circumstances. We want friends and lovers who will be there for us if things go wrong, and are suspicious of "fair weather" friends, and friends who are only calculating their advantage. With possessions come distrust and meanness. Paul Piff of the University of California, Berkeley,[9] showed through a series of experiments giving people notional credits to distribute, that wealthier people are less inclined to give to charity, and that even encouraging people to think of themselves as wealthier than they were, led their generosity to decline—those at the bottom turned out to be 44 percent more generous with an equivalent body of credits than those at the top. The richer participants could be made more compassionate by showing them suitably compassionate messages. But Piff's conclusion is that greater compassion is a survival tool for the poor; having more money means that you may have more reason to resent others, either because they want a share of your money or because they make you feel guilty.

3. Capitalism Promotes Mindlessness

The third set of critiques follow on from these. If capitalism can only see some things as valuable, the implication is that it is mindless, the enemy of culture, reason, and reflective wisdom. This has been the traditional conservative response to markets. The rule of buyers and sellers pushes high culture to one side. Majority taste predominates over minority taste, the desire of the many ignoramuses over those of the few aesthetes. This was the complaint of successive generations of romantics, aristocrats, and reformers in response to the arrival of factories, mills, and railways, and later to mass advertising and mass media. Democratizing the market meant dumbing down, fast food, the lure of glitter and baubles rather than wisdom and reflection. And markets inevitably meant clamor, noise, and the barking pressure to buy, to spend, to borrow, a spirit opposite to that of the temple, the library, or the museum, and opposite to the stillness needed for reflection or deep thought.

This critique has taken many forms. In his novel *Sybil*, Disraeli provided one, describing Wodgate, a Black Country town derived from the real life Willenhall in Staffordshire, and the effect of mass availability of new products:

> On Monday and Tuesday the whole population of Wodgate is drunk; of all stations, ages, and sexes; even babies who should be at the breast; for they are drammed with Godfrey's Cordial. Here is relaxation, excitement; if less vice otherwise than might be at first anticipated, we must

remember that excesses are checked by poverty of blood and constant exhaustion. Scanty food and hard labour are in their way, if not exactly moralists, a tolerably good police. There are no others at Wodgate to preach or to control. It is not that the people are immoral, for immorality implies some forethought; or ignorant, for ignorance is relative; but they are animals; unconscious; their minds a blank and their worst actions only the impulse of a gross or savage instinct.[10]

A century and a half later we worry not so much about savage instincts but about the impact of vastly greater flows of information on our ability to think. We may be more aware of the cornucopia of choices available to us, and the possibilities we have forgone, but this may not have brought much enhancement in our ability to absorb or use information, and as businesses concern themselves ever more with the struggle for scarce attention,[11] breadth is won at the price of depth: as Nobel Laureate and Artificial Intelligence expert Herbert Simon put it, "a wealth of information creates a poverty of attention."

Related arguments went, and still go, even deeper. They warn that a capitalist system lacks moral mindfulness, and, worse, that its very mechanisms corrode moral sense. Capitalism doesn't just destroy what is truly valuable. It makes it harder for people to recognize that this is happening; it blocks off the very routes along which a society might choose to make its way to a different social order. Justice can be blind too. But its blindness allows it to judge fairly. Capitalism's blindness by contrast excludes fairness.

So the investor and the trader deliberately cultivate moral blindness; they take it as a mark of weakness or lack of professionalism to care about the consequences of actions, to join the dots on chains of transactions. Within the market, mindlessness manifests itself in the common defense of the seller of damaging goods: "I'm just responding to a demand, and if I didn't, someone else would," an argument as common for arms industries as for the sale of heroin, and almost a model of mindlessness.

Capitalism doesn't just ignore reason, it colonizes it, eroding people's ability to think and judge, as they learn the habits of buying and selling, of calculating but not thinking. It drives people into excessive spending and debt (William Cobbett the English journalist and campaigner, constantly urged his readers to ask, "can I do without it?"). Capitalism encourages mindless aggression as well as addictive behaviors, like gambling. Seen in this context, the web becomes just the latest form of chosen slavery. Bernard Mandeville's fable of the bees reinforces the point: a market works because we become mindless, herd-like, automatons. Within it, mindless behaviors are common. Investors and traders have been compared with boy racers on a motorway who are only aware of their speed relative to others, driving faster and faster, until one makes a mistake and then all pile up in a disastrous crash, a story repeated again and again in bubbles, and the hysterias of speculation that take hold of markets for shares or housing. Samuel Taylor Coleridge used the fitting metaphor of the fever to describe these market dynamics, and this captures well the folly that is seen every time markets boom: as Chuck Prince, the chief executive of Citicorp, put it just before the crash in 2007: "when the music stops, in terms of liquidity, things will be complicated. But as long as the music is playing, you've got to get up and dance."[12]

The mindlessness of markets reveals its own irrationality within organizations. Capitalism is made up of many large organizations that want to elicit loyalty and even love from their employees and their consumers. These large bureaucracies are full of people who have sacrificed freedom for security, fun today for future reward, their own identity for a share of a larger corporate one. But the ideology of the market denies commitment or indeed anything that might get in the way of accumulation.

There are parts of any economy where this contradiction matters little. Sectors full of start-ups, populated by relatively young people without the encumbrances of children and mortgages, can embrace to the full a fluid world without any lasting attachments, the world celebrated in business books. But most of the economy isn't like this. It depends on commitment, care and, yes, mindfulness—which is why so many firms devote such efforts to creating their own cultures, myths, and meanings. Richard Sennett quotes a modern boss who commented that in his firm no one owns their role and no one has a right to a future: "past service in particular earns no employee a guaranteed place."[13] This is a way of thinking that runs contrary to our nature. In any other institution, from a family to a club, a school to a political party, we assume that the past has some bearing on the future, that loyalty matters: it is an odd celebration of mindlessness to deny it.

If capitalist organizations can be mindless, then so can investors. Max Weber viewed the investment mind-set as unnatural: "a person does not 'by nature' want to make more and more money,"[14] and Karl Marx wrote of the trap the capitalist himself falls into, as he

> relentlessly drives human beings to production for production's sake . . . as such he shares with the miser the passion for wealth as wealth . . . competition forces him continually to extend his capital for the sake of maintaining it, and he can only extend it by means of continual accumulation.[15]

In its purest forms, as Marx recognized, capitalism is not just, or even primarily, a system for people to get rich. Rather, capital exists to beget capital, and should not be taken out of circulation. Every gain should be reinvested, put to work and made productive. To jump off the treadmill is to admit defeat. This attachment to insecurity that can be found among many of the practitioners of Wall Street or the City of London is psychologically peculiar, and clearly not healthy for personal relationships or indeed for happiness.[16]

Another, more recent, strand of the mindlessness critique targets the organization of the world by numbers: the idea that only what can be measured can be managed leads to any number of pathologies, worse too when it's mimicked by governments. Depending only on numbers, or the rules of profit and loss, means deliberately ignoring other kinds of judgment: judgment of worth, of beauty, of dignity, or of justice. It means institutionalizing mindlessness, mechanical decision making over serious thought. The tendency to abstraction, and a widening gulf between the real economy of food and computers, cinemas, and haircuts, and their virtual representations turns out to be very risky. A modern economy depends on representations, but it can also fall victim to them. Anthropologist Karen Ho has written about how neoclassical economics is engaged in the "conscious attempt to make the real world conform to the virtual image." It is precisely this "move to greater abstraction and virtualism" in economic thought that is creating a prescriptive model for reality, a virtual reality that is reductive, but also encourages the dislocation of decisions. Within business, disaggregation and outsourcing take what were more durable relationships and turn them into market transactions. The people making the critical decisions become much less likely to know what's really going on and what the service they ostensibly run actually feels like. Instead, they operate through mediated data and mediated messages—often clever, but also often mindless as we discover when the numbers on a screen add up in the virtual world but no longer add up in the real one.

Capitalism's history is bound up with successive innovations in measurement to close the gap between reality and representation. What matters is measured, and in the clichés of management consultants, anything that can't be measured can't be managed (a dictum that one hopes they never apply to their own lives). But measurement is always a struggle because value is never objective; it has to be wrenched out of the facts. Max Weber defines capitalism as depending on the "valuation and verification of opportunities for profit" which involved the "valuation of total assets . . . at the beginning of the profit making venture, and the comparison of this with a similar valuation . . . at the end."[17] But the numbers aren't objective. The flows of money into a shop or a factory are facts: but how they relate to the inputs of energy or labor, the relative contribution of the worker and the shopkeeper, are not. The answers are both technical—how to organize accounts for a complex system like an aircraft factory, a videogames studio, or a massive retailer like Walmart—and also political, about competing claims for rewards that reflect the relative power to choose of each player, how easily they can walk away and do business with someone else.

Unreliable measurement is the Achilles' heel of a modern capitalist economy. Standard & Poor's notoriously gave high ratings to investment banks just before they collapsed in 2008. Greece's economy appeared to be thriving shortly before it went into meltdown. The professions charged with measurement claim to favor sobriety, prudence, a bias toward what is hard and objective, and auditors profess to be neutral, cautious, and beyond influence (though some have been willing accomplices in inflating the numbers for their clients' benefit). Their fetish of measurement is often criticized as somehow inhuman, a form of blindness. But oddly an opposite phenomenon is also criticized—the tendency to equally mindless over-estimation and hysteria. Capitalist systems need tools of estimation that make it possible to peer into the future, and judge future returns: the business plan, the forecast, and the scenario are some of these, and futures markets try to put a price on future prices. These estimations aim to be objective, but capitalism is by its nature a culture of optimism and hope that constantly reaches away from reality and then falls back, in necessary cycles of exuberance and disappointment. Its congenital optimism is surely linked to the ways in which hope is functional—it is hope that gets the worker to work, the investor to invest, the manager to expand. Just imagine what capitalism would look like in a fatalistic culture. Optimism also helps people to strive and succeed: according to one famous study, self-reported cheerfulness at college entry predicted income sixteen years later, controlling for many other variables, including parents' income. The most cheerful children of well-off parents earned $25,000 more per year than the least cheerful.[18] But institutionalized optimism also drives an endemic bias to exaggeration, inflated numbers, and unwarranted confidence.

This optimism has been inextricably linked to capitalism's expansive character. Hope is hope for an expansion of things, of profits and money, but also an expansion of spheres, the idea that anything and everything can be bought and sold. As Karl Marx predicted, capitalism tends to break free from constraints, and its nature is expansive. Nineteenth-century capitalists bought politicians, art collections, landscapes, and universities with equal relish. Contemporary capitalism is equally at ease with corporate sponsorship, luxury products, and old masters, as well as software programs and space travel. Its methods have spread into healthcare, land management, and charity (and even "philanthrocapitalism," the surreal idea that the rich are the people best placed to solve the problems of poverty and inequality).[19] Finance has become a major source of political party finance (helped by rulings like the "Superpac" decision in the U.S. Supreme Court which greatly eased the dominance of U.S. politics by the rich). The result is that capitalism's values and cultural expressions—whether diamond-encrusted heads, corporate art, advertising videos or avatars, or generous tax breaks for venture capital—define our culture. But the other result is a constant tide of complaint that these very things are the antithesis of true culture and mindfulness.

4. Capitalism Makes People Miserable, Not Happy

Capitalism's most powerful moral claim is that it meets human wants and needs better than any alternative. It connects desires to productive capacities, and by doing so makes people happy. Around 135 countries have reasonably complete data sets going back forty years. In these, GDP per capita doubled; life expectancy climbed from fifty-nine years in 1970 to seventy in 2010, school enrollment went up from 55 percent of all primary and secondary school-age children to 70 percent. The pessimistic view that the world is going to the dogs requires that these, and many other measures like them, are ignored.

But against this optimistic account is the longstanding complaint that the pursuit of exchangeable value poses as the ally of the pursuit of happiness—but actually deposes it. The representations of value undermine the reality. Capitalism imprisons the worker on a treadmill of work, as the breadwinner sacrifices his life to the corporation in the hope of promotions that may never come. The consumer becomes trapped on a treadmill of ever greater consumption, jumping from anticipation to anticipation but never being truly satisfied, while the small investor is imprisoned by the hopeful dream that his stocks will suddenly shoot into the stratosphere and make him wealthy without the inconvenience of work. All are vulnerable to that ill-defined but ubiquitous epidemic of the modern world—depression.[20]

Yet looked at in the round there is little doubt that capitalist prosperity does correlate with growing happiness, with nations appearing to become happier as their income rises to $10,000 per capita. There are also some increases in individual happiness well beyond that level, certainly up to around $60,000, according to recent surveys such as Gallup's very large 2009 survey on U.S. citizens. Beyond that, more money doesn't increase the experience of happiness: but it does improve stated satisfaction with life, presumably because it improves people's sense of relative success.[21]

This success has always been ambiguous. Nineteenth-century Britain may have led the world in industrialization, but it was also believed to suffer from high suicide rates, and this encouraged many critics in continental Europe to ascribe them to too much freedom and overly high expectations. Ever since the knowledge of happiness has been the most direct challenge to economics, prompting critics to warn, like Avner Offer for example, that "affluence breeds impatience and impatience undermines well-being," or like Franco Berardi that capitalism has become an "unhappiness machine" widening the gulf between the capacity of the brain and the expanding volume of information and pressures that are bombarding it.[22]

Richard Easterlin was one of the first economists to look systematically at the evidence showing that growth did not reliably lead to happiness. In a recent survey of the data, Easterlin reported that

> [in] sixteen developed countries with time series at least 21 years in length, there is no significant relation between the rate of economic growth and the improvement in life satisfaction. In seven countries transitioning to free market economies with time series that are at least 14 years in length and include a measurement before or close to the beginning of transition, there is no significant relation between the rate of economic growth and the improvement in life satisfaction. In thirteen developing nations spanning Asia, Africa, and Latin America with time series at least 10 years in length (the average being 15 years), there is no significant relation between the rate of economic growth and the improvement in subjective well-being. Pooling the data for all thirty-six

countries above, there is no significant relation between the rate of economic growth and the change in life satisfaction.[23]

Other research seems to confirm the picture with a leveling off as income rises.[24]

Yet the evidence isn't quite so straightforward.[25] One reason for the leveling off of the correlation between happiness and economic wealth is simply that each marginal increment of income produces a smaller absolute increase in happiness. When mapped on a log scale, there is a fairly close fit between income and happiness. More detailed analysis also suggests why the data come out as they do. The Gallup World Poll asks people what emotions they experienced the previous day. People in relatively rich nations report themselves as more likely to have felt love and enjoyment and less likely to have experienced anger, depression, or boredom. Patterns over time are similar, with trends toward greater happiness (the United States is a particular exception).

So growth has some impact on happiness. But what is surprising is how little. A good case study was the crisis of the late 2000s. In the UK in 2007, average life satisfaction levels were 7.3; in 2008 the figure rose to 7.5; it fell marginally to 7.4 in 2009 and was back up to 7.5 in 2010, following the most severe recession in several generations and a sharp rise in unemployment. In the United States, the Gallup daily poll found a drop of only 2 percent reporting being happy the previous day (from 89 to 87) during the course of 2008. Why was this? Why should a downturn make people happier, even if only marginally? It's possible that people had to spend more time with friends or family and quite enjoyed doing so; that low interest rates kept the majority feeling prosperous; that expectations had become more realistic; or that they felt more fellow-feeling than at the height of the boom. Another answer is simply that all measures of happiness tend to be fairly slow to move; measures of unhappiness, perhaps surprisingly, don't move in tandem with measures of happiness and may be more sensitive. Unemployed people in the United States are 20 percent more likely to report worry on any given day than people with jobs, but they are only 5 percentage points less likely to report happiness.[26] Recessions, it turns out, increase stress and anxiety a lot—particularly where debt is involved.

Another answer is that we quickly revert to a set point of happiness, even after serious shocks like illness, disability, or the death of a spouse, a challenge both to political action and to the promise of the market.[27] It also simply could be that so many of the factors shaping happiness, like genetic makeup or childhood experiences, sit well beyond the reach of any conceivable market.[28] Some influences can be bought: physical attractiveness for women and height for men correlate with reported happiness, and can be influenced by consumption of the right makeover or shoes. Even blood pressure roughly correlates (inversely) with happiness at the level of whole nations, and in principle is amenable to influence by what we buy and consume. Yet much of what matters most for happiness is beyond the reach of money.

The claims that capitalism causes misery are at best unproven. But so is the claim that capitalism reliably grows well-being. This is strange since economics has built a grand edifice of theory and analysis around the ways in which individual choices work to maximize utility, which originally meant happiness. Through buying things in the market we satisfy our wants and needs, and thus become happy. So work is a means to consumption, and consumption is a means to happiness. More money means more consumption which should mean happiness. But not always. Korea, the miracle economy of east Asia, is a good example of how capitalism can apparently corrode well-being. In the 1950s, it had a GDP lower than much of Africa but over the next few decades vaulted ahead to the ranks of the most prosperous nations. Per capita GDP in Korea increased from $800 in 1970 to $19,000 in 2008. Yet according to the OECD, the level of life satisfaction among Koreans decreased from 61.1 percent to 47.3 percent between 1990 and 2002.[29] Egypt is another example: in late 2010, just before the regime fell, only 9 percent of Egyptians were described as thriving, less than Palestine and Yemen, despite 5 percent growth that year. The figures had fallen in previous years for all but the richest, again despite strong economic growth.[30] Progress should mean longer lives, lived more richly, with more fulfillment. Yet although money and consumption can serve time, they can also degrade it. Indeed recent research suggests that the very freedom and choice associated with developed markets may be antithetical to happiness. Comparing data from many countries, economic freedom turns out to correlate negatively with life satisfaction (once other factors such as income, health and trust are controlled for).[31]

Recent research has also looked at more micro evidence on the relationship between market economies and happiness, and this seems to confirm that at least some aspects of consumer culture are likely to make us less satisfied while promising the opposite. One of the leading investigators of the relationship between consumption and happiness concludes that "people who strongly orient towards values such as money, possessions, image and status report lower subjective well-being."[32] Symptom and cause are interwoven: blocked relationships and dissatisfactions lead people to focus on material goods, which then renders them less able to make and keep good relationships. A "materialist value orientation" develops through "experiences that induce feelings of insecurity and exposure to social models that encourage materialistic values."[33] If you show young men extremely attractive women, they will judge others more negatively. In one study eighty-one male dormitory residents watching a popular TV show, whose main characters were three strikingly attractive females, were asked to rate a photo of an average female (described as a potential blind date for another dorm resident). They rated the target female as significantly less attractive than did a comparable control group, and another study found that men who were exposed to photographs of physically attractive women subsequently became less satisfied with their current heterosexual relationships.

The initial impressions of romantic partners—women who were actually available to them and likely to be interested in them—were so adversely affected that the men didn't even want to bother. Self-assessments of attractiveness also change. "Women who are surrounded by other attractive women, whether in the flesh, in films, or in photographs, rate themselves as less satisfied with their attractiveness—and less desirable as a marriage partner." These pressures may be reaching ever younger, as advertisers target girls younger than age thirteen, urging them to buy makeup and fashion as the easiest route to popularity and happiness. Consumer research shows that too much attention to materialistic values and possessions has a negative impact on psychological well-being.[34] The effects on self-esteem are fairly obvious. But there is also a more general effect on attitudes.[35] The more that people attach importance to material objects the more they risk feeling let down, since the new fashion, makeup, or perfume is unlikely to achieve all that it promises. Too much attention to material things may also get in the way of other relationships. This was the finding of a study to examine the empirical links between watching, wanting, and well-being in UK children.[36] It discovered that children who spend more time in front of the TV or computer screen are more materialistic. Children who are more materialistic tend to have lower self-esteem, a lower opinion of their parents, and children who have a poor opinion of their parents also argue with them more, and have a lower opinion of themselves.[37]

There are also clearly reinforcing links between materialism and anti-social behavior. Children who communicate less with their parents, or receive negative messages from them, tend to focus more on money.[38] They then become more vulnerable to the messages from business. Much advertising depends on creating insecurity from upward social comparisons that leave slim women feeling fat, beautiful people feeling ugly, and successful people feeling inadequate.[39]

Here the different types of capitalism have different effects. Spending per capita on advertising has been four times greater in the United States than in mainland Europe, twice as great in the UK. What effect does this have on the mood of a society? Does it lead to a more materialistic orientation—to choosing harder work so as to earn more cash rather than more time with family or friends? It appears so. Does it then disappoint in terms of happiness? Again, it appears so, with a tendency to make up for disappointment with addictive behaviors. Robert Frank explored some of these patterns in the United States.[40] He asked people to consider a choice between two worlds. One, world A, is a world where you earn $110,000 per year; others earn $200,000.

The other, world B, is a world where you earn $100,000 per year; others earn $85,000. A majority of Americans, it turns out, choose World B. Why? It could be envy, but it's also a recognition that the visibility of those richer than us that makes us dissatisfied. The very dissatisfaction that can act as a spur for hard work and risk-taking can also just end up as a trap, particularly in an environment where it's hard to avoid media that offer Porsches and Patek Phillipe watches, luxury holidays and sports cars. H. L. Mencken once defined a wealthy man as one who earns $100 a year more than his wife's sister's husband.[41] The same pressures that drive some to work harder drive others to debt. We know that happiness isn't just achieved by owning things, or earning more. Learning to be happy often means learning to sustain emotional connections, and learning how to teach others about our needs, and ourselves about how to meet the needs of others. Yet capitalism often encourages a narcissistic preoccupation with self that is one of the least likely routes to happiness.[42]

5. Capitalism Threatens Life

The fifth family of criticisms of capitalism are the most devastating of all: they cast capitalism as against life. The relentless pursuit of exchangeable value pits capital against living labor. Marx wrote of it as a vampire; dead labor feeding on living labor. William Blake portrayed it as the bringer of satanic mills. In this view it is like warfare, a force of thanatos, of death masquerading as healthy activity. If capital became primary that had to mean that nature was forfeit. So were people, who came to be seen as disposable commodities to be bought for a time and then discarded. No wonder that life expectancies fell sharply in the early stages of western industrialization, and then again in recent times in China, where the most dramatic industrialization in history was matched by a marked fall in lifespans.[43] There too nature was an early victim of the march to profit, capitalism's ruthless appetite only being matched by the equally rapacious appetite of the communist state before it discovered markets.

This idea of capitalism as against life may seem far-fetched. But just compare a typical market, like a market for vegetables or fish, with the places that are most typical of capitalism like that. Markets are full of life, vibrant, busy with people interacting with others in a rough equality, and they have been for thousands of years, from the first gatherings in towns like Jericho and Uruk. Even the stock exchange floor has some of these qualities. Compare then the iconic places of capitalism: the big corporate headquarters, the central business districts, the cities built to be dominated by cars, and the vast factories churning out consumer products. All can seem the opposite of life; repetitive, cold, soulless, with none of the quirks and sociability of living places. Their aesthetic merges with that of totalitarianism (the headquarters of firms like Goldman Sachs are oddly deliberate in doing this too, with decor full of harsh blacks, with little or no color, no detail, no humanity, almost a cult of ugliness). All of these places choose to show off a culture of abstraction that reflects the difference between capitalism and markets—with capital most at home in a cold modernism, with art that is devoid of any representation, let alone any people, and advertising that hints at all sorts of qualities, but never quite describes what is being sold and why. Where markets are grounded in direct interaction and the give and take of humanity, capital is remote and distant, and its ethics as well as its aesthetics reflect this.

This matters because all of us can immediately distinguish places that are living from those that aren't; and capitalism's public relations problem is that although we may like its products, and their uses in our everyday lives, as a system it stands against much that we hold dearest. It can seem to stand against life and against the principles of life. Nature is cyclical, where capitalism accumulates and hoards. Nature achieves harmony from plurality, whereas capitalism's architecture is often almost willfully hostile to beauty, made up of bleakly repetitive tower blocks and industrial units that deny the patterns of variation that make forests, gardens, or seas appealing.

There have been attempts to reconcile nature and capitalism. The idea of sustainability was first defined by the Brundtland Commission of the United Nations in 1987 as "development that meets the needs of the present without compromising the ability of future generations to meet their own needs." More recently ecological metaphors have been gradually introduced into economic thinking, often indirectly through the shifting currents of complexity theory. The theories describing capitalism have come to seem a bit more like life, its market patterns compared to the natural world, with a similar code of power laws, randomness, chaos, and complexity. Later I describe how ecological ideas are being used to make production less wasteful, more circular, and more at home with nature. But the criticism still hits home: capitalism in its purest forms is abstract, and whatever is truly abstract can easily come to stand against humanity and nature.

THE VICES OF NATURALISM IN BOTH CRITICS AND ADVOCATES

One of the stranger features that much of the criticism of capitalism has shared with the advocates and apologists is a claim to deduce conclusions from facts about human nature. Capitalism claimed to express a fundamental human nature that is acquisitive, selfish, venal, and materialist. Predation may be nasty, but it's natural and unavoidable. Valuing everything in terms of money may be coarse, but it fits with our character as avaricious calculators. And if consumers sometimes behaved in mindless ways, that was just their expression of freedom.

The critics countered with a similar structure of argument. They claimed in contrast that human beings are "truly" kind, altruistic, compassionate, cooperative, and spiritual. If they are violent or selfish, this is just the consequence of flawed social institutions, or brutalization. Set them free and they will naturally revert to kindness.

Each argument implied its conclusions. The first, founded on a view of human nature as made up only of self-interest, requires systems built entirely around punishments and financial incentives. The latter, founded on altruism and generosity, can survive with voluntary work and compassion (and even taxes can be made voluntary). One is dog eats dog; the other is dog helps dog (oddly, given how rarely dogs do either of these things).

These polarized arguments already look strange today, as strange as some of the theological arguments of the distant past. It's hard to believe that anyone could seriously adopt such one-sided views of human nature and then deduce a whole political and economic philosophy from them, when we know that human nature is all of these things, and more. Both reflect a strong yearning for the world to be a simpler place than it is, more explicable and more meaningful. We know better now that self-interest matters but not exclusively. Financial rewards motivate some people some of the time, but not all of the people all of the time, and feeding financial motives can be counterproductive. Much of social psychology has tried to calibrate better the qualities of human nature, with subtle lessons about the balance of financial reward and moral commitment that appear to work best for different roles.[44]

Social psychology is far from being a settled science. But it has steadily carved out more realistic views of human nature; of the heuristics we use to make decisions; of the biases in perceptions and decision making. Its healthiest instinct is to observe, not to assume. What do people appear to value in the way they live their lives? You can choose to look at how they spend their money, which is the preferred method of economics. But you can just as easily look at where they spend their time, or where they devote their love and attention. The first emphasizes housing and food, cars and clothes as all-important. The second emphasizes the world of family and friends, enthusiasms and beliefs. This economy of time and love, as I will show, may be the more important one now and in the future.

If there is a lesson from the two centuries of polarized argument, it is surely that our nature is neither fixed nor fluid. We can find patterns that connect us back to our evolutionary origins, and we are often driven by hunger for food, or sex or fame (I like the comment of the boxer, who never quite made it to the very top tier, who was asked what he might have achieved if he had stayed clear of the girls and the booze: "I was only in it for the girls and the booze"). But these drives are only partial; we suppress them, divert them, and contain them all the time, and every institution, from the family to the firm, exists in part to do this. The monastery; the army; the school; and marriage all are institutional means of molding people, and none takes nature as given. Instead, through encouragement, reward, punishment, and the influence of peers, they mold people into something new. At their best they reinforce our better nature: they make us more creative, more compassionate, and more diligent. At their worst they reinforce our nastier natures, making us more violent, more hateful, and more greedy.

The rainbow coalition of critics have for two centuries hurled ferocious arguments against capital and capitalists, as well as bombs and bullets. A million slings and arrows have been thrown at the juggernaut, forests of pamphlets and newspapers, and innumerable sweaty demonstrations and angry strikes. Seen from the vantage point of the present, they both won and lost. They lost in that capitalism survived and even triumphed. But they won in that with each step forward it had to change.

Chapter 6

· · · · · · · · ·

Anticapitalist Utopias and Neotopias

ONE OF OSCAR WILDE'S MOST FAMOUS QUIPS suggested that "a map of the world that does not include utopia is not worth even glancing at, for it leaves out the one country at which Humanity is always landing. And when Humanity lands there, it looks out, and, seeing a better country, sets sail." For most of capitalism's history there has been intense interest in what would follow it, and much utopian thinking to imagine its successors. Capitalism had grown up so quickly, almost suddenly in some countries, turning lives and assumptions on their head, that it seemed plausible that it would be replaced by something as dramatically different again. Surely the system that had turned the world upside down would itself be turned upside down?

For two centuries the visionary alternatives did precisely that: they turned capitalism upside down. Many identified the most distinctive features of capitalism and imagined its diametrical opposites. So where capitalism empowered the capitalists and disempowered the workers, socialism and communism would put them in charge. Workers' councils would run enterprises. Profits would go to the people who had done the work, not to distant investors. In place of private property, the utopias suggest common property. In place of money they suggest a society with no money. In place of profit, they propose no profit. In place of no accountability, they propose new requirements to justify.

104

As I show in chapter 9, this technique of inversion, turning a pattern of relationships or power on its head, has also become a tool for more practical social innovation—transforming peasants into bankers, patients into doctors, or students into teachers. So have the methods of extension that are also common in utopias: taking an existing idea and stretching it to its limits, or translation, taking an idea from one field and transplanting it to another.

The very plasticity of capitalist culture has continued to encourage utopianism, the restless imagination of possible worlds. Yet the vast majority of imagined worlds fail to make sense in capitalist terms and rub up against its assumptions. When Arthur Miller was asked whether his play, *The Death of a Salesman*, was about one man's experiences or about the Depression, he replied that "the fish is in the sea, and the sea is in the fish." Any system as complex and pervasive as capitalism is both inside us and outside us, and one of the tasks of utopias is to take the fish out of the sea.

Some utopias are fully formed imaginary societies, with every detail colored in, from the clothes people wear to the precise laws. Some are practical experiments, often on a large scale, like the communes inspired by Thoreau in nineteenth-century America, or the Kibbutzim in Israel. Others are generative ideas that begin as apparently impossible but then, at least sometimes, come to life. The principles expounded by political thinkers from John Locke to John Rawls, who hoped that a few guiding ideas could generate, if not a utopia, then at least a good society, were of this kind. The idea of universal human rights promoted by Rene Cassin was certainly utopian, but became enshrined in the UN Declaration; so was the Webbs' idea of free healthcare for all, first mooted at the beginning of the twentieth century and then made a reality forty years later. More recent ideas proposing that everyone on the planet should have a fixed and equal allocation of carbon are certainly utopian now, but may become tomorrow's common sense. All try to articulate ideas from which much else could be deduced. All embody the very radical idea that the future can influence the present, and not just the past; that we are made by our creativity as well as our learning. And all are expressions of what Ernst Bloch called "the principle of hope," an impulse that lies in the very nature of humanity, and that sometimes animates action and sometimes substitutes for it.

The most memorable utopias present coherent and consistent alternatives to the present, new societies appearing as if by decree. They serve as devices for what the Russian formalists called "making strange," helping us to see the oddness of the present. The origin of the tradition can be traced to Plato's *Republic*, but in its modern form began with Thomas More's *Of the Best State of a Republic, and of the New Island Utopia*, a book written in 1516 describing a fictional island in the Atlantic Ocean, which set the tone for the form. Although it long predates modern capitalism, some of the themes found in later anticapitalist utopias can be found there. It promises a system without money or property. Work is to be shared. The working day is limited, and there's also the eccentricity that so often seems to come with utopias: everyone has to go to bed by 8. The worst evils of society, such as poverty and misery, are banished. Even better, the utopia has few laws and therefore no lawyers. It rarely sends its citizens to war, but hires mercenaries from among its war-prone neighbors.

The tradition of utopian writing gathered pace in France before and after the revolution. A good eighteenth-century example is Louis Sebastien Mercer, who presented a utopian counterpoint to the excess and hierarchy of monarchical France, with taxes fixed at 2 percent of income but voluntary contributions of much more thanks to the public-spiritedness of the people. In place of finery, the people were dressed in simple clothes, enjoying pedestrianized cities. Public provision was impressive, with clean water and public health.

A few decades later, Claude-Henri de Saint-Simon described a utopia of the productive, with power taken from the idle rich and clerics, and an economy built around workshops. Science (the basis for the "religion of Newton") and industry would together shape the society. Unluckily he included the royal family among the idle, for which he was arrested, and his plans for a European Union were premature. But his perspective was of its time, as was his hope that science would shape utopia as reason unfolded over all things. "The most absurd of beliefs places the golden age in the past," he wrote, "it is the future alone which holds it in store. Giants will return, not giants in stature but giants in reasoning."[1] Hayek later described his ideas as the religion of the engineers, with good reason. Saint-Simon viewed the French revolution as a wasted opportunity to spread industrialism that had instead gone down the cul de sacs of law and rights. And so in his utopia, public revenues would be removed from the army and police and invested into productive activities and public works (with a "Chamber of Invention" developing ideas to be overseen by a second "Chamber of Execution"). The world was seen as plastic—there to be molded by reason and experience, but with an unmistakable direction of change toward a better world.

A more overtly political variant can be found in Etienne Cabet's utopia of Icaria, an extreme land of reason incarnate, which promised absolute cleanliness and absolute symmetry, helped by laws to specify everything from food to dress, and with all citizens engaged in government (as well as voting), supported by a Department of Statistics to provide them with the facts they needed. Icarian societies spread in working-class communities all over France, and then in the United States, where communes were set up in Texas, Louisiana, Illinois, Missouri, Iowa, and California.

France at the time of the revolution had experienced the full malleability of the world, and had seen just how much could be transformed in a very short space of time. After the restoration, the persistence of so much of the Napoleonic legal code disproved the reactionary claims that reform was futile and against nature. But France had also experienced the limits of reason: the failed attempts to legislate a ten-hour day, ten-day weeks, and an array of new festivals and honors, all infused with the same spirit as many of the utopian novels, proved that not everything is plastic. Wishing a new world did not make it happen, and even when it was legislated it wasn't guaranteed to stick.

England's equivalent utopias, popular in the nineteenth century, tended to be less urban, more rural, and more overtly nostalgic. Their vision of a world after capitalism was closer in spirit to the world before it. W. H. Hudson wrote one of the popular variants describing a future in which cities would be remade into rural paradises, with crafts replacing industry, market gardens growing up to replace the factories and railway stations. But the most influential was William Morris, whose *News from Nowhere* promised a world of folk festivals and crafts, with the railway tracks pulled up by citizens happily reverting to a medieval Eden, without paid work. Samuel Butler's *Erewhon* (an anagram for nowhere) was just as popular. In this country, illness was considered a crime. Sick people were thrown in jail; sickness was their own fault. Even sad people were imprisoned, for grief was taken to be a sign of misfortune and people were held responsible for actions that made them unfortunate. People who robbed or murdered, on the other hand, were treated kindly and taken to hospital to recover. No machines were allowed in *Erewhon*, as one of their philosophers had warned that machines could rapidly evolve and take over the world.

There are thousands of other examples of often elaborately constructed worlds, with legal codes, institutions, and leaders. Nikolai Chernyshevsky's *What Is to Be Done?*, published in Russia in 1863, and Edward Bellamy's *Looking Backward* were both huge best-sellers. These labors of love represent a unique outpouring of hope as well as of frustration with the present. They worked in the spirit of Schiller's injunction to his contemporaries to rise "on wings bravely high above your time" so that "faintly in the mirror may the future dawn."

Capitalism, in full flood as the nineteenth century progressed, plays an ambiguous role in these utopias. It's more often the enemy than something to be built on. Karl Marx was unusual in seeing capitalism as a necessary stage of progress, a rocky landscape that had to be passed through on the way to the sunlit uplands of socialism. To the extent that there was a utopian strand of capitalism, it was to be found less in books and more in events. The promise of plenty was celebrated in grandiose cornucopias like London's Great Exhibition of 1851 with its great palaces of glass, Chicago's in 1893 with its phosphorescent and neon lights, its 27 million visitors (and its spirit of indefatigable optimism only partly marred by the mayor's assassination just before it closed), or Paris in 1900 with 50 million visitors, talking films and escalators. Each in its way was utopian and each punctuated another phase of restless expansion with visions of public and domestic bliss, high-tech entertainment and transport. But their visions were essentially reduced to things, an accumulation of stuff that would transform life.

It was natural that when capitalism did come to promise utopias they would be more personal than collective ones, and, that when its imagination did take flight to paint a whole world, the results were ambiguous. The science fiction of 1980s cyberpunk, for example, was in some respects a deliberate extrapolation of contemporary neoliberalism and capitalism, glamorous, individualistic, oppositional, immersed in brands and virtual realities, and taking the world of global corporations as a given. It certainly portrayed an interesting and exciting world, but it wasn't one that most people would choose to live in.

Too much confidence in a materially and technologically fueled progress troubled as many people as it enthused, and made many all the more eager to turn the clock back to a rural idyll of communal living and life amidst nature. In the nineteenth century, the aristocracy, who were as baffled by capitalism as the workers, found themselves well placed to describe these ideals, a more egalitarian version of their country estates. Prince Kropotkin wrote of a return to communal village life, a world without a state, and advocated mutual aid and association, which all living creatures found the "best arms for the struggle for life." Voluntary cooperation and exchange would replace a corrupted world of money and power. Tolstoy wrote in a similar vein and tried to create a small paradise on his lands in Russia, arguing not for a violent revolution but a moral transformation, the regeneration of the inner man since, as the title of one his books asserted, "the Kingdom of God is within you." These were visions of societies without industry or technology, a simpler, more honest equality, grounded in labor, but rather than the miserable and demeaning work of the factory, it would be the soul-enhancing work of the craftsman or the farmer.

This was a common theme in many of the utopias. They wanted work to remain as the spine of daily life, but hoped that it would no longer be work for others, no longer be grinding toil, and no longer be turned into a commodity. Karl Marx criticized the utopians, but he too wrote of a future where we would hunt in the morning, fish in the afternoon, rear cattle in the evening, and criticize after dinner (though, as the feminists pointed out, he was never clear about who would cook the dinner). This new age of leisure, achieved thanks to the wonders of automated production, would leave us with the freedom of pharaohs, freedom that would be used not for idleness but for creative work. Work in capitalism was alienated work, where "activity appears as suffering, strength as powerlessness, production as emasculation." But work in the future would be reintegrated with our true selves and our deeper needs as human beings. And if there was a fear that too little competition and work would "make men dull," the answer William Morris forecast was "the production of what used to be called art, but which has no name amongst us now, because it has become a necessary part of the labour of every man who produces."

The more that twentieth-century capitalism turned into a boom for bureaucracy, thanks to the burgeoning power of managers, time and motion studies, and Frederick Taylor's advocacy of a separation of thought and action, the more the utopians went the other way. James Burnham encapsulated this fear best, with his account of why Henry Ford and Joseph Stalin were engaged in a parallel enterprise to stifle human freedom in a world dominated by planners and managers, it mattering little if the domination came from capitalist corporations or communist state agencies. Their hierarchies and even their buildings looked much the same. Agriculture had trapped people in oppressive toil 10,000 years ago after the freedoms of hunter-gatherer societies were lost. Now capitalism was intensifying the subjection, but hopefully paving the way for true freedom.

If for some that freedom meant true work, honest, creative, and no longer alienated, for others it mean the escape from work. Paul Lafargue (Marx's son-in-law) wrote of "The Right to Idleness," and many others have hoped that progress would free us from the necessity of work, not impose a new kind of work as the answer.

Either way the freedom to be more utopian generally meant being less connected. Where capitalism brought railways and telegraphs, broadband networks and satellites, most of the utopias take their cue from Thomas More and depict islands. For example, Ernest Callenbach's *Ecotopia* suggests a blockaded new country, made up of parts of California, Oregon, and Washington State, and finding a new way of life through adversity. Fiction predicts reality in that blockaded and isolated Cuba, deprived of oil, was forced to adapt urban agriculture to feed itself, and then became a model for radical Americans trying to green their cities.

Many of the writers either began with practice or went on to put their utopian visions into practice. A century after Thomas More, Gerard Winstanley and his co-conspirators set out to make a utopia on St. Georges Hill, a radically egalitarian community without hierarchy or property, that was ultimately crushed by the landowners and the army. But two centuries later the conditions for utopia had improved. The Garden City movement is one of the better examples, inspired by a utopian novel (*Looking Backward*) and founded by Ebenezer Howard, they were imagined as self-contained communities of around 30,000, mixing homes, workshops, and agriculture in the surrounding fields. Howard's vision, set out in *To-morrow: A Peaceful Path to Real Reform* in 1898, was of a network of such garden cities, all as satellites of a central city of around 50,000, linked together by rail. Two were built during his lifetime, Letchworth Garden City and Welwyn Garden City, both in Hertfordshire, England, and his ideas proved very influential across the United States, from Woodbourne in Boston to Jackson Heights in Queens, as well as further afield, from Argentina's Ciudad Jardín Lomas del Palomar to Colonel Light Gardens in Adelaide, South Australia.

In retrospect, it's striking how many of the utopians were also practical. William Morris's written accounts of the future might have been far-fetched, but he was successful as a producer of textiles and wallpapers (even working on commission to Queen Victoria). The arts and crafts movement began as an alternative to capitalism, providing useful products for the people (though it ended up making them mainly for the wealthy). Robert Owen combined imaginative musings on the future of cooperation with ownership of one of Europe's most productive and successful manufacturing enterprises in New Lanark near Glasgow. At their best the utopians broke free from the constraints of nature in both their thought and their action. Interestingly, although Karl Marx was keen to denounce the naïveté of some of the utopians, who hoped to wish a new world into being, he also admired others and wrote that "in the utopias of a Fourier, an Owen etc, there is the anticipation and imaginative expression of a new world."[2]

The most recent utopias revive many of the same themes. There are extreme versions like Ivan Efremov's *Andromeda*, published in 1958 and setting out in laborious detail a harmonious classless world, in which the planners have remade the world as almost a parody of urban zoning (and in which dissidents are dispatched to an "island of oblivion" to rehabilitate themselves). More often the visions are milder, messier, and more real, sometimes situating their utopias after an apocalypse has brought down industrial civilization as people pick up the pieces. Again we see a yearning for cooperation, for village-scale communities and work that is meaningful. And the most recent utopias provide a mirror to waste, presenting an ecologically sustainable world in which things are reused and recycled, buildings look the same from the air as the land did before they were built, and emissions from factories are drinkable water.

One of the best representations is Ursula LeGuin's *The Dispossessed*, based on Anarres, a moon of the planet Urras, where revolutionaries have created a society without government or coercive authoritarian institutions. Here the language has been shorn of possessives; people are judged by what they do and what they do for others, not what they own. This is a poor society, in a materially barren environment. The novel's main character, the physicist Shevek, gradually comes to understand that the revolution that brought his world into being is stagnating, and that power structures are forming where there were none before. The result is an ambiguous utopia that doesn't pretend that a perfect society is possible.

Today visionary utopias can be found in the anarchist and socialist traditions, in the movements around the World Social Forum (slogan: "Another world is possible"), on the edges of all of the major religions, in the radical subcultures that surround the Internet, and in moderated form in thousands of civic ventures across the world. They can be found in the detailed philosophies of movements such as permaculture, which promotes holistic ways of farming. Different variants can be found in the subcultures of open software, which value technology as the agent of freedom and democracy, suspicious of any kind of concentrated power, private property or profit, making heroes of hackers and cyberguerrillas (and demonstrated, for example, in Europe's Pirate Party). Periods of crisis bring all of these groups new adherents looking for meaning, a way to make sense of the chaos and confusion of an economic system that takes pride in the blindness of the invisible hand.

But their weakness and the weakness of much contemporary anticapitalist literature (such as the writings of David Korten, Wendell Berry, Alain Lipietz, or Michael Albert) is that they offer little account of how their visions might be realized and how powerfully entrenched interests would be overcome. In books like *Looking Backward* and *News from Nowhere*, too, the utopias are spread by the power of example; others copy what so evidently works. In reality change is never so simple. As a result, the visions float in the air, appealing, self-contained, but without much chance of traction. Sometimes they inspire practical acts—a food box scheme here, an organic farm there, a web cooperative—and are in this sense close modern equivalents of William Morris and others, who combined utopian thinking with small-scale practical action. But they remain marginal, finding modest niches within the market economy but doing little to threaten the power of capital head on. They're given the freedom to be moles, digging their own molehills: but without the power to change the shape of the field.

Perhaps this impotence also stems from the paradox that all utopias are personal visions yet aspire to be collective ones. Their elements which are general—the desire that everyone should be fed, housed, happy, and free—are also the ones that are most banal, while their elements, which are most interesting and specific, by contrast, are the ones that are likely to jar the reader. Every utopia has to call into existence the public necessary for its creation; yet having called forth a public there's no certainty that it will choose the utopia prescribed for it.

So what of the utopias and their use for thinking of a world after capitalism? The very act of imagination that they are part of is useful in itself: it warns against permanence, the delusions of fixity that all institutions create, with their great buildings, their apparently timeless constitutions and rituals. Priest and paleontologist Pierre Teilhard de Chardin was right to comment that "the Utopians . . . though their flights of fancy may make us smile . . . have a feeling for the true dimensions of the phenomenon of man." We need to be reminded of our own hopes, as well as of the plasticity of the world. The root of wisdom is uncertainty (which is why St. Theresa was canonized for her doubt). It's easy to become psychologically enmeshed with the fatalist juggernauts, the fears of ecological or nuclear doom, the assumption that we are imprisoned by a market we cannot resist because it is our nature, the pessimists' certainty that all attempts at progress are futile. It's the plasticity that utopian thinking makes possible that we should cherish, and it may be more natural to a generation brought up on software, programs, and games like Sim City, where worlds can literally be invented and reprogrammed.

Modernity makes it possible to imagine new worlds in their entirety: other planets with life forms based on elements other than carbon or modeled virtual worlds obeying their own generative rules. At a more everyday level the imagination of possible worlds opens up new ways of thinking. So, for example, designing a workplace or a town without any text or writing forces attention to visual languages, which may then be useful in helping new migrants, or children with learning disabilities. Designing a town without any place for cars may open up new ways of thinking about architecture. Designing a whole educational curriculum through play and games may provide new insights into motivation and learning. The important point is that the very extremism of possible worlds feeds back usefully into the more prosaic and incremental world of everyday practice. The physicist Wolfgang Pauli once said of an unimpressive theory that "it's so bad it isn't even wrong," meaning that it wasn't sufficiently sharply defined to prove either true or false. Good theories aren't always right: but they can be useful. Utopias tend to be wrong, but useful even in their wrongness.

The best visionary thinking is where poetry collides with prose—the beauty of ideas with their realism. British musician and composer Brian Eno wrote well that "we feel affinities not only with the past but also with the futures that didn't materialise, and with the other variations of the present that we suspect run parallel to the one we have agreed to live in." And at their best, we look to utopias to do what all thinking about the future should do, which is to "disturb the present."

But utopias are not in themselves good tools for transforming systems. They are too pure, and usually too complete. The best human creations emerge and unfold. A common lesson in urban planning is that the more fully formed the plans for a new community or housing estate, the more detailed the specifications and the architects' images, the less likely it is that the community will succeed. It's the incomplete plans that work best, because they leave the greatest space for residents to fill them in.

The same is true of whole societies. And the critique made of Saint-Simon nearly two centuries ago remains valid. Without a sense of the dynamics of a system, it's not possible to design or even imagine what might come after. Most healthy change is evolutionary, and has room for trial and error. What we need are not utopias—fantasies of "no place" (the strict meaning of the word in Greek), but rather neotopias, new places, embryos of the future ready to be grown and adapted. First, however, we need to understand the dynamics of change, the contexts within which we act to change systems or shore them up.

Chapter 7

· · · · · · · · ·

The Nature of Change

How One System Becomes Another

BUDDHISM was the first great system of thought to recognize the fluidity and impermanence of things. The Buddha warned against excessive attachment, which was bound to end in disappointment and suffering. But he saw no inherent virtue in this constant change: it was just the way the world was made.

Capitalism is change incarnate, and the first system whose advocates came to embrace perpetual revolution, and to celebrate the idea that "everything that is solid melts into air" (Karl Marx deserves the credit for identifying this as a defining character of capitalism, but many others happily adopted the insight and made it their own). The constant search for value requires destruction of the old; a ruthless lack of sentiment in stopping or closing anything that is unproductive, and a cultivated hunger to seek out new things or ideas that might create value.

Yet, for all its fixation with change, capitalism, and the economics that has evolved around it, has lacked any theory to explain how it too might change. There are many theories to explain how a traditional society could become capitalist, or how free markets could be introduced into a communist economy. But economics can't explain what might come after that.

This is the great paradox of capitalism's intellectual life. Its theorists can give lengthy and compelling accounts of how change might take place within a market economy, with businesses waxing and waning, and technologies and production systems stumbling in and out of life. If you extrapolate current trends, it is not hard to show that the global economy will treble in size by 2050; that China will have standards of living not far from those of the United States, and a greater capital stock. More sophisticated forecasters can also point to less obvious dynamics and patterns—for example showing how energy efficiency declines in the early stages of development before rising again, or why China's labor force (and probably its growth rate) will decline after 2020.

But capitalism's theorists, and the discipline of economics, can give few accounts of it as a living system, or of how it might undergo nonlinear changes. Its advocates assumed it to be the end of an evolutionary line. The only future they could imagine was a more extensive and more intensive capitalism: what Friedrich Hayek called "catallaxy," a complete market economy, a society where everything is turned into a commodity to be traded.

So the task of understanding the longer term dynamics was left to the critics. They took up the challenge with enthusiasm and devoted extraordinary creativity to describing the many spades with which capitalism might dig its own grave. Liberals (both in the nineteenth century and today) tended to see world history as made up of only two stages: a primitive one and a progressive one, the latter made up of ever-expanding freedoms under representative democracy and widening markets. The radicals by contrast tended to see history as made up of three stages. Two of the stages were shared with the liberals. But a third stage was always posited which represented a further progress toward socialism, communism, or a withering away of the state. These stages, or epochs, were believed naturally to follow on one from another, by analogy with the human body and its predictable stages of organic development. The implication—at least in the harder line sometimes taken by Marx—was that people had little option but to be observers of these great currents of change: "are men free to choose this or that form of society? By no means" he wrote.[1] They could choose to hasten the progress from one stage to another; but they couldn't shift history from its predetermined path.

In the classic Marxist account, technology was given the decisive role. It was destined to drive change, becoming revolutionary through the contradictions that would emerge between the forces of production, the technologies used by factories, and the relations of production, which governed the relative power of owners and workers. Technological change would make the workers ever more productive: but the relations of production would guarantee that owners took the lion's share of profits, leaving the proletariat ever more impoverished and ever more miserable until they had no option but to revolt. In the twentieth century's revised accounts it would be the empowerment (and, in some accounts, the proletarianization) of the knowledge workers that became the decisive factor. Either way capitalism would spawn its own gravediggers.

Crises would tip the system into chaos, and then into a new order. Marx had forecast a falling rate of profit that would force capitalism into ever more severe crises. It would be prone to overproduction, its warehouses packed to the rafters with unsold goods (and it was only half a century later that capitalism did indeed suffer a disastrous crisis of overproduction, otherwise known as the Great Depression). Its ideal of competition would give way to vast monopolies: again, a prediction that came true, embodied in figures like John Rockefeller, who lobbied to eliminate "wasteful competition" (though in time antitrust legislation kept the worst excesses of monopoly in check). Financial capital would fall out with industrial capital. Inequality would widen (again this has happened as the ratio of the world's richest 20 percent to the poorest 20 percent has risen from around 5 to 1, to 75 to 1). The "reserve army" of the unemployed, the people kept out of work to "encourage the others," maintaining a downward pressure on wages and working conditions, would become ever angrier.

As forecasts go, which is admittedly not a very high bar, Marx's were not unusually inaccurate. But he misread the ability of capitalism to respond to threats and pressures, and in particular he misread how well it would be able to spread wealth as well as hoarding it. That the distribution of wealth was often forced on it by striking workers, or reforming governments, is one of the paradoxes of history. If capitalism had been left to the capitalists it probably would have destroyed itself. Instead, the capitalists were bullied into saving themselves.

Nor were some of the more profound layers of Marx's account of change borne out. Marx suggested that capitalism would be superseded precisely because of its peculiar mix of progressive power and cruelty. The latter would so alienate the workers, so strip them of identities and attachments, that they would ultimately discover and implement "true humanity through this historically imposed social nakedness."[2]

Instead the workers found not only identities, but also reasonable wages as well as votes and respect. The result was that Marxism was pushed to the edges, to protest parties, or to the pacified academic arguments of a theoretical Marxism that has merged into the abstractions of literary theory, becoming, as the philosopher Jacques Derrida put it, a ghost. The world's leading Marxist nations, China and Russia, became state capitalist with a vengeance, and they did so in part because Marxism itself spawned such ugly dark mirrors of real markets, like the blat system in the USSR.[3]

DYNAMIC INSTABILITIES

Yet the Marxist method of seeking out the dynamic instabilities, the contradictions and tensions, remains a powerful tool for making sense of change. We cannot begin to imagine a world after capitalism, or even an evolved capitalism, without first mapping out the places where societies and economies are being stretched, traumatized, or unraveled.

One factor is demography. In some accounts, capitalist meritocracy would steadily reduce the incentives for people to have children, sacrificing income and pleasure for the relentless labor of family life. Hence the sharply declined birth rates across Europe and among white Americans, now well below replacement rates, and the clear evidence that global economic growth rates have declined in step with fertility. The decline in fertility rates from 5 to 2 that took 130 years in the UK (1800–1930) took twenty years in South Korea (1965–1985) and could be even faster elsewhere (in Iran it fell from 7 in 1984 to 1.5 in 2010).

At some point the resulting demographic imbalances threaten to undermine the generational contract upon which any society or economy depends, with a growing group of the elderly demanding ever more from a shrinking group of younger workers. This argument takes us once again to that litmus test of responsibility, the savings rate. That these rates have almost collapsed when they needed to be closer to 30 percent to cope with aging is a stark symptom of a capitalism that has lost the ability to protect its own future. Ironically China, despite its high savings rates, may be even more at risk, as the one-child policy transforms it from a young to an old country faster than has ever happened before in human history. The one-child policy may have guaranteed a more intense commitment of love from parents to child; but it in no way guaranteed the inverse, and today's young Chinese face the prospect of having to support not only their two parents but also four grandparents.

According to the UN 2008 Revision, population growth rates are assumed to decline and eventually to turn negative,[4] as they already have in Japan and a few other countries. In this case world population will start declining before long,[5] a dramatic reversal of several centuries of growth, with the central projections now pointing to a world population in 2100 back to less than six billion. No one can be sure what an economy would look like through a long period of population decline, but it's reasonable to expect that it would struggle to avoid conflicts, resentments, and pressures to run down capital rather than building it up.

Another strand of critique has emphasized capitalism's vulnerability to success. Extraordinary productivity gains in manufacturing have had the odd effect of reducing its share of GDP. The more successful a sector is, the more it disappears from the radar, at least in statistical terms. A sector based on technologies that halve in price every year will have to double its markets not to lose ground. An economy apparently full of stuff has surprisingly relegated the makers of stuff. Japan and Germany still have manufacturing industries that account for over a fifth of their economies. But they are the exceptions among developed economies. In most, manufacturing has shrunk, to 13 percent of GDP in the UK (compared to 35% in 1960), just ahead of 12 percent in France and the United States. The result of the manufacturing productivity boom (helped by outsourcing) has been to leave economies ever more dependent on services, which are inherently harder to grow. Services are not immune to productivity jumps, and big investments in IT and logistics in the 1990s led to correspondingly big jumps in retailing (exemplified by Walmart)[6] and in banking (exemplified by the replacement of branches by ATMs). But much of the service economy is unlikely ever to emulate the dramatic gains achieved in information technology and manufacturing. Hence the argument that growth rates are bound to fall in the long-term, and that the faster capitalism evolves, the faster it closes off its own sources of growth.[7]

There's a matching vulnerability in consumption. Capitalism has been extraordinarily successful at meeting at least some material needs. In the developed economies, few go hungry or homeless. Material plenty and excess have become problems—obesity, alcoholism, gambling, and drug addiction are vices of prosperity (even if they tend to hurt the relatively poor more). Having successfully met peoples' material needs, capitalism is threatened if they then lose interest in working hard and making money, turning instead to new age counseling, midlife gap years, and three-day weekends. If people trade in money for time, work for leisure, the system's vital resources dry up. What can an industrial civilization mean without industry?

Nearly a century ago, John Maynard Keynes considered this possibility and predicted that

> assuming no important wars and no important increase in population, the economic problem may be solved, or be at least within sight of solution, within a hundred years. This means that the economic problem is not—if we look into the future—the permanent problem of the human race.[8]

The economic problem he was referring to is the problem of material satisfaction, and that has indeed been solved for much of the world which now has enough food, housing, and energy for everyone. The permanent problem is the problem of how to live, how to use scarce time in the best possible way.

This is the paradox of the more optimistic accounts of capitalism's future. Mainstream forecasts predict that over the next forty years China's income will rise tenfold and even the United States and Europe will see per capita incomes double. If these forecasts are right, current tendencies to react against satiation and excess will be even more marked. Slow food, voluntary simplicity, and organic lifestyles have spread from affluent minorities to a wider population, and there are already signs of reactions against the excesses of consumerism in China (just as these appeared in Japan within a generation of the great postwar boom). Capitalism's only response to this contradiction may be to invest ever more hysterically in creating new needs nudged by anxiety about status, or beauty and body mass, a perverse result that may make developed capitalisms more psychologically troubled than their poorer counterparts. Again this could be an unsustainable strategy for survival, a cure worse than the disease.

All accounts of capitalism's self-destructive tendencies pale into insignificance next to the ecological critique. Many past civilizations—from the early cities of Mesopotamia, to the Mayans, destroyed the environment on which they depended. Sometimes this happened so slowly that people barely noticed that they had to travel ever farther for food and water. Prisoners of their own misguided beliefs, they found it hard to diagnose their problems let alone to act. And then, too late, ecological collapse usually coincided with conflict, and took the once proud civilization back to subsistence. Mayan civilization, for example, is now thought to have collapsed from the combination of overpopulation, drought, and then social conflict.

In the modern versions of this story, too, blindness plays its part: communism collapsed because it didn't let prices tell the economic truth, and capitalism will collapse because it didn't let prices tell the ecological truth. That truth is complex since the carbon intensity of the economy is declining globally at 0.7 percent per year. But with population rising at roughly the same rate, and often dramatic growth in GDP, the net effect is an accelerating depletion of environments.

The Global Footprint Network, drawing on the work of the Stockholm Environment Institute, claims that we use the equivalent of 1.5 planets now. Like our predecessors we may be doomed because our institutions with the cognitive capacity to understand what is happening lack the power to change it, while those institutions with the power to change things lack the cognitive capacity to think their way out. A previous generation of ecological critiques didn't fare well: when the Club of Rome published its famous 1972 book *The Limits to Growth*, arguing that the world would soon run out of resources, its critics showed that they had greatly underrated the impact of technology and innovation. Then the critics were vindicated; ecological pessimism was overdone. But capitalism cannot always escape, Houdini-like, from the traps of its own making.

Many of these dynamics echo those we know well from the natural world. Evolution can drive arms races between predators and prey. But in the short run predators have a tendency to destroy themselves. If wolves eat too many sheep, they go hungry as the number of sheep falls (phenomena that are captured mathematically in the Lotka-Volterra equations).[9] Large predators turn out to be particularly vulnerable to the disappearance of their relatively large prey (and then once predators wane, "trophic cascades" swirl through whole ecosystems). Successive crises of capitalism have been interpreted as crises of overexploitation: too much exploitation of arable land leads to dust bowls; too much exploitation of workers leads to revolt; and too much degradation of nature ultimately destroys the biosphere on which our lives depend.

Yet perhaps just as powerful as the ecological arguments are the claims that capitalism is culturally doomed to fail or to disintegrate. A generation ago the American social scientist Daniel Bell wrote one of the best, and most original, dialectical analyses that drew in spirit at least on the Marxist method. For Bell what stood out were the "cultural contradictions of capitalism."[10] Capitalism rested, he argued, on a foundation of moral duty and obligation that it did little to sustain. It required people to be willing to work hard, to make sacrifices, to delay gratification and save money even if they didn't stand to benefit.

Yet the culture of modern capitalism tended to destroy precisely these traditional norms. By encouraging a restless attention to self-interest, by promoting material acquisitiveness as the heart of human nature, and advocating that consumption now is the most reliable road to happiness, capitalism corroded the willingness to work hard, to pass on legacies to children, or to avoid excessive hedonism, even though these were the very wellsprings of capitalist success. The corporation depended on hard work and delayed gratification: armies of people willing to put up with the slings and arrows of daily work in the patient hope of future reward, who took comfort from the stability and order of great structures that gave them a modicum of respect. But capitalism was ushering in a culture that valued the eternal now—pleasure and the path of least resistance. Individualism was at odds with responsibility, and democracy made things worse by encouraging an unhealthily rising sense of entitlement to welfare and a diminishing sense of obligation to pay for it.

Daniel Bell had in mind the counterculture of the 1960s and 1970s which he found distasteful. The children of the corporation men of the 1950s had taken to drugs, free love, and rock music, and a sometimes narcissistic pursuit of the self, where they hoped to find meaning (and often found, instead, their rather disappointing self). In France during the same period, business leaders and commentators worried about the new "allergy to work" that had infected so many young people. A few years after Bell's work appeared, Japan in the 1990s was an even clearer case—its slacker teenagers happily rejecting their parents' loyal work ethic that had done so much to drive the economic miracle. Theirs was a secular hedonism, of manga and sneakers, Walkmen and later iPods. They came to be described as "shin jin rui," a new breed of people. In a rather different way, a later generation in the United States also confirmed Bell's point, though not in the behavior of the hippies so much as in the behavior of the middle class. Between 1950 and 1990, the personal savings rate had averaged 10.5 percent and the lowest ever rate had been 7.3 percent. Prudence and responsibility meant living within your means and saving for your retirement or to help your children through college. But by 2006, the net savings rate had become negative,[11] a symptom of ballooning credit and a population no longer able to control their impulses to spend.

Bell didn't explore some of the most important cultural contradictions of capitalism, however. Repeatedly over the last century, the most powerful economic institutions have worried that, thanks to prosperity, the most able and educated were defecting, rejecting capitalist work for work in the arts, or public service, or dropping out entirely because of their sheer embarrassment and shame at the roles the market offered. Aristocrats in previous centuries had seen trade and production as grubby occupations, incompatible with dignity and self-respect, but here were the cream of modern meritocracy coming to similar conclusions. The anxiety reached a peak in the 1960s, when Marvin Bower, a director of McKinsey and president of Harvard Business School, spoke for many when he lamented the "weak attraction of business to elites."[12]

As wildcat strikes fizzed across the western world, everyone could see the production line workers in revolt, contrasting the ideology of freedom in consumption with the reality of subordination at work. But their anger was, far more than in previous eras, matched among their managers who had been brought up in a culture of rough equality, in which democracy and self-determination were treated as self-evidently good things. Yet inside the firm, they were expected to act as despots. Capitalism, once again, simply didn't make enough sense.

In retrospect, it is interesting to see what happened. In some cases a harsher market discipline put paid to the complaints. Workers were given a choice of buckling down to work or joining the unemployment lines that started lengthening in the 1970s. Revolt was an unaffordable luxury when, as Fidel Castro was reported to have said, the only thing worse than being exploited by multinational capitalism was not being exploited by multinational capitalism. Most manual work became more tightly controlled, monitored, and specified, greatly helped by new generations of technology that could track productivity in detail and in real time. But at the higher ends of the labor market business responded in a very different way. For the more elite knowledge workers, the same technologies offered the prospect of dramatically greater autonomy and creativity. The reality of daily life in big businesses might be no less hierarchical and bureaucratic than before, but at least now there was an official creed, promoted by figures like the business writer Tom Peters, that portrayed it as a world of exuberant liberation, where the individual could reign supreme, finding full expression for their passions. The complaints of an earlier generation of dissenters were absorbed, and woven into a new hybrid which made a virtue of change, fluidity, and even insecurity, with an ever greater emphasis on intrinsic motivations for work rather than extrinsic ones[13] echoing an earlier generation of psychologists who had worked to humanize the industrial workplace and office.[14]

In Bell's account, religion provided the moral underpinning for capitalism and a large part of the extrinsic motivation to work hard and suffer the slog of the factory floor, corporate bureaucracy, and career disappointment. Yet sometimes religion could appear on both sides of the cultural contradictions. An economic system that had its roots in the hard grind of Calvinism risked ending up with the ideals of motivational speakers, daytime TV, and mega-church pastors, so many of whose self-help million sellers promote the appealing idea that you can get anything that you want if you believe strongly enough and dispel all doubt. Visualizing possibilities makes them happen, and makes you rich. The more extreme purveyors of positive thinking took elements of truth—that people with optimistic personalities achieve more than pessimists—and distorted them into cults where it's impossible to air doubts. Such industries of fanatic positivity have the odd side effect of implying that any failure must be the individual's fault, the result of not believing enough. But they also corrode the motivation to stick with the hard grind that is usually the precondition for success in life or work.

This positivity has a particularly intriguing importance for capitalism. Capitalism is inherently optimistic. It is predicated on the willingness of investors to bank on things working out, and on millions of savers trusting in strangers more than in their mattresses. Every major business venture and every new technology depends on a leap of faith. By definition there can be no certain confidence that anything radically new will succeed. So capitalism institutionalizes the adventurers' spirit, seeking out new lands and conquests, hidden wealth, and admiring those who pull it off. It succeeds when exuberant optimism overcomes cautious prudence. And when optimism dissipates, the economy freezes in its tracks. Money stops flowing. Savers withdraw their money. Bankers learn again how to say no. Capitalist optimism is the polar opposite of prudence and sobriety—and the fear is that over time the first, reinforced by a mass culture, weakens the second, which is grounded more in the everyday virtues of the family.

Such cultures may move cyclically—with periods of luxury and laziness followed by periods that value simplicity, authenticity, and true living. As George Orwell put it, we strive to avoid the ease that we long for. Part of us becomes uncomfortable with comfort, perhaps a throwback to when too much ease made us liable to drop our guard against saber-toothed tigers.

Many cyclical patterns of this kind overlay the more linear patterns of economic growth and technological advance. For our purposes, perhaps the most important are the ones that involve creativity and predation. These have not been much theorized, but they have often been observed. Cycles of creativity seem to follow a fairly consistent pattern. They usually involve a first phase of openness and possibility, when new ideas flourish and are embraced. That's then followed by a phase of routinization, when the new ideas are implemented and institutionalized. After some time there then follows a phase of decay and stagnation. Finally, after a crisis or shock the system returns to openness. This is the pattern to be found, for example, in theories of "product life cycles."[15] A related model can be found in the work of C. S. Holling, the pioneer of resilience. In ecological systems, periods of apparent optimization (when everything has found its niche) tend to be unstable, and are succeeded by periods of creative destruction with spare energy, that allows opportunities for predators and parasites, before returning to order.

These cycles of creativity intersect with cycles of predation. The expansive culture of creative periods opens up more opportunities for predators, as constraints are removed in a spirit of liberalization and freedom. But predators tend to overreach—and tend to be blamed when crises hit. By overreaching they destroy their prey, and end up harming themselves. The settlements that result from crises usually rein them in with rules and restraints. The patterns have been extensively mapped and modeled in the natural world, but they are also found in history. Many historians have shown the cycles whereby states periodically overreach and overtax, prompting revolts; the cycles whereby elites take too much until something snaps; the cycles whereby farmers overgraze and end up with dustbowls.

In the next chapter I look at how creation cycles and predation cycles can intersect. But first I turn to a more comprehensive framework for thinking about change within which both can fit.

HOW TO CHANGE THE SYSTEM

In Tom Stoppard's trilogy on Herzen, *The Coast of Utopia*, Herzen advises his son, and the audience, to sail toward the coast of utopia but not to imagine that there is a true paradise to be found on land. I've suggested some of the imaginative utopias, and the ideas, that have promised an alternative to capitalism.

I've also described some of the dynamic properties of capitalist systems that constantly throw them away from equilibrium. But how far do any of these add up to a change in the system, or a change of the system? What makes a whole society decide that it needs to shift, and not just the people involved in pockets of experiment? How are predators of all kinds overthrown?

These sorts of change are rare but not unknown. The transitions into democracy, from market economies into communism and then from communism to market economies, are ones that we can readily bring to mind. In each case predatory elites, and predatory systems, were transformed, and very visible events symbolized the change: vast crowds gathered in city squares, grandiose pronouncements greeted with exhilarating emotions and fears, and the vortex that sweeps unknowns into celebrity, and celebrities into oblivion. Others are more piecemeal: the creation of welfare states, socialized healthcare, consumerism, privatization, and deregulation. And others still are partial and potential, like the shift to a circular economy.

There is a vast literature on how change happens, and many have tried to come up with a single "theory of change." There are good reasons why we should want to know. Without a theory of change our efforts to better things may be futile—trying to change what can't be changed, trying to do fast what has to be done slowly or trying to do slowly what has to be done fast is bound to lead to disappointment. Everyone would like to find a point of leverage, the single key to unlock change, and many accounts of change like to focus in on a heroic leader, a miracle cure or a silver bullet from which all else follows. The lever may be a technology—like the stirrup or the contraceptive pill—or a person, like a Napoleon or Henry Ford. Yet even if such explanations can be convincing in retrospect, they are little help to anyone wanting to make a change. As Karl Popper put it, "the most striking aspects of historical development are non-repetitive . . . the fact that we can predict eclipses does not provide a valid reason for expecting that we can predict revolutions."[16]

Indeed all attempts to find a single theory of change are doomed. As the many theories described earlier in this chapter make clear, change takes place in different ways in different fields—from families and consumption, to governments and technologies. It would be surprising if there was a common shape to all of them, not least because people learn (at least some of the time—as Hegel commented, the clearest lesson of history is that people don't learn the lessons of history). The rhythms of change are very different for, for example, slow-moving, capital-intensive energy infrastructures, political constitutions, sexual norms or fashion. And because change always involves competition and conflict between the newcomers and the incumbents, and between predators and prey, what worked in one situation won't work in another.

What I suggest here is not a single theory of change. Instead, it is an overarching account that aims to sharpen how we think about what will come after capitalism by starting with two simple questions: why, most of the time, do things stay the same; and why, some of the time, do things change?

THE FOUR FORCES OF CONSERVATISM

Within most systems, changes are usually modest. Other things being equal, life repeats itself. In evolution successful mutations are very rare. The rhythms of the typical day, the routines of sleep, meals, travel, or work show us to be creatures of habit, and children observe their parents' repetitions and learn to copy them. Humans are creative and curious yet our default is laziness, and we generally seek out easy, not difficult, paths. That's why institutions, too, are built around repetition and patterns that change only incrementally—the primary school, the factory, and the shop survive both by adapting and by not changing. When change happens, we usually start with single steps rather than jumps. Innovations are rarely dramatic "out of the box" leaps—though they can look so from a distance. Much more often they are a combination of incremental steps.

The reasons aren't only a lack of imagination, laziness, or dogma, though these can all play a part. Instead there are reasons for inertia that any reformer needs to grasp. The first reason why things tend to stay the same, and why even predatory systems can survive for long periods of time, is efficiency. Within any system, whether it is an industry, a school, or a city, many different elements have over time come to be "optimized" around each other: they have adapted and adjusted to get along, like people's steps finding the most convenient paths across fields or parklands. The practical details of how businesses operate; how professions are trained and rewarded; how laws are made; how families organize their time, and a million other ways in which daily life is organized, have evolved in small increments, and in tandem with each other. This is certainly true of capitalism as a form of life. Each of its elements, like the idea of personal credit, mass advertising, the factory, or the idea of being paid by the hour or by the year evolved gradually, falteringly. Over time people became ever more confident in using these tools and as they did so, the tools became more useful.

Any new approach, however well designed, may appear quite inefficient compared to the subtle interdependencies of an existing social or economic system. When cars were first introduced in the 1880s they were inefficient by almost any standards. As a way of getting from point A to point B, they were unreliable and costly. Seen in context they were even more inefficient: wholly unsuited to an ecology of stables and horse fairs, carriage drivers, and men armed with shovels to remove the monumental scale of horse refuse. It was only the persistence of inventors and drivers, both groups enthused by the dream of the car, that helped the technology to advance to a state where it could plausibly offer an efficient alternative to the horse and carriage.

These patterns are even clearer in energy, the lifeblood of industrial capitalism. Energy systems are slow to build and slow to change, because they require so many things to be aligned. An oil-based economy needs not only oil prospectors, oil wells, refineries, and distribution systems, but also machines designed to use oil and skills to make oil work well. Any competing technology, however apparently attractive, starts with a profound disadvantage because it lacks these complementary factors.

Even public sectors which by many standards are highly inefficient build up their own logics: like the military bases in the old Soviet Union that propped up local economies, or the vast U.S. prisons built in the 1980s and 1990s that did the same. For any system to change, there has to be a widespread consensus that it is no longer efficient and that its internal efficiencies are outweighed by its larger failings.

The second reason that change is difficult is the power of interests. In any successful social or economic system many people have a high stake in stability. Predators defend their privileges with honest conviction that the people they prey on would do worse without them (a remarkable proportion of the top 1 percent in any society are convinced that the 99 percent benefit from their success). The risks of change appear great compared to the benefits of continuity—and this applies as much to peasant farmers nervously contemplating new models of farming as it does to managers responding to globalization, or civil servants contemplating a new deal around performance-related pay. Most will have sunk investments of time and money in past practices that they are loath to discard or cannibalize. In stable societies the most acute tensions will have been papered over or settled in compromises—another reason to fear changes that may bring these to the surface. Meanwhile, the interest groups that are the greatest beneficiaries of the status quo will have learned how to work the system to their own advantage and how to make themselves indispensable. Capitalism only won a grip in societies when already powerful interests saw that they would gain more than they might lose, when nineteenth-century landowners for example remade themselves as commodity producers, or late twentieth-century communist officials saw that they could become rich.

The third factor is mind. Any social system comes to be solidified within peoples' minds in the form of assumptions, values, and norms. The more the system appears to work, giving people the security and prosperity they crave, the more its characteristics will become entrenched, and the more they become part of peoples' very sense of identity.[17] Stability breeds inertia, since the system appears to be telling the people within it that what they do and how they think is right.[18] As Joseph Schumpeter wrote, "social structures, types and attitudes are coins that do not readily melt. Once they are formed they persist, possibly for centuries."[19] We've already seen how often predator ideologies have taken hold, not just among the winners but among the losers too, who accept that it's merely natural that, while they are poor and powerless, others are billionaires. Minds do change, however, and some of the most vivid histories of industrialization have documented how peoples' minds were changed, often forcibly, first to make them reliable and disciplined workers, and then to turn them into active consumers. Politics has rarely been far behind in this, since much of the business of government is really about shaping how people think—and what they categorize as good and bad, legal and illegal, just and unjust, part of the nation or outside it.

The fourth factor that inhibits change is the bond of relationships. The personal relationships between the movers and shakers in the system create an additional stabilizing factor in the form of social capital and mutual commitment. Real-market economies are animated by networks of contacts and favors, from the golf club to the sauna, as well as by more visible transactions. Similarly, much of the business of government rests on personal relationships that may count for more than formal organograms: these networks of favors and debts may be all-important for getting things to happen within a stable system, but they are likely to seriously impede any radical change that will bring in newcomers. Most people would rather not rock the boat or get a reputation as a trouble-maker: saying what you really think may leave you socially isolated.[20]

All of these forces present huge impediments to change, and all can be seen in every real capitalist economy. Despite the commitment to change that animates entrepreneurship, capitalist economies are devoted to stability. They have tried to optimize arrangements, for example around how people are hired for jobs, or how pensions are organized in a long process of mutual adaptation. Powerful interest groups have solidified their stakes in the system—and not just bankers, and the other beneficiaries of large surpluses, but also people with a pension, or a permanent job. The market has become simply part of how we think: it's natural that a firm losing money should sack workers, natural that city roads are covered with advertising billboards, natural that the nightly news should tell us that our currency's exchange rate has changed by a minute fraction. And personal relationships hold markets together: how else to explain the huge investment in conferences, networks, clubs, and the continuing vitality of face-to-face interaction in a world where technologies should have made it obsolete?

Together these four forces explain why systems are designed as they are, and why the rules take the shapes that they do. And because ideas and interests evolve in tandem, it's not possible to say which rules the world: both do, but they only do so because they mobilize each other.

The magnetic pull of what is, as opposed to what might be, helps people ignore or wish away the deeper structural challenges of demography, productivity, or ecology. As the German philosopher Arthur Schopenhauer put it, new truths are first ignored, then violently opposed, and only later come to be treated as self-evident. Indeed, change may only be possible when the people change (as the saying goes, "if you can't change the people, change the people"). Thomas Kuhn's classic account over forty years ago of scientific change, which popularized the idea of the paradigm, applies just as well to other forms of life. Kuhn showed that even in the apparently rational world of science, better theories do not automatically displace worse ones. Evidence and facts are not enough. Indeed, when existing theories fail the natural response is to work even harder at trying to get the theory to work. Existing theories have to be clearly failing on a large scale, and their adherents have to have either died or given up, before the new theory can take over. We need to feel naked, and vulnerable, before we're willing to adopt unfamiliar new clothes.

These problems of change pose a challenge to all reformers. Precisely because in human societies so many intricate elements adapt to each other, any radical change is likely to cause performance to deteriorate in the short run, even if it then takes off in the longer run. The beneficiaries of ending predation may lose before they win. New models are bound to take time to optimize their performance—and adapt to the environment around them. A succession of writers about change—from Joseph Schumpeter in the 1930s to Donald Schon in the 1970s and Amitai Etzioni and Clay Christiansen in the 1990s—have emphasized this point: that reformers and innovators have to hold their nerve—and hold onto their supporters—through difficult periods of transition when things may appear to get worse rather than better.

So how can things ever change? Within societies and economies, some kinds of change happen all the time. Modern capitalist societies are unique in that they devote scarce resources to discovery—to research and development, to the creative arts, all exploring the frontiers of the new. These bring with them the disruption that always comes with innovation: the failure that accompanies most new ideas; and the destruction and loss of old skills and jobs that accompany ones that succeed, just as the apple that Adam ate from the tree of knowledge disrupted an earlier, optimized society. But truly far-reaching social changes only take place when all four of the great inhibitors of change shift, or, to use dialectical language, when they run into contradictions that are sufficiently acute to unravel them.

WHAT DRIVES CHANGE?

First, what turns efficiency into inefficiency? We've already surveyed many of the dynamic factors that can do this—from demographics and productivity effects to the impact of new knowledge. The reasons may be external (a rising power over the frontier) or they may be more internal (resource depletion).

Problems can be felt at many levels. In business, profitability is the litmus test of efficiency, and rare moments of genuinely systemic change are marked by dramatic gulfs between the falling profitability of the old and the vast profits of the newcomers, particularly when, like J. P. Morgan or Bill Gates, they bring with them radically new models of production, organized in temporary monopolies. For whole economies, the symptoms of crisis are slow growth, falling profits, and financial failure. These in turn make it harder for governments to raise taxes, and to legitimate their actions. Political parties find it harder to win votes. Slow growth then tends to exacerbate tensions and intolerance. Europe in the 1930s and the United States in the 1970s both serve as warnings: when system performance deteriorates, people become angrier, they look for scapegoats and realize that they will have to fight harder for a share of a shrinking cake.

These crises of performance also manifest themselves in the personal stress felt by millions as they see their cherished values or norms less validated by experience. So although people are adept at explaining away uncomfortable results and avoiding "cognitive dissonance,"[21] and although elites generally try to police taboo ideas, at some point they recognize that the status quo can't survive. When this happens, each of the forces that contributed to stability starts to unravel.

Crises of efficiency are invariably also crises of interpretation, and during periods of waning performance one of the most bitter sites of struggle is how efficiency should be defined and categorized. The most radical changes happen not just when material realities change, but when the categories change: in the mid-nineteenth century economic success came to mean not just high prices for producers but also low prices for consumers, as producer interests came to be seen as predators rather than as pillars of society. Later on, reformers challenged the idea that the efficiency of individual firms was all that mattered, emphasizing instead the efficiency of the public realm, and the need for investments in public health, schools, and infrastructures: ruthless factory owners came to be seen as predators, just as landowners had been a few generations before. In 1833, the British parliament spent more on the Queen's stables than on children's education, but by 1880, schooling was compulsory for 5–10-year-olds thanks to a consensus that better education was vital to support an industrial economy. In 1858, the appalling stench of the River Thames (known as the "Big stink") brought government and parliament to a halt but also prompted the creation of a comprehensive system of public water and sewers. Forty years later, during the Boer war, half of all volunteers were deemed to be medically unfit, and by World War I the same was true of a third of conscripts, prompting demands for universal healthcare. Similar shifts occurred at the end of the twentieth century, as societies and firms looked for new approaches to efficiency that took account of ecological waste, the waste of excessive consumption, or the failure to achieve happiness and well-being, and started to see oil companies more as predators on nature rather than as pillars of a mobile society.[22] Many of these struggles are still unresolved. For example, should energy efficiency be thought of in terms of units produced for each dollar, in terms of sustainability, or in terms of the energy achieved for each unit of energy invested? Fossil fuels usually achieve a ratio of between 20:1 and 100:1 by this measure, whereas solar power is closer to 10. In a world worried about energy security and climate change, ecological inefficiency matters more; in a possible world once more glutted with gas and oil, or unconcerned about the long-term future, economic inefficiencies may matter more.

As efficiency, however defined, decays, the second force of conservatism can switch, as people cease to believe that their interests are protected by the status quo. During the good times, predators are rich not just in money but also in friends seeking patronage. When things turn sour they start to look more like pariahs. Groups on the edge, such as voluntary organizations, trade unions, small businesses, and professions may be weather vanes, during some periods fully co-opted into power, and during others opting out. Weak power becomes strong as social networks mobilize the many, allowing social movements to embrace, bypass, and absorb the reactions of strong power.[23] Such shifts are more likely to be quick when there are visible, easily identifiable winners; conversely, as Machiavelli pointed out, change is harder when the losers are concentrated and the winners are diffuse.[24] Either way, as efficiency declines rising interests gain confidence while declining ones get angry.

This is also when battles intensify over meaning and understanding, the third force of conservatism, and when people change their minds. As Eric Weil put it, "revolutions erupt when man is discontent with his discontent." As fatalism and acceptance dissipate, critics become more visible and try to reshape mind-sets: in particular the young, marginal, ambitious, and annoyed start to advocate radical change and to directly challenge their older colleagues who, having been most socialized into the status quo find it hardest to imagine how things could be different.[25] Artists, writers, poets may come to the fore during this phase, using stories, images, and metaphors to help people break free from the past, while others cling even harder to fixed points in their identity, responding to the cognitive fluidity of the world around them by ever more ferocious assertion of their nationality, religion, or values. The art historian T. J. Clark captured this well:

> Art seeks out the edges of things, of understanding; therefore, its favourite modes are irony, negation, deadpan, the pretence of ignorance or innocence. It prefers the unfinished: the systematically unstable, the

semantically malformed. It produces and savours discrepancy in what it shows and how it shows it, since the highest wisdom is knowing that things are pictures that do not add up.[26]

Art is at home in the periods of flux, less so in the periods of consolidation that come later. But it's at these times that it liberates by showing predators for what they are, and providing a public witness for private feelings. These, too, are the times when people feel the need to rub out of their eyes the dust that history has thrown into them.

Rubbing out the dust doesn't come naturally to institutions. Periods of systemic crisis are particularly difficult for governments whose habits emphasize order, conformity, and playing by the rules. The people who have prospered from the system and sit at the top of bureaucratic or political hierarchies may be the last to see its deficiencies. Ever more sophisticated accounts may explain why the status quo can be saved, or why only modest reform will be enough. The president of the New York Stock Exchange notoriously declared in September 1929: "it is obvious that we are through with business cycles as we have known them," and his counterparts eighty years later more than matched him in myopia. Such periods, when old systems are in crisis but the new isn't strong enough to be born, can continue for many years, as governments respond with feverish fixes to paper over the cracks. The same is true in big businesses. The vice of past glory is that it gives leaders the leeway to make mistakes, and continue making mistakes (one definition of power is the ability to get away with mistakes). The histories of colossal failures, such as General Motors, or Citicorp, are marked by intricately complex myopia, with decision makers imprisoned by past successes.

But when efficiency, interests, and mental categories shift, the social capital that holds the system together tends to come unstuck too, and people peel away from previous commitments and relationships, and find new partners and allies.[27]A few individuals who sit on the edges of multiple networks can suddenly become powerful arbitrators, signaling to the suggestible majority which way the wind is blowing. How the pieces of the kaleidoscope land depends on tactics as well

as strategy, the personal qualities of leaders as well as grand historical forces. The sparks may be moments of cruelty, or offended dignity (like police brutality). But ultimately what matters is the power
of organization: whether there are organizations with the means to
make the most of changing minds and relationships, to concentrate
them and win decisive battles, to bolster their supporters' confidence
when things look difficult, and then to surge forward when they find
breaches in the enemies' defenses.[28]

The tipping points in the past came when insurgents took command of coercion (the military and police) or communication (the TV
stations). Today the centers of power are more diffuse, ranged across
politics, media, and finance.

So all four forces of conservatism can become forces for change, and
as they do so, material factors and ideas evolve in tandem. Most explanations of long-term social change focus on one or the other. From
Hegel onward, some have sought out the ideas that are being realized
in the world, transforming how people think, see, and act, for example
the idea of human rights, natural contracts, or transhumanism. Since
Marx, the dominant explanations have been materialist—falling profits and overproduction, or diminishing energy supplies and climatic
pressures providing the causal prompt for shifting power structures.
But on their own, both types of explanation fall down. Material factors
only become forces for change once they are interpreted in the right
way. Poor harvests, low growth, high crime, and climatic instability can
all be interpreted as just bad luck, or inevitable, rather than as symptoms of fundamental failings. Some societies can survive for a long
time in denial of their weaknesses, if those with power are convinced
that change would be worse, and those without power are unable to
concentrate their minds and their forces. Indeed, almost any crisis can
be interpreted as proof that the status quo needs to be reinforced more
vigorously rather than overturned (and whenever the economy slumps
into crisis, arguments break out over whether the solution is more
capitalism—lower taxes, and fewer regulations—or less).

But anyone seeking to accelerate change and weaken predatory
power has to work on all four dimensions: bringing to the surface

inefficiencies and failures; peeling away interest groups, and help-ing people to redefine their interests; changing mind-sets, the frames through which people see or think; and nurturing the relationships and friendships that sustain alternative options. The most successful social movements do all of these things, rather than relying only on the power of argument and ideas.

INSTITUTIONALIZING CHANGE

We now expect governments to institutionalize economic change. True conservatism has been banished from economic policy. Govern-ments invest a significant share of GDP in new knowledge to speed up the emergence of new industries and firms. They support institutions to transfer technology, they subsidize firms to take up new technolo-gies, and they finance demonstration sites. Most prefer a bias to the future rather than to the past (even if the industries of the past make the strongest claims for support and subsidy).

In the social and political fields there is little comparable. Social research and development is very modestly funded if at all. It happens despite official systems, not because of them. But there have been some exceptions, political leaders who made a virtue of social experimenta-tion and enterprise. One was Franklin Delano Roosevelt, who in May 1932, in the depth of crisis, asserted that

> the country needs, and unless I mistake its temper, the country de-mands, bold, persistent experimentation. It is common sense to take a method and try it; if it fails, admit it frankly and try another. But above all, try something.[29]

Yet this is opposite to the stance taken by most states. For them there is comfort in plans, policies, and strategies rather than trials and pilots. As I show in chapter 8, although there is a scattering of institutions for innovation within society and government across the world, these are relatively weak, and rarely last long. The pressures of time make it hard for governments to experiment—democracy in its contemporary forms can be the enemy of democratic experiment. A mayor or prime minister with a four-year term is unlikely to be patient with an experiment that may take two years to start and another two years to run its course. So the temptation is either to avoid risk, or to act fast, to experiment on the whole city or nation, with bold plans for reform put through in a rush.

Sometimes there may be no choice. But more often the public interest is better served by careful experiment and incremental change that builds on success. Orchestrating this kind of change has become one of the most important, albeit rare, skills of modern government. It has to start with good diagnosis, understanding the real causes of problems rather than their symptoms, and close observation of daily life—how people really experience such things as hospitals or policing (which is hard, since as Keynes put it there is nothing a government likes less than being well-informed, since it makes the business of decision-making much more complicated). The orchestration of change then requires tools for multiplying the options—allowing public servants, business, or civil society to dream up or discover many competing solutions, from the people succeeding against the odds, the positive deviants,[30] to the iconoclasts and entrepreneurs (again this is particularly hard for governments, since it is by definition unpredictable). Successful change then requires methods for testing which ideas actually work, and finally for growing the ones that do. Parts of this process are highly rational, like randomized control trials, and legislation to spread new models. Others are purely creative, closer in spirit to jazz saxophonist John Coltrane's comment that "the inspiration is out there, you just need to grab it." Yet government bureaucracies are not well-designed for innovation—it's too messy, and too risky. Their instinctive response to the need to innovate is to command it, or to create lots of jobs with innovation in the titles. A better response is to support intermediaries that can work with a very different culture than public bureaucracies, and take more risks. That's why scientific innovation is pushed out to arm's length bodies: ministers and senior officials don't have to fear being held to account for experiments that fail.

Far-reaching change nearly always involves alliances of the bottom and the top, of the bees and the trees, where the bees are the powerless groups and individuals buzzing with ideas, and the trees are the great institutions with power and money but few ideas. True revolutions from either the bottom or top alone are much rarer than creative alliances between factions with access to power and money, and outsiders with energy and passion.[31] This is as true of political revolution as it is of radical social enterprise and economic change,[32] and any society wanting to institutionalize a capacity for change needs intermediaries to connect the bees and the trees, the inside and the outside. This linking of insiders and outsiders also happens in places, through what the great historian of cities, Peter Hall, called milieux,[33] and what the musician Brian Eno called "scenius," the collective form of genius, where new ideas grow through a heady mix of mutual admiration, competition, and criticism, often concentrated in leading cities. They could be found in eighteenth-century Edinburgh, nineteenth-century London, and twentieth-century California, and in pockets everywhere. These milieux need to be open, but not too open; grounded in particular disciplines, like architecture or design, but not rigidly; and encouraged by intelligent customers and patrons. The ability to imagine the new turns out to be a highly social activity, as dependent on journals and magazines, meeting places and websites, commentators and critics, as it is on individual imagination.[34] The great nineteenth-century industries rested on a "technological public sphere" of clubs, learned societies, and associations, where inventors and engineers shared their thinking, and these have their direct counterparts in fields like high-performance computing or solar power today. The societies that can nurture these kinds of collective creativity, from slow food to speed dating, are likely to adapt most easily, because they have created the space for the future to be conceived and tested. Those that are uncomfortable with the presence of living alternatives are likely to find change more jarring, more costly, and more painful.

Entrepreneurs play a critical role in bringing ideas to life, and not just business entrepreneurs—rather, entrepreneurs of all kinds who are looking for adherents, resources, and commitment, whether for a campaign, a political party, or a religion. They are as likely to be entrepreneurs against capitalism as within capitalism. Either way they thrive off the areas of failure, the points of friction and stress, the places where capitalism no longer works. In business, these are the spaces of waste, the unmet desires, the unrealized opportunities that can be exploited by applying a new piece of knowledge or technology. They are the places where productivity or profit is stagnating, or where consumers are dissatisfied or just bored. Beyond business they are the places where we see people or things unused and inert.

The orchestration of change can use sophisticated technologies—such as Internet-based "crowd-sourcing" and challenge prizes that encourage the public to submit their own ideas[35] or more sophisticated variants that mobilize specialist communities to improve and refine ideas.[36] But it can also be very low tech. A century ago Britain's Royal Navy "crowd-sourced" tens of thousands of ideas from the public using only paper and the postal service.[37] In India, the Shodh Yatra organized by the HoneyBee Network uses walking as a tool for change. In one week, walkers (farmers, scientists, and researchers) travel hundreds of kilometers across rural India to unearth, share, and disseminate solutions to local issues including conservation, organic farming, and biodiversity as well as health and nutrition. During the day, walkers pass through farming land—usually accompanied by local farmers and laborers who discuss and reflect on their farming practices. In the evening, walkers stay in villages and hold meetings with local residents to share insights and knowledge of innovations from other parts of India. There are also prizes, such as biodiversity competitions, recipe competitions, and a felicitation ceremony for creative villagers. Walking in groups remains a surprisingly powerful tool in highly developed societies too—what you see and discover together with others can change you fast, and create a pressure from your peers not to suppress the imagination once it's been sparked.

There are in principle an infinite number of directions social systems can take. But history suggests that at key moments evolution is highly selective. Only a relatively few models turn out to be sustainable, with an affinity to the prevailing technologies and values. That's why change often looks like punctuated equilibrium, or like pulling a jellyfish with a rubber band, with sluggish small steps interspersed with sudden surges that reveal new interdependencies and systemic efficiencies. What determines which ones will succeed? There are innumerable factors—but technology is bound to be one of the decisive ones, and so in the next chapter I turn to the role of technology in social change and, potentially, in creating a world after capitalism.

Chapter 8

· · · · · · · · ·

Creative and Predatory Technology

THE GREAT MAJORITY of economic growth—and of human progress—has come from new knowledge and its application. Much of the legitimacy of capitalism draws on its association with a tide of new stuff that makes life easier and more pleasurable: jet planes and refrigerators, mobile phones and video games. If an earlier era of capitalism was concerned with mobilizing capital, increasingly today's capitalism is concerned with how to mobilize, orchestrate, and channel new knowledge. But how to do so? And how to ensure that new knowledge creates genuinely life-enhancing value?

Almost every aspect of human life has been shaped by the progressive mastery of technologies. Our ancestors observed natural phenomena—like fire, light, motion, or electricity, and then found ways to replicate, channel, or amplify them. Much of this observation and invention happened at one remove from commerce: the discovery of gravity, the circulation of the blood, and electricity were not motivated by commercial gain. But modern capitalism grew up closely entwined with technology, and the culture of eighteenth-century England brought the practical arts, manufacturing, and science closer together, in the application of steam power, electricity, chemistry, and communications.

A good example is the world's first modern laboratory, which was founded by Sir John Lawes at Rothamsted in Hertfordshire in England in 1843. Lawes had created the world's first factory for artificial fertilizers. With his partner Joseph Gilbert, he combined systematic experiment into the crop yields of different organic and inorganic fertilizers with a hugely successful business sense. His legacy is a world with a dramatically greater capacity to feed itself, and a capitalism that is so adept at implementing, and then rapidly improving, physical things in its search for value. As a result of capitalism's history it is bound up with an optimistic view of technology, and with materialism: seeing the world as made up of things, and seeing human needs as primarily material. While many of the nineteenth-century utopias decreed that invention should stop, and that the factories should be mothballed and railways pulled up, the futurology of capitalism has mainly been a futurology of technology, offering a cornucopia of the providers—with ever smarter gadgets, networks, and implants turning more of life into a commodity, and ultimately displacing human intelligence altogether. Its utopias and dystopias were ultimately about stuff, which is why they came to be called science fiction, the utopias emphasizing how technology would provide countless new wonders, the dystopias emphasizing the new possibilities for predation that leave humans enslaved to dictators or robots. Many of the dreams and nightmares of science fiction later materialized—drone robot warriors, prosthetics, handheld electronic devices, and lasers all made the march from fiction to fact. Today, too, it is the constant tide of new technologies that fuels confidence in capitalism's ability to solve its own problems, from climate change to mental illness. In some accounts it transcends humanity itself, ushering in an age of ubiquitous intelligence. Ray Kurzweil, for example, has forecast an imminent moment when biology will be superseded by technology, as machine intelligence passes a point of no return, soaring away from the imperfections of merely human brains (the "rapture" for nerds).[1]

Seen in the round, innovation of these kinds is a solvent against predation, and cultures of innovation tend to favor democracy over autocracy, newcomers over incumbents, the young relative to the old. Many firms, and many governments, proclaim themselves to be in favor of more innovation, and like to be seen to side with the new against the old. But a moment's reflection shows that simply being in favor of innovation is not a very coherent stance to take. Some innovations are unambiguously good (like penicillin or the telephone); others are unambiguously bad (like concentration camps or nerve gas). In the field that John Lawes pioneered, some products were unambiguously good, some benefited one group and harmed others, such as pesticides which killed parasites but also polluted the water supply. And a few inventions were more predatory than productive, like genetically modified "terminator" seeds deliberately designed not to propagate, so that the farmer has to buy new ones every year.

If you stand back and take a broad look at technology, it's obvious that some innovations support predation, making it easier to control, exploit, or conquer. Technologies for war, or for surveillance, are by their very nature contrary to the spirit of the golden rule. There is no missile system, directed energy weapon, or security camera for which it makes sense for others to do unto you as you would do unto them.[2] Computer viruses are very obvious predators, secretly stealing your credit card details, often to support organized-crime syndicates. New fields of technology bring new patterns of predation as well as empowerment. The "Internet of Things" with its arrays of sensors is a good example. Almost any action may now be generating data to be matched, mined, and commercialized, without your knowledge or consent. Cameras and sensors on machines, or attached to billboards, can assess the age, gender, and ethnicity of people walking by, with "glance counters" to measure how much attention they are paying. You cannot help but generate data for them, and you may not mind since there is no immediate harm to you. But something of you is being taken without your permission and without any reciprocal benefit to you.[3] An even clearer example is the industry of surveillance exemplified by firms like Amesys, Gamma, VASTech whose technologies were found by the people of Egypt and Libya when their regimes fell; SS8 and Vupen make viruses to take over computers and smartphones, recording every action, again mainly for governments.[4] Firms like Huawei now sell communications infrastructures around the world that are designed to let the state monitor Internet traffic, a radically different model from the idealists' hopes for a medium that would keep Big Brother at bay. There are subtler technologies of predation too—mass broadcast television couldn't help but tempt advertisers and dictators alike to manipulate their viewers, and games now provide a new array of tools to grab attention and transmit messages. Other technologies are more obviously compatible with the golden rule—like mobile phones that only become valuable if others have them, oral rehydration therapy yellow fever vaccines, or new crops enriched with vitamins. Others sit in between, like cars that simultaneously provide value to their owners but also take away clean air, space, and peace from people who don't have them.

Then too there are technologies of predation that benefit people but leave nature worse off. How you view these depends on how human-centric your world-view is. To some eyes large-scale mining whether of the land or the oceans is by its nature predatory (even when it doesn't come with the messy combination of displacement, abuse, and occasional windfall payoffs to indigenous communities). To others it's just the good fortune that humans enjoy thanks to their evolutionary superiority.

Leaving these bigger questions to one side, the everyday arguments about technology soon turn to questions of predation and power: Is widespread access to data likely to empower or disempower the individual? Will genetically modified crops damage the livelihoods of other farmers? Is it right that the dominant forces in the World Wide Web are unaccountable to their users? Market dynamics make these questions unavoidable. Information technology, even more than past technologies, has tended to generate monopolies. Even if the monopolist's technologies are not predatory, their behaviors often are, driving up prices, squeezing out competitors, and manipulating standards.

So it's unwise, and almost certainly incoherent, just to be in favor of innovation or in favor of science. Instead we should want to favor good innovation, innovation that serves human ends. But that turns out to be a more radical starting point than you might imagine. Most organized innovation in the past was guided by the interests of states and then more recently of big business. For states the priority was, and is, state interest more than public interest: hence the disproportionate investment in military and security technologies, missiles rather than mental health. For big firms too, the motives have been mixed: sometimes to create more and better drugs or cars, sometimes to extract more value from the public without giving much back.

It's common to ascribe capitalist innovation to market dynamics: the restless search for new ways to meet wants and needs, and that's the story that most people immersed in capitalism tell themselves. But the facts don't quite fit. Not one major technology associated with modernity was developed without substantial government involvement: pharmaceuticals, computers, the Internet, mobile phones, and commercial aircraft all prospered thanks to state patronage.[5] Nor is capitalism so obvious a partner of technology. There have been places and times when commerce played a leading role in generating new technologies, and today much of the invention of the future lies in the hands of corporate laboratories and spin-offs. But just as often that role has been played by the military, by bureaucracies, or even by monastic orders. This was as true in the fourth century when the citizens of Antioch invented artificial streetlights, as it was a thousand years later when Giovanni di Dondi built one of the first mechanical clocks working as a professor at Padua, and in the nineteenth century when the British government funded Charles Babbage's difference engine and the U.S. Congress funded Samuel Morse's experimental telegraph.

Even today, in typical OECD countries, public investment in research and development is roughly comparable to private investment, and much of the dynamism that's achieved in innovation comes from the connections between the sectors, not just from the dynamism within the private sector. The same appears to have been true in the past, and the great historian of technology Arnold Pacey suggested that the most creative societies may have been those "in which many types of institutions were active and in dialogue with each other," cutting across the different sectors and professions.[6]

The time when business dominated technology in a pure capitalist model may turn out to have been brief. A simple measure of this can be found in the listings provided by *R&D Magazine* in the United States of the one hundred most innovative commercial products introduced in the previous years. In 1975, forty-seven out of eighty-six domestic innovations had been produced by Fortune 500 companies, forty of them with no outside partners. By 2006, big firms had produced only six of eighty-eight innovations and mainly had partners. Fifty were products of researchers at U.S. government laboratories, universities, or public agencies. Twenty-five came from private firms, of which at least fourteen involved federal funding. All but eleven depended on some public funding.[7] Similar patterns have been found in other countries, with a growing norm of cooperation between firms, and dependence on public support.[8] Globally too, many of the most exciting projects for innovation are collaborative, including a new generation of public private partnerships such as the International Aids Vaccine Initiative (IAVI), Medicines for Malaria Venture, or the Global Alliance for TB Drug Development, in which public funds and philanthropic money guarantee to buy quantities of drugs if they meet specified standards.

More surprising perhaps is the mismatch between growing sums invested in technology and deteriorating results. The jury is still out on whether there really has been a slowdown in innovation over the last few decades. But in some industries the gains from innovation have declined—pharmaceuticals being the clearest case in point. In others, old technologies have persisted much longer than expected: like cars that are in their essentials not dissimilar to their predecessors of a century ago, or jet planes based on 1960s technology that have outlived the Concorde. In 1970, the U.S. Congress promised that cancer would be defeated in six years; forty years later no one expects victory soon. And in many fields new gains seem to require both more financial investment than in the past, and more work.[9] With each decade that passes, a greater proportion of scientific and technological work is conducted by teams rather than individuals, and the chances of young researchers making breakthroughs diminishes (the growth rate of scientific journal articles is around 5.5 percent a year, suggesting a corresponding reduction in the fraction of existing knowledge that anyone can master).[10]

LONG WAVES OF CHANGE

John Kenneth Galbraith once said that the only function of economic forecasting is to make astrology look respectable. But long-range forecasts have not been as inaccurate as the shorter range ones. There are some steady patterns to be found, whether in the long-term nature of economic growth, the changing composition of economies, or the makeup of occupations. A century ago the first attempts were made to construct a theory of economic and technological change that could make sense of these patterns. The Russian economist Nikolai Kondratiev proposed long cycles averaging fifty years, with expansionary periods fueled by new technologies and bringing with them low interest rates and rising prices, followed by periods of stagnation as the opportunities for investment dried up. His model parallels many other accounts of creative cycles—which mirror the cycles of life, starting with periods of openness and experimentation, leading to formalization, deployment, and growth, and then stagnation. These patterns appear to reflect something real: as the historian Eric Hobsbawm put it, they have "convinced many historians and even some economists that there is something in them, even if we don't know what."[11] But almost every dimension of them remains contested: exactly when the cycles happened; whether they are getting shorter; why they happen; and whether they are useful for prediction or only for retrospective understanding. Orthodox economics was never convinced (Allen Meltzer, a professor at Carnegie Mellon, commented in 1991 that "there are very few ideas in macroeconomics that serious economists agree on, but doubting the existence of the Kondratiev is one of them"). Nor was Stalin convinced: he executed Kondratiev. But Joseph Schumpeter, in probably his greatest work, *The Theory of Business Cycles*, built on Kondratiev's ideas to suggest that capitalism followed a regular rhythm, with concentrations of technological advance leading to surges of innovation that in turn led to the emergence of new industries. Others have tried to link the economic waves to a deeper pattern of successive revolutions in physics; each time the new knowledge makes possible new industries that then wipe out older ones, bringing with them slumps and mass unemployment, particularly as phases of product innovation are succeeded by phases where profits are mainly grown through process innovation.[12] The new industries tend to be oligopolies (think of General Motors or General Electric in the 1920s, or Intel and Google today), and their success in raising productivity in the short term spells disaster for workers with older skills in older industries, which in turn shrinks consumer demand.[13] In other words, the most exciting periods of advance are also potentially the most dangerous socially.

Most writers agree on a rough periodization of five cycles, from the original industrial revolution of the 1770s, to the age of steam and railways in the 1830s, to the age of steel electricity and heavy engineering at the end of the nineteenth century, the age of oil, cars, and mass production in the early twentieth century, and an age of information and telecommunications after the 1970s. In this view we are now at the turning point of the "fifth Kondratiev," the point where the contribution of computers and networks begins to wane, and when we might expect to see the beginning of another wave, perhaps fueled by clean, low-carbon technologies or genomics.[14]

These waves are strongly shaped by what Richard Lipsey has called "general purpose technologies" that really do transform everything around them.[15] These become fundamental to many areas of life, like computers or cars. Sometimes this is immediately apparent, as in the case of railways which between 1830 and 1870 boosted labor productivity growth by 0.14 percent per year.[16] More often the potential isn't immediately apparent. Writing was invented to record trades; steam engines began their life extracting water out of English mines; computers were invented to help fire anti-aircraft guns more accurately at their targets. Only gradually did the wider potential of these technologies become apparent. Other technologies look likely to be transformative, such as lasers that are used as bar codes, for CDs, surgery, or cutting diamonds, but don't end up contributing to far-reaching cultural or institutional change.[17]

There's plenty of controversy about how meaningful it is to talk about general-purpose technologies. Cotton-making technologies, for example, achieved explosive growth (from 2.6 percent of Britain's GDP in 1770 to 17 percent in 1801) on a scale that's never been matched: but it was the organizational model and mind-set as much as the technologies that ended up changing the world. More recently, the organizing principles of the Internet—the languages of HTML, URLs and so on—have arguably been as important as the underlying technologies.

Either way, it is inherently hard to judge which ones will turn out to be decisive in shaping the future of the economy and society, and it's just as hard to judge which ones to back, and many governments in the past have gone astray, placing big bets on what looked like sure-fire exemplars of truly transformative technology—such as Minitel in France (a forerunner of the Internet) or the Apollo missions in the United States.

History suggests that it's unwise just to back technologies: better to create the conditions in which they can be played with, since the ways in which technologies transform the world around them is itself a creative process, a way of representing things as well as applying them. As Brian Arthur wrote in his brilliant overview of technological change,

> innovation is not so much a parade of inventions with subsequent adoptions: the arrival and adoption of computers or canals, or DNA microarrays. It is a constant re-expressing or re-domaining of old tasks—accounting, or transportation, or medical diagnostics—within new worlds of the possible.[18]

Doing that requires that powerful interests can't block innovation. Innovation is always disruptive and troublesome, particularly if it involves "re-domaining," and many do their utmost to strangle new ideas at birth. Joel Mokyr tells how Swiss printers successfully lobbied for laws to ban improved printing presses, how Dutch guilds opposed advances in shipbuilding, and how French paper makers burned machines that would have accelerated pulp production. Their equivalents today are just as eager to dismiss or destroy challengers—just look, for example, at the music industry's response to Napster.

Governments play an important role in preventing powerful incumbents from crushing newcomers, even if they can't, for example, know which overlaps of "cogno, info, nano and bio" technology will be most productive. At their best they protect the space for creativity, and for the complementary innovations that are necessary for the full value of transformative technologies to be realized. Such a stance of openness, not just to individual technologies but also to the ideas and ways of life that they bring with them, is hard for government bureaucracies used to plans and targets. It also runs counter to the temptation in much writing about the future of capitalism which is to default to a view of technologies flowing out of the labs and into society, whether they're jetpacks or prosthetic limbs. Instead, as we've seen, technologies evolve in tandem with the societies around them. The car makes it possible to live in suburbs and to shop in supermarkets, and these in turn shape the ways in which cars are designed. The radio was thought to be a technology for point-to-point communication and only through trial and error became a mass broadcast medium. Electricity required a host of complementary innovations, from domestic appliances to regulators, to realize its full potential, and these took many decades. Containerization transformed freight transport, but only took hold after several false starts, and then turned out to require new regulations and working practices (and often entirely new ports) to realize its full potential. The mobile app only emerged some time after mobile devices had become ubiquitous, and then required the public to change their habits as well as providers to accept entirely new business models. Each innovation involved a different way of thinking and seeing as well as a different way of doing. That takes time. But once achieved, it creates enormous value.

It is the interaction of a technological potential and a present desire that determines the shape of a technology, let alone the shape of a society. So the radio responded to the desire for connectedness of fairly new industrial urban societies, but if it had been invented two centuries previously it might only have been used as a military technology, or to transmit the word of god (rather as as the communist regimes used it as a means of propaganda). In a previous era Chinese

Buddhists played a particularly important role in developing technologies, from bridges made of iron chains (the building and repair of bridges being a pious duty) to printed books (to spread the image of the Buddha). These might have evolved rather differently if militarists or investment bankers had been in charge.

This story of co-evolution involves both creativity and predation. Any new technology becomes a potential tool for both. The factory made it possible to remove workers to one-industry and one-company towns, making them easier to exploit. Oil drilling, telegraphs, and railways each brought new imbalances of power and control while also opening up productive capacity. This double character of technological potential, both predatory and productive, has been even clearer with the array of communications technologies, most of which have their origins in the military. Writers interested in cables and computers in the 1950s and 1960s were able to present them either as wicked tools of Big Brother states and corporations, or as forces for liberation. Both interpretations were right, and in the succeeding decades the information economy produced both new hierarchies, from the Pentagon's automated battlefields to Microsoft, and looser horizontal networks. They made possible, in other words, both firewalls and hackers, and any account that emphasizes only one is misleading.

As they spread, technologies become more useful both for provision and predation. Long time-series data show that technologies improve their performance partly thanks to time and partly thanks to their growing scale of production. This is what is known as the learning curve that results from doing more: the more we do something, the better we can do it and at lower cost. These patterns are roughly power laws, though some technologies, including IT, have followed much faster paths, with the exponential improvement of Moore's law and Metcalfe's law.[19] But they also become more useful because of what changes around them, as technologies prompt complementary innovations as well as new ideas about what it is to live or how we might solve the problems of life. The internal combustion engine could have been used for many things: only in a particular kind of consumerist society could the car have become the dominant application, growing in interaction with its related social innovations: the city organized into suburbs dependent on cars; shopping reorganized around supermarkets designed to be visited in cars; driving schools to teach people how to avoiding crashing into each other; road markings and rules to govern behavior. The technology itself is only a potential. It becomes valuable through use, and through constant response to use.

It's more than a century since an electric car, *La Jamais Contente* (The Never Satisfied), became the first vehicle to go over 100 kilometers per hour at Achères, near Paris in 1899. But it failed to generate an equivalent momentum of use and improvement to the internal combustion engine, and so turned out to be an evolutionary dead end. Others stumble on social or psychological hurdles. Lewis Paul, the inventor of the cotton spinning factory in the 1730s and 1740s, ultimately failed because of discipline, not technology: on some days only half his employees turned up. His successors succeeded not just because they changed the technology but also because they changed the people. Here again we see that technologies don't simply diffuse in a linear way; and they don't simply spread because they are useful. They spread when people change and when whole systems are reshaped around them.

Perhaps the most influential theorist of the connections between technological change, the economy and wider societies, is the Venezuelan economist Carlota Perez, who is a scholar of the long-term patterns of technological change and how they intersect both with social change and with the financial cycles that have repeated themselves again and again during capitalism's relatively brief history. Her analysis is a new variant of the many accounts of creative cycles that turn open, dynamic fields into routinized ones, and then into stagnation and decline. It's unusual in that it suggests how cycles of creation may connect to parallel, but distinct, cycles of predation.

In Perez's account, which builds on Kondratiev and Schumpeter, the cycles begin with the emergence of new technologies and infrastructures that promise great wealth. These then fuel frenzies of speculative investment, with dramatic rises in stock and other prices whether in the canal mania of the 1790s, the railway mania of the

1830s and 1840s, the surge of global infrastructures in the 1870s and 1880s, or the booms that accompanied the car, electricity, telephone in the 1920s, and biotechnology and the Internet in the 1990s and 2000s.

During these phases of technological exuberance, finance is in the ascendant and laissez-faire policies become the norm. Letting markets grow freely seems evidently wise when they are igniting such visible explosions of wealth. During these periods some investors and entrepreneurs become very rich, very quickly. Exuberance in markets may be reflected in exuberance and laissez faire in personal morals—a glittering world of parties, celebrities, and gossip for the rest of the public to hang onto and experience vicariously. Entrepreneurs take wild risks and reap wild rewards. The economy appears to be a place for easy predation, offering rewards without too much work, and plenty of chances to siphon off surpluses. But it also rewards entrepreneurs with a predator-like hunger to find new opportunities who play a creative role in finding new uses for technologies.

The booms then turn out to be bubbles and are followed by dramatic crashes. The years 1797, 1847, 1893, 1929, and 2008 are a few of the decisive years when crashes took values tumbling. The stock market crashes brought with them the dramatic bankruptcy of many of the most prominent companies of the booms, like so many railway companies in the later nineteenth century. Sometimes currencies collapse too, and sovereign default by governments is also common.[20]

After these crashes, and periods of turmoil, the potential of the new technologies and infrastructures is eventually realized. But that only happens once new social, political, and economic institutions and regulations come into being that are better aligned with the characteristics of the new economy, and with the underlying desires of the society. Once that has happened, economies then go through surges of growth as well as social progress, like the "belle epoque" or the postwar miracle.

These patterns can be seen clearly in the Great Depression and its aftermath. Before the crisis of 1929 the elements of a new economy and a new society were already available—and the promise of technologies like the car and telephone encouraged the speculative bubbles of the 1920s. But they were neither understood by the people in power, nor were they embedded in institutions. Then, during the 1930s, the economy transformed, in Perez's words, from one based on

> steel, heavy electrical equipment, great engineering works (canals, bridges, dams, tunnels) and heavy chemistry, mainly geared towards big spenders . . . into a mass production system catering to consumers and the massive defense markets. Radical demand management and income redistribution innovations had to be made, of which the directly economic role of the state is perhaps the most important.[21]

What resulted was the rise of mass consumerism, and an economy supported by ubiquitous infrastructures for electricity, roads, and telecommunications.

These patterns only become obvious in retrospect. During the 1930s, it wasn't clear which institutional innovations would be most successful. Fascism, communism, and corporatism were all contending solutions, and for a time looked like plausible answers to the problems of mass unemployment and urban alienation. Nor was it clear which would most accord with the wishes of the society, the willingness to commit and engage. The course of history could have taken a very different turn. The political and social models of fascism and communism fitted well with the characteristics of the emerging technologies of their times. They were certainly compatible with the telephone (and found ways to use it as a tool for surveillance as well as communication). The new energy sources became a defining feature of communism (which Lenin defined as "soviets plus electrification"). Their social models were equally compatible with the ideas of modern management which became so decisive for firms after World War II, to such an extent that James Burnham in a very influential book published in the 1940s forecast a world no longer divided into left and right but dominated by managers and managerialism.[22]

Yet in their different ways fascism and Stalinism overreached (though the USSR achieved sophisticated computing and space travel with a GDP barely a quarter that of the United States, and enjoyed several decades of reasonable growth before it imploded). Instead, after World War II, in much of the developed world a new model of development crystallized with radically different institutions and policies, and elements as diverse as suburbs and motorways, welfare states and macroeconomic policies, which then underpinned the extraordinary growth of the 1950s and 1960s. This was an economy "based on low cost oil and energy intensive materials (especially petrochemicals and synthetics), and led by giant oil, chemical and automobile and other mass durable goods producers. Its 'ideal' type of productive organization at the plant levels was the continuous flow assembly-line . . . the 'ideal' type of firm was the 'corporation,'"

> including in-house R&D and operating in oligopolistic markets in which advertising and marketing activities played a major role. It required large numbers of middle range skills in both blue and white collar areas . . . a vast infrastructural network of motorways, service stations, airports, oil and petrol distribution system.[23]

Seen in the light of what came next, the Great Depression was both a disaster and a great accelerator of reform. It helped usher in new economic and welfare policies in countries like New Zealand and Sweden that later became the mainstream across the developed world. In the United States it led to banking reform, the New Deal, social security, and unemployment insurance (both backed by big business)[24] and later the GI Bill of Rights. In Britain it was the depression, as much as war, that led to the creation of the welfare state and the National Health Service in the 1940s. Predatory extremes were reined in (in the United States, marginal income tax rates peaked at 91 percent in the 1950s prompting Kennedy to call for rates to be cut to 65%),[25] and the dominant spirit in many countries emphasized fairness and fair chances.

In retrospect, the new ideas provided answers to the most compelling questions of the era: how to achieve security in a market economy (a question that was answered by welfare states and jobs for life); how to open up opportunities for women (a question answered by introducing technologies into the home and then by more open labor markets); how to avoid depressions (a question answered by Bretton Woods, the new tools of macroeconomic management and free trade); and how to avoid totalitarianism (a question answered, at least for some parts of the world, by democracy and the new creed of universal human rights).

None of these answers was wholly new. All existed as possibilities, and promising elements already existed in some places and some institutions. But only after World War II did they take shape and turn into the governing rules for societies and for the world system.

Perez, like the other advocates of cycles, points to repeated patterns. Phases of entrepreneurial exuberance are followed by phases of consolidation and oligopoly. Industries become more ordered; the products and services they provide become more settled, and more reliable, alongside dominance by just a few firms. Bureaucracy wins out over buccaneering risk-takers. This happened to the Hollywood film industry, telephony, and cars in the 1920s and then to software and computing sixty years later. Firms like Apple and Amazon are attempting a similar consolidation today, using business models that integrate vertically and lock in their customers. For them there are the benefits of monopoly; for their customers, the benefits of stability.

Perez doesn't fully explore the political economy of these cycles, but her work is suggestive of how creation and predation influence each other. During the upswing periods, and then the periods of deployment, large surpluses are created. These justify greater freedom for creative entrepreneurs—with laissez-faire policies and low taxes. But the very same freedoms are also used by predators to extract rent. In other words, predators benefit from the successes of creators. The public tolerates huge gains for a minority because, on balance, they seem to be benefitting too.

Then, sooner or later, crisis hits, caused in part by the excesses of the predators. Profits and surpluses shrink. The public becomes less tolerant of predators, who are seen to have taken without contributing. Their excesses come to be blamed for the crisis—and the threats to everyone's living standards. Less capital then flows to creators. Rules and regulations are tightened up, as are redistributive measures. Predation doesn't disappear: instead it takes different forms—more about large organizations rather than rentiers, and usually with more overt compromises with the public interest. But the risk then is that the measures to constrain predation may also constrain the hungry, predator-like search for new opportunities on the part of creative entrepreneurs.

The number of variables involved in any cycles of this kind makes it unlikely that anyone could forecast them in detail, or that they would follow a fixed timescale of the kind proposed by Kondratiev. But the more that we understand cycles of this kind, the more we may be able to avoid the excesses and errors common at each stage.

SCIENCE SYSTEMS

The settlements that Perez suggests evolve out of crisis are likely to touch many aspects of life. To succeed, they have to offer plausible answers to the dilemmas of life as they're experienced at that time: how to be happy, how to extend our lives, how to reduce our damage to the environment, how to stop waste, how to maintain our friendships and amplify love.

In the 1930s and 1940s the primary concerns were about peace and economic security, reducing the burdens of labor in the home and achieving a modicum of autonomy and mobility. These in turn influenced the priorities for science and technology. Several generations later, our societies have chosen to invest between a fiftieth and a twentieth of their income in discovery (research and development accounts for 2.6 percent of GDP in the United States, 3.3 percent in Japan, and 4.5 percent in Israel). But the priorities for spending are not so clearly linked to public priorities. Mental health is greatly underfunded relative to physical health. Warfare continues to be dramatically better funded than peace. And innovation in physical stuff—nanotechnology and pharmaceuticals, next generation aerospace and new materials—is far better funded than innovation in services, let alone social ideas.

In this respect the world's science systems are all children, direct or indirect, of the ideas recommended in the 1940s by Vannevar Bush, who saw science in very materialist terms. Bush was one of the influential shapers of a very new kind of strategy (and later achieved retrospective fame when his vision of the "Memex" materialized fifty years later in the Internet). He had been in charge of the Office of Scientific Research and Development which ran defense research in the United States, including the Manhattan Project to build a nuclear bomb. In 1945, just as the war was coming to an end, and encouraged by the success of the Manhattan Project and the work of the National Committee for Aeronautics (NACA, the precursor of NASA), Bush wrote a report to the president titled "Science: The Endless Frontier." The report made the case for systematic peacetime investment in technology: "New products and new processes do not appear full-grown. They are founded on new principles and new conceptions, which in turn are painstakingly developed by research in the purest realms of science." Bush recommended a new National Science Foundation to drive basic research and a healthy flow of public funds into technology. He advocated channeling money to younger researchers along with the freedom to pursue their own ideas—in contrast to the hierarchical European universities where their job was to serve and admire the old professors. And he helped institutionalize stronger channels to link research, invention, and applications.[26]

Before the twentieth century, much of the work of invention had been left to amateurs. Marconi, Bell, Daimler, and Edison all worked from home laboratories. But firms like DuPont had shown just how much could be achieved through systematic investment. Bush's ideas were intended to take the whole system—from universities to businesses—to a higher level of activity. Over the next half century his plans achieved extraordinary success, and around them an ecosystem of institutions emerged, from venture capital and technology transfer to university labs and commentators. Frederick Terman at Stanford's Department of Electrical Engineering translated Bush's vision into what became Silicon Valley, with a recipe that combined generous defense contracts, a culture of technological creativity, and strong encouragement for spinoffs from universities. The United States made most of the world's new technologies (even if it wasn't always the best at using them), and other countries ran hard to catch up. The systematization of innovation wasn't always beautiful to watch: Schumpeter lamented,

> the business of teams of trained specialists who turn out what is required and make it work in predictable ways. The romance of earlier commercial adventure is rapidly wearing away, because so many things can be strictly calculated that had of old to be visualised in a flash of genius.[27]

But it largely worked, and seen from the vantage point of today, it was prescient to apply common resources to the pursuit of knowledge and in systematic ways. It was also prescient to encourage innovation in innovation itself, from the peer review of the National Science Foundation (NSF) to the more experimental approach of ARPA which hired outstanding individuals and gave them great leeway to decide what should be funded and how, bringing together communities of researchers around particular challenges cutting across universities, small start-up firms, and big firms. Some of the big strategic gambles also turned out to be wise: the National Institutes of Health (NIH) funded the early days of genetics and molecular biology, and public funds supported both the Strategic Computing Initiative in the 1980s, and Sematech, a grand corporatist venture to retain U.S. leadership in microprocessors.

There were always critics of this highly interventionist stance, that some have called the world's most serious "developmental state." Milton Friedman in his influential book *Free to Choose* saw no justification for government funding for scientific research via the NSF. But the critics were silenced by the larger purpose which animated the funding. Throughout the Cold War and its aftermath the United States felt itself to be in a struggle, which could become a struggle to the death, and technology was likely to be decisive in determining who won (a view shared by the USSR). This more than any commercial or economic logic justified the vast investments in technology. It was a lived value—survival—that counted for more than monetary returns.

For other countries the pressures were different, and the questions they had to answer specific to their times and spaces: yet for them too economic logic was only a limited part of the story.[28] There were periods when everywhere wanted its equivalent of a Silicon Valley, and paid advisers to help them create a Silicon Wadi, Glen, or Fjord. Most failed. The successful strategies ended up very different from each other, in part because the questions they were answering were different. Israel, Taiwan, Finland, Denmark, Singapore, Korea, all shaped systems that fitted their own cultures and characteristics. Israel, which has the world's highest spending on research and development as a share of GDP, has set up many incubators in the public sector and then spun them out, as well as funding up to 90 percent of technology development costs within firms in exchange for royalties on future earnings. Finland shaped its strategy, partly out of necessity, around the particular circumstances of one firm, Nokia, having poured money into research even in the depths of recession in the early 1990s. Taiwan built a dominant position in semiconductors thanks to a concerted industrial strategy, a powerful public vehicle to implement it (ITRI was founded in the 1970s and by the 1990s accounted for 0.3 percent of GDP), and a pioneering science park in Hsinchu as well as dynamic universities.

Yet perhaps the most interesting feature of this list of new exemplars is that each had a different reason for caring so much about technology, often, as with the United States in the 1940s, because of geopolitics as much as economics. For Israel it was survival against the far more populous Arab countries surrounding it. For Taiwan it was survival against China. For Finland, it was the need to break free from the shadow of the Soviet Union, and, even more, from the spillovers of its economic collapse. For Singapore, it was the paranoia of a rich city-state surrounded by poorer and much larger neighbors, and becoming ever more anxious as its citizens' birth rates declined far below replacement levels. For South Korea it was the pressure of sitting uncomfortably between Japan and China, and next to north Korea, a country that turned unpredictable aggressiveness into a strategy. What each was seeking was a motor—the key to faster economic growth—but also an answer to what they felt to be their most compelling need. And, in each case, fear justified generous public funding and stimulated a strong sense of common purpose.

We can learn many lessons from these examples. One is the importance of necessity or stimulus. In the past technologies developed faster when there was a stimulus, or when "the achievements of one society stimulated people elsewhere to make different but related inventions."[29] So when Europeans heard of the gunpowder invented in China that prompted the invention of the cannon; when modern Japanese manufacturers learned about the transistors that had been invented in the United States, they invented new generations of consumer products. More recently the same has happened with hybrid cars and renewable energy, and cities equipped with wifi and broadband. Well-defined problems can prompt more innovation than vague ones, and necessity really can be the mother of invention.

Another lesson concerns the mobilization of finance. Leonardo da Vinci was able to invent helicopters (to contribute to entertainments rather than transport) because there were patrons willing and able to finance him. The discovery of knowledge has to be paid for: in universities or in research laboratories. It's perhaps not surprising that firms which invest most in innovation, tend to produce the most innovative products and to grow fastest. But capital markets are wary of innovation: it's too uncertain, and too destructive. Rapid turnover of shares militates against financing long-term innovations, and even investors with deep enough understanding of technologies to judge future prospects will be vulnerable if their short-term numbers fall behind the pack. This is what justifies states to share the risks: subsidies, tax credits, collaborative R&D, or public purchasing that rewards firms to innovate.

Governments have also learned more about the importance of skill. Knowledge and ideas don't float free: to become valuable they need to be applied and adapted. One interesting finding from the study of innovation is that much of the impact of spending on research doesn't come from the research itself, but rather from the PhD students who then go into businesses. Advanced technology doesn't issue solely from knowledge that is widely available, but rather from deep craft: the subtle, often tacit understanding of how things work and how they work together. Tinkerers and tweakers play as big a role as inventors.[30] This deep craft tends to cluster in places, in organizations, and in networks. This was certainly true in eighteenth-century England which was unusual in providing status, rewards, and money, to engineers,[31] and in the early stages of the industrial revolution:

> even the ordinary millwright . . . was usually a fair arithmetician, knew something of geometry, levelling and measuration, and in some cases possessed a very competent knowledge of practical mathematics. He could also calculate the velocities, strength and power of machines, could draw in plan and section.[32]

The implication is that the most successful places in the next few decades may also be the ones that don't just honor inventors, but also happen to have concentrations of the right skills, perhaps for neuroscience or personal care, synthetic biology, or low-carbon aerospace. Israel is a good example—a strength in axiomatic set theory provided one of the spurs to its immensely successful IT industry. Google's engineers exploring the boundaries of search, Emilio-Romagna's providers of care for young children, and England's Formula One carmakers are all exemplars of deep craft, as are fashion designers and games programmers. A recent study of the Apple iPhone 4 illuminates the point: only a very small share of value came from the assembly of its parts and components, and even their production accounted for only a quarter of the value created: the great majority of the value was captured by Apple, reflecting both its investment prior to manufacturing, and the value of the brand it used to effectively combine the elements.[33] That in turn resulted from a geographically, and organizationally, concentrated skill in design (Apple has rarely pioneered new technologies) and logistics, combined with unusually effective and exclusive business models (such as iTunes).

These deep pools of skill, each in different ways engaged with demanding consumers, then need to be stimulated by wider peripheral vision. Governments regularly commission futurological surveys that purport to show how technologies will spread through their societies, transforming life as they go. Finland's parliament even has a committee for the future. These have become an important space for long-range thinking and imagination. Management consultancies often publish synthetic overviews of future trends to help with their marketing. But perhaps even more important than these are the exercises to imagine possible worlds, the creative utopianism that happens as much in literature, cinema, and games as it does in the dry reports of futurologists.

The linear view of innovation as a river flowing out from basic science has been partially discarded. The technologies that thrive are often the ones that tap into hopes and desires, capturing the imagination of investors and consumers. The hoopla of the dotcom boom, and the equivalent investment booms in biotechnology and clean technology, combined show business and serious business, playing on the fear of being left behind as much as any rational assessment of what might make a profit. Germany's huge investment in solar power (which, through the device of feed-in tariffs, may end up benefiting industry in China more than in Germany) was prompted by the power of the idea as much as by business plans. The rising importance of the silver economy, meeting needs not just for care and health but also for experiences and meanings in old age, is also about ideas as well as things, connecting new concepts (like active aging) and public demands with emerging technologies such as mind gyms, monitoring devices, and prosthetics.

How much of this is by its nature capitalist? Only a subset of innovations that can create lived value can also predictably create monetary value, and most of the value of innovations spills over. Some technologies and service models quickly find a fit in the market place. A world suffering from the wrong water in the wrong places at the wrong times will prompt radical innovation to save and process water, and generous rewards for the best ideas. Existing systems for personalized healthcare provide a ready home for genetic tests. Nutrigenomics and pharma foods are likely to find ready buyers keen to boost their health with every meal. The cultivation of 100-kilometer^2 solar plants in the deserts of Morocco, and equally vast wind farms being built in central China, fit well with a world of high oil prices and ecological anxiety. Single electron gate processors using graphene nanotechnology could find a place in millions of electronic devices.

But other technologies struggle to find a place, like smart energy grids and meters, which are eminently rational but not so easily aligned with desires and corporate incentives, except where entirely new towns and cities are being built; or videophones, first marketed in the 1960s but only widely taken up decades later; or smart cards, the focus of repeated experiments to make use of them from the 1980s onward. Some may work perfectly well in technical terms (like driverless taxis), but stumble on attitudes and legislation (driverless trains are already in operation in Copenhagen, but that's not enough to assuage public fears). Some may just meet the needs of people who with little money to pay: like insecticide-covered mosquito nets, or drugs for malaria.

Perhaps the biggest challenge for the people responsible for shaping and running innovation systems is a widening mismatch between the juggernauts of technological innovation, selling ever more stuff, ever more cars, ever more handheld devices and smart drugs, and what people actually want, the compelling questions they are asking of their lives. Technology systems that are founded on a materialist economy, and a materialist view of how change happens, find it hard to adapt to an economy where value comes as much from relationships as it does from things. This shift is not the consequence of technologies, though it is aided by them (particularly, of course, the social media). Rather this shift is the consequence of a stage of development: of patterns of need and demand to which technologies are at best a partial answer.

This matters because science has to legitimate itself: it has to persuade voters and taxpayers of its merits. In the past, states could prioritize their own needs—primarily for military prowess and surveillance. Or they could ally with big business, and prioritize meeting its needs. But democracy has slowly penetrated into science systems, and we may soon see more overt devices to engage the public in setting priorities for research and innovation, with their hopes and fears mobilized much more directly as factors shaping the direction of change.

One of the marks of a civilized society is that it provides free resources for discovery, exploration, and experiment, whether in the arts, science, or society. But a mature innovation system needs to go further, aligning both ends and means. That requires it to align three things. The first is awareness of the needs and aspirations of its people—and the greatest challenges they face in order to thrive and survive. The second is the capacity of the best and most creative minds that is mobilized in search of answers. The third is a system for turning the ideas they create into practice. This kind of alignment is all too rare. Even when societies are aware of where innovation is most needed, their creative resources are all too often diverted to the needs of powerful interests, or to trivial tasks. Yet alignment of this kind will surely be one of the great tasks of this century, and the mark of a truly intelligent society.

HOW TECHNOLOGY FOLLOWS IDEAS

If technology does become more responsive to public needs rather than state needs and business needs, the influence will be partly mediated through ideas. Although technologies sometimes appear as a "deus ex machina." coming from outside to transform our lives for better or worse,[34] a more accurate account shows that technologies, from the steam train and the steel mill to the microprocessor, were often preceded by new ways of thinking and seeing. The technologies didn't change society; instead they were simultaneously the product of a new kind of society, and the means for it to be realized. So for example, the clock co-evolved with new ways of thinking about the ordering of time, which, over many centuries, prepared the way for workers to clock in and out. In the same way, the World Wide Web co-evolved with a technological imaginary that dates back to H. G. Wells, and Vannevar Bush's proposal for a Memex, so that millions of people were familiar with the idea of a global network of computers long before it materialized.

Francis Bacon expounded some of the new ways of seeing that became integral to capitalism, and its ability to seek and exploit value, long before these ways of seeing were embodied in machines. The most important of these was the method of breaking problems down, and then reconstructing them. This was the method used by the pioneers of military drilling methods, the pioneers of statistics and the pioneers of manufacturing.[35] Later these methods became part of how capitalism thinks, with time and motion studies, and the mechanization and automation of all things. And, later too, they became the organizing principle for laptops and cars, automated ports, and hospitals.

If anyone wants to shape the future it's as likely to be through ideas that generate technologies as it is through the technologies themselves. Very different ideas now sit on the cusp of ideas and technological possibilities at the dawn of a networked, low-carbon economy: ideas of circularity and reuse, self-management and personalization, simplicity and closed loops, networks and self-organization, many of which are almost the inverse of Francis Bacon. These all point toward a future economy that is less rapacious on other systems.

Some areas of technological advance may chime with deeper desires, such as the movement toward "transhumanism," or synthetic biology. The nineteenth century brought a shift from natural chemicals to synthetic ones, and we are now witnessing an even more rapid development of synthetic life forms, some of which may replace or combine with the human body. Transhumanism raises immensely challenging questions of equity and morality: but it responds to an aspiration for life, and is likely to be a priority for at least some national innovation systems.[36] The same is true of brain science: the rapidly burgeoning knowledge of how the brain works intersects with peoples' desire to be happier, smarter, and better company, and is likely to drive a flood of new products and services, many of which will be just as ethically complex as those associated with transhumanism.

Other areas of technological advance may founder because they cannot offer sufficiently convincing accounts of the question to which they are the answer: space travel and colonization, for example, never quite convinced publics and politicians that they warrant the massive investment that would be necessary to go beyond space shuttles, satellites, and occasional unmanned vehicles exploring the universe.

The important point is that ideas play a decisive role at every stage. Significant technologies only spread when they awaken desires—enough to persuade researchers to devote their lives, investors to invest, governments to subsidize, consumers to spend. To do so it's not enough that they are useful (surprisingly many technologies are not very useful in their early days). They also have to be meaningful, to capture imaginations. In the next chapter I therefore turn to what may be the most important ideas animating the next phase of capitalist development.

Chapter 9

. . . .

The Rise of Economies Based on Relationships and Maintenance

Only in relationship with the other am I free.

DIETRICH BONHOEFFER, *CREATION AND FALL/TEMPTATION*, 1959

FOR MORE THAN FORTY YEARS, technological forecasts and futurology have highlighted the rising importance of information and knowledge, and much of my own career has been shaped by this movement of both ideas and practice.[1] The idea that a significant slice of the economy has become "dematerialized" is now commonplace, and most forecasters expect the future economy to be composed of ever more intangibles, of flows of data and knowledge, with every object fitted with transmitters, objects talking to objects as well as people talking to people. Ultimately, in some visions, every part of every human body may have its own URL, an identity in cyberspace. It's entirely likely that, with further advances in processing power, the real world and the virtual world will become much more integrated, with teenagers hosting parties on wall-sized screens in their bedrooms, and buildings, cars, and trains overlaid with layers of data, images, and sounds.

But here I emphasize a less familiar story. The largest sectors of the next stage of capitalism will not be information, or telecommunications, or computer manufacture. The stories of successive waves of technology surging through the economy and daily life are relevant, but only partial. The data for the last two decades already tell a very different story, and the data for the next two decades are likely to do so too. The paradox of stuff is that the very brilliance of a capitalist economy in achieving productivity gains means that the economic significance of physical technologies is almost bound to decline. The more they succeed, the more they shrink as a share of jobs or of GDP.

Instead we are witnessing the emergence of an economy founded more on relationships than on commodities; on doing rather than having; on maintenance rather than production. The ideas that animate this emerging economy are about service; empathy and emotional intelligence; consumer voice; and providing things with people rather than only to and for them. The services that result will be supported by sophisticated communication networks and rapid flows of information. But to emphasize the infrastructures alone misses the point, rather as it missed the point in the 1900s to see only the electricity networks, rather than the mass consumer goods that they were making possible. Instead, as in the past, the everyday uses of technology will be more social, more concerned with love and friendship, than their inventors ever imagined.[2]

Successive forecasters predicted that technology would replace human interaction, and turned out to be wrong. In every creative industry, contrary to expectations, consumption of electronic forms has risen in tandem with consumption of the live direct experience. Today's teenagers go to stadium concerts as well as listening to iTunes; their parents go to live sports matches as well as watching the replays on cable. The more we consume at one remove, the more we seem to relish unmediated experiences, just as the more we travel virtually the more we also travel physically. Peter Drucker forecast that by the 2020s "the big university campuses will be relics" and will probably be equally wrong and for similar reasons.

What drives these changes has less to do with technology and more to do with needs and wants: our compelling needs in satiated material economies are no longer ones for more stuff. They are needs for companionship, friendship, love, and care. They are needs for a better environment, needs for healthier minds and bodies, and these needs become economic facts as they pull technologies away from the visions of their inventors and investors toward what people really want. The car, the telephone, and electricity had the impact they did because of the ways in which they caught peoples' imagination, the freedom they signaled, the effortlessness and the sociability they promised, and these in turn pulled their technological development. The same was true of technologies such as the mobile phone, twitter, and SMS which spread much faster than the ones expected by the experts (such as ISDN).

At least in the rich quarter of the world most people's material needs are largely satisfied; the great majority have enough to eat (often too much), a roof over their head, enough energy to heat their homes, clothes for their backs, and shoes for their feet. There are significant pockets of material poverty in even the richest countries.[3] But the satisfaction of material needs is no longer the compelling task it once was. There are only so many new products that we can buy. Not surprisingly, many of the most upmarket sectors now emphasize smaller quantities rather than larger ones; leanness; simplicity; and the virtues of products built to last.

Putting relationships at the heart of things is not in itself new. Many of the ideas that animated the science of human resources and marketing were designed to overcome deficiencies in market-based, money-based exchange relationships. But these were always sideshows.

In some fields they may still feel like sideshows. In the medium term the economy of commodities has vast forward momentum. Forecasters expect that by 2050, India will have 350 million cars in service; China will have 500 million. We should expect to see several more generations brought up with the lust for things, from flat-screen TVs to iPads. But seen in the long view, an economy built around things, a cascade of ever cleverer, and more disposable, products, is being replaced by an economy based on relationships and maintenance. Once our material needs are satisfied these are what matter most for our lives: it becomes worse to be lonely than to miss out on another pay raise; worse to have no one to turn to for comfort and support than to miss out on the next gadget.

So we see new industries growing up around experience, and others around relationships. Some of these are illegal and therefore unmeasured—serving desires for sex or drugs. Some are very exclusive, like concierge services to guide the rich through their complex lives. Others are open to everyone, like booming industries for dating or escorts and the websites promising to reunite you with your old friends, or to construct a family tree. Feminist sociologist Arlie Hochschild described some of these as the "commercialisation of intimacy," but that may be too harsh. Certainly commerce is offering intimacy, but it's filling a gap, our need for others, rather than corrupting something that already exists.

If we go further and ask which parts of the economy are growing and look best set to grow, the answers suggest a marked change. What's striking is not the increase of cloud computing or gene therapies, but rather the shift from an economy made up of things, their manufacture, sale, and consumption, to an economy based more on relationships and maintenance. This can be hard to see through the chaotic exuberance of marketing and business news. As always older models consolidate alongside the emergence of the new. Modern capitalism grew up around mass production—the manufacturing of Ford and Toyota, Boeing and later Microsoft—and the dynamic of these ideas is not yet spent. That dynamic continues to take products from being exclusive to being commonplace, and it continues to toy with personalizing what were once standardized, albeit within tight constraints and on highly controlled platforms: Amazon, eBay, Apple are the dominant names of this economy. They have taken to a new level some of the keys to economic success in the twentieth century: reaping vast economies of scale, using very tight central control and very precise specification, and segmenting markets as far as they can.

But it's less likely that these are the harbingers of the new, or to be more precise, they may point us toward the infrastructures of the future but not to the activities that will happen on them. The reasons have partly to do with the dynamics described earlier. The productivity miracle of capitalist manufacturing reduces the GDP value of industry after industry, even as it boosts the capital values of individual firms. The paradoxical combination of rapid advance, and rapid shrinking, happened to farming, and then a few generations later to industries like steel, and then in accelerated form, to microprocessors.

Manufacturing remains a great source of wealth—but it is condemned to decline not just as a share of employment but also as a share of GDP by its very success in improving its own productivity. The same may well be true of search engines, retail websites, and games. Their market capitalizations may be vast, but they may be misleading signals of where the economy is heading. By contrast services are likely to grow and, ironically, the less successful they are in achieving productivity gains the more they will grow as shares of GDP and employment.

This has certainly been the case in recent years. Almost all recent EU jobs growth has come from services[4] and the same is true in the United States. Looking to the future, industries delivering outcomes such as care, health, and love, or the pleasure associated with tourism, look well-placed to grow. These form part of a relational economy where value resides in the quality of relationships more than in the consumption of things. The private doctor, therapist, and counselor, and the shopkeeper or hairdresser who charges more but knows you well, are all turning relationships into value. But during the industrial age these were marginal sectors, displaced by the economies of scale of mass production and retailing.

HEALTH, CARE, AND THE RELATIONAL ECONOMY

In advanced economies more people are already employed in health and education than manufacturing. Health has been the second most important source of new jobs in the United States in recent decades, and healthcare spending has increased from less than 5 percent of GDP in 1960 to about 17 percent of GDP now. The conventional wisdom (repeated by the Congressional Budget Office [CBO]), as well as most other researchers, attributes this long-term cost growth to "the emergence, adoption, and widespread diffusion of new medical technologies and services."[5] But this explanation obscures more than it illuminates. Most of the spending turns out not to be associated with particular technologies, let alone cures, but rather with the repetitive, labor-intensive, and continuous maintenance of long-term conditions such as diabetes and heart disease. Other, once fatal, conditions such as some cancers and AIDs have now become chronic conditions that can be coped with over long periods.

The CBO periodically releases seventy-five-year healthcare spending projections. Current projections forecast that total U.S. spending on healthcare will rise from 16 percent of GDP in 2007 to 25 percent in 2025, 37 percent in 2050, and 49 percent in 2082. This latter figure may be a joke, or designed to shock. But it contains a grain of truth. Elsewhere too, forecasters expect relentless upward pressures on spending: in the European Union, aging is predicted to drive public spending up by about 4 percentage points between 2004 and 2050,[6] while in China even larger growth is expected. One factor is the availability of new knowledge; another is changing demand. In the UK, for example, an eighty-year-old today is twice as likely to have cataract surgery, knee replacement, or coronary bypass as they were in 1990.

Aging is not the only factor driving these changes. A UK government foresight panel suggested obesity alone would affect the majority of men and women, and could indirectly cost as much as half the current health budget. A generation of couch potatoes, glued to social networks as teenagers, could, it is feared, reverse trends to rising life expectancy if it turns out to be plagued by mental and physical ill health.

Some of their demands for care may result from objective problems. But some will result from greater awareness and higher expectations. For several decades objective improvements in health have coincided with evidence of rising concern about health, with the "worried well" becoming as important a pressure on health systems as the sick. Health is part of a larger emergent industry loosely concerned with well-being, both physical and mental, and that includes the many services that try to make us well or keep us well, from gyms and massage salons, to health enhanced foods and tests. What economists call "positive elasticities of demand" create strong grounds for expecting spending on these to grow. Given the choice, richer populations usually want to spend a higher proportion of their income on services like care and education. And, given the choice, wealthier consumers tend to want to pay for more personalized services, ones that treat them as a person rather than just as another consumer.[7]

The bad news is that data from OECD countries show a roughly inverse correlation between spending on health and mortality, and a roughly inverse correlation between growth in spending on health and improvements in mortality (the correlations hold even if the United States is excluded). These are signs of systems badly in need of radical innovations.

Some improvements may come from overhauling existing institutions—for example encouraging hospitals to adopt the methods used by the Narayana Hrudalya hospitals in India which combine intensive measurement of results, extreme specialization, and peer review, and achieve better results at far lower costs. But in the long run the hospital or family doctor, the primary school and the university are unlikely to retain their dominant position as ways to provide health or education, just as the supermarket and the fast food chain are not guaranteed to remain as dominant forms for retail or restaurants. Instead we may see radically new models grow up alongside the older forms, making use of new capacities, such as far more widespread access to information; personal health records; or personalized curriculum vitae automatically linked to the databases of educational institutions).

The most promising methods either organize knowledge much more intensively or else mobilize society's capacity to complement that of doctors and nurses. Sweden's patient hotels point the way to a different kind of hospital—situated next to hospitals they provide a pleasant environment for the patient and an extra bed for a spouse or parent: although they involve greater capital cost, they achieve better clinical outcomes at lower overall cost, mobilizing a social capacity—the love and care of the family—to support healing. When every home can be relatively cheaply filled with devices for monitoring blood pressures or other vital signs, as well as high-speed video links to tutorials on self-care or educational games, very different kinds of service become possible. Portable devices can compare health status—such as blood glucose levels—with expected parameters, and warn when they are going awry. Wristbands can track pulse rates, motion, and sleep patterns. Care itself can be organized over the phone, by email, or through video clinics, with support from specialist doctors and nurses enhanced by support from other people suffering from similar conditions, rather than depending on general-purpose family doctors or accident and emergency rooms. All of these will achieve their greatest impact if they turn not just patients but also their spouses and parents into active managers of care rather than just passive recipients.

Some of the pressure for change will come from the need to save money.[8] To drive productivity improvements some of the tools used in business services are likely to be adopted: breaking down "service journeys" into modular elements and then recombining them using web and other technologies. Specialists can be concentrated in a clinic and call center focused on just one condition, like diabetes or multiple sclerosis. Here again we see some of the themes of twentieth-century capitalism—economies of scale, concentration, and segmentation—but now allied to twenty-first-century ideas about networks, mutual support, and the sharing of time.

Finance can also be reengineered to encourage more relational services. Health insurers can incentivize their customers to change their diet or join gyms (for example, cutting their premiums if they can show improvements in their body mass index); municipalities can reward social housing providers who do better in supporting older people at home, and reduce the pressure on hospitals or residential care homes; and employers can be incentivized to deal with their employees' low-level mental health problems. In all of these cases, tools that reveal the long-run pattern of costs and benefits will open up new opportunities to invest for prevention.

Health and care are already the dominant sectors of this evolving service economy, and they will benefit from a flood of new products, from smarter pregnancy and HIV tests to automated insulin dispensers. Some will promise much but deliver little. Anti-depressant drugs turn out to have little or no effect on moderate depression (placebos do just as well), though that has done little to diminish demand.[9] But many of the most interesting innovations combine technology with much more powerfully orchestrated networks of support. Large-scale examples are being organized by nongovernmental organizations supporting self-management and mutual support, for example through Expert Patients Programmes, or e-tutoring, or the 200,000 members of the online mutual support network for Sweden's diabetics. Patients like Me brings together 150,000 patients to share experience and gather data (which is then sold, in anonymized form, to pharmaceutical companies and regulators). That there are more than 10,000 apps on Apple's store is another symptom of demand for new ways of organizing healthcare. Small-scale examples that combine the best of technology with social support include Canada's Tyze, which organizes an online network of support for isolated older people, allowing friends, family members, and professionals to coordinate their care: who will visit to cook a meal, remind about prescriptions, or do the shopping. It's a very simple technology of connection but one that involves little or no exchange of money.[10]

Robots may in time form part of the mix, automating mundane activities so as to free up people's time for activities that really do create "relational value." The Care-o-bot developed by the Fraunhofer Institute in Germany could eventually become a useful aid for the vulnerable housebound elderly (and at the other end of the age range, South Korea aims to provide robots to teach children in kindergartens, one for English, another for gymnastics and dancing).

The end of life is likely to be a particularly important focus for innovation. In the United States, some estimates suggest that 50 percent of Medicaid is spent on the last three weeks of life, often in ways that do little to enhance the final days of the patient, or their friends and family. Most people die in hospitals, tied up with tubes and with their bodies pumped full of drugs. Yet most would rather die at home and with more control over the timing and manner of their death. The hospice movement grew up in Britain in the 1950s and 1960s as one answer, and made palliative care rather than clinical care the priority. The movement for legalizing voluntary euthanasia drew on similar frustrations with systems in which death had become so mechanized and inhuman that the relationships that matter most at the time of death had been pushed to one side.

Huge sums are invested globally in medical research and development, and with good reason. Yet less than 0.5 percent of this research addresses the behavioral and social factors that explain well over 50 percent of mortality (and most of that 0.5 percent focuses on compliance—getting patients to take their drugs). A very different kind of health economy is coming into view—but for now the management of innovation funding has barely begun to catch up.

GREEN ECONOMY

Health and care share common features with the other great source of new jobs and wealth, the industries loosely labeled green. These too contain many advanced technologies, and the "Cleantech" field has excited venture capitalists and angel investors in very much the same way that biotechnology did twenty years ago. Energy-efficient light bulbs, hybrid cars, and biodegradable cleaning products are becoming mainstream alongside water-based paints, roof tiles that reflect the sun back only when it's hot, and biodegradable pesticides. Biomimicry is being taken seriously in design, adapting methods from the natural world and applying them to materials and objects. Countries like South Korea have overhauled their economic strategies to prioritize the greening of industries such as cars and steel.

But it would be a mistake to see the green economy solely as a new wave of high-technology products pouring into the marketplace. A large proportion of activity in green industries involves rather more mundane technologies in repetitive tasks, and is often more akin to a service. The collection and processing of waste for recycling is one example. Large-scale off- and onshore wind farms are another. Retrofitting old homes, one of the keys to reducing carbon emissions in big cities, is technologically trivial, but remarkably hard to organize effectively (although the economic returns to the home owner may be substantial, people are generally reluctant to undergo the hassle). The same may be true of urban farming and the various movements to change the way we make food and consume it, replacing ever more exotic and distant imports with local production and seasonality. Most of these are labor-intensive, and all of them require continuous care and attention.

These shifts in the forms of production are mirrored in the evolution of consumption. One-off purchases of gadgets, clothes, and cars still dominate mass advertising. But wealthy societies have learned the disappointments of shopping: that more income and stuff are unreliable sources of well-being. And so we see constant innovation around the edges of consumption: products and services in which the consumer has to work harder (such as advanced cooking or dangerous sports); consumer goods that attempt to embed values of ecology or fair trade; and products that try to give their buyer the feeling of being a member of a club.

So far I've described discrete new models and ideas. But the brand new cities being built around the world have to rethink from scratch how to organize schools, libraries, parks, or healthcare. For some, technology is in the ascendant. South Korea's New Song Do aims to be the first city with more soft architecture than hard, with cameras and ambient technologies woven into the physical fabric of street lights and walls, a step up from the cities like Shenzen with their millions of CCTV cameras. Its vision of the future is one in which people appear as an afterthought. Others are consciously green: like Harmaby Sjostad in Sweden, Vauban in Freiburg in Germany, Masdar in Abu Dhabi, or the eco-city being built in Tianjin in China. Their aim is to be low-carbon exemplars of the future, and to achieve that goal they have substantially repudiated dependence on the car. In some cases, such as Vauban, there are strict rules regarding behavior—a far cry from the libertarian utopias of a few years ago—and there is little of the ostentatious consumption of the big urban developments of the 1990s and 2000s. Their vision of the future is one in which there is a good deal of civic activity, with support for volunteering, mutual support, and the arts, and allotments for food. They can be criticized for the gap between the hype and the reality, and for the lack of public input into their design. But they represent serious answers to serious questions.

To the extent that they embody a view of the future direction of economic change, it is toward an economy in which commodities no longer dominate and unnecessary consumption is reduced. All of the eco-cities are pushing the boundaries of reductions in energy use. The world's twenty largest megacities account for some 75 percent of energy consumption; within them, buildings account for about 40 percent of energy use, and typical buildings are used only 40 percent of the time. So there is great scope for large reductions in energy use: not just through better materials, insulation, and monitoring, but also through new ways of organizing work by bringing together office workers from many companies to share facilities and space, and work more from home or on the move. The drive to cut unnecessary use of resources is also encouraging the reuse of old buildings, rather than the automatic instinct to demolish and rebuild (the vast Shanghai Expo in 2010, China's great showcase of economic strength, made a point of reusing various century-old warehouse buildings), as well as much higher levels of recycling, whether of paper or glass, plastics or metals.

A more circular economy (to use the language proposed by Chinese President Hu Jintao at the 16th Communist Party Congress) would have quite a different feel and texture to one based on consumption and commodities. It may be more labor-intensive, and it certainly requires more labor on the part of the individual. The circular economy is also likely to be more local. If energy and carbon costs mount up, the economic logic of ever longer distance trade may be turned on its head. The successors of today's 3D printers and fablabs may allow us to manufacture close at hand. Energy may be re-localized in local generators making use of anaerobic waste, rather than being shipped in oil tankers and distributed over great distances from coal-fired stations. Cars may be provided for short-term rental in public transport systems (as is already done for bicycles in cities like Paris and London) rather than being assumed to be a private possession (Hiriko in Bilbao aims to be the world's first example of a public transport system based on electric cars). Food may be grown once again in parks, reservoirs, on roofs, and balconies: Havana became a model for this because it became necessary to grow 80 percent of its own food in response to the

U.S. blockade, prompting many other city-dwellers to wonder whether they wouldn't prefer to live in cities that were more self-sufficient, and even edible, with streets and parks full of fruit-bearing trees, nut bushes, and nutritious leaves. The vision of localized production may seem irrational and inefficient when seen through the lens of modern economic analysis: however, it responds not just to a larger imperative of climate change, but also to aspiration (who would have guessed that foraging for wild food would become an urban fashion?).

The net result of the various possibilities outlined above is that in both health and the environment it is possible to see a new economy taking shape that is very different from the visions of futurologists who could see only the hardware, and people adapting around the hardware. Instead, this economy is a response to needs and problems as well as technological possibilities. Like other parts of the modern economy it is heavily dependent on data and extensive networks, and, at least in part, on science. But its value comes from relationships: the value of being cared for, or maintained, rather than the value that comes from commodities that can be produced, consumed, and then discarded. Both health and the environment bring with them blurred boundaries between production and consumption—as in all intimate relationships, the consumer or user also makes and provides, whether that's through separating their waste or selling energy from their home back into the grid, or managing a chronic disease.

Both fields, healthcare and the green economy, are, partly for these reasons, reinvigorating the household as a place of economic activity. It has always been economically significant, but it was previously seen as outside the economy, and as too complex and ungovernable to be seriously analyzed or influenced. In an earlier stage of capitalism its only overt role was as the place of consumption—providing an insatiable demand for labor-saving white goods, and branded consumables—while its invisible role was as the source of successive generations of competent, and pliant, workers.

Demographic change and fiscal crisis mean that public policy has had to turn its attention back to the household. Much of the interest in behavior change is about what people do in the privacy of their own home, from helping children with homework to cutting energy consumption. It's also brought policy innovations such as nurse-family partnerships that provide intensive support for young mothers in poor areas to improve the chances for their children, green concierges who help streets or housing blocks to cut energy consumption, eldercare mutuals in which older people help each other out—and all are concerned with value in the household. Such an economy tends to become more personal, since any kind of relationship or support needs to be tailored to the very different needs of individuals; it tends to involve more intensive feedback; and it tends to focus attention not just on the sale of things but also on pathways (for example, through parts of the life cycle, from early childhood into adulthood, or from retirement into old age) and service journeys (whether of a patient through a health system or a passenger through an airport).[11]

Rethinking these journeys can then become a rich source of creativity. Often the decisive innovations change what sociologists describe as the 'scripts' governing behavior. An example from the private sector was the rise of fast food retailing which created a new script for having a meal. Where the traditional restaurant script required the customer to choose what they wanted, to be served by waiters, to eat their meal, and then pay for it, the self-service/fast food script requires them to choose, pay, carry food to their table, eat, and then clear up. Many innovations are attempting to embed similar new scripts, from personalized learning in schools and self-managed healthcare, to scripts that encourage residents to take more responsibility for cleaning their streets—and these are likely to be critical to future productivity gains in public services as well as private ones.

This attention to the household has potentially revolutionary implications. It suggests that the most important thing to be valued in a modern economy (for people at least, if not for markets) is no longer things, but rather time, or, more precisely, the quality of time as it is experienced. Much of modern economics treated household time as largely irrelevant.[12] To shift an activity from the household into the paid-for economy was an unambiguous gain for GDP, even if there was no obvious gain to human well-being. Turning attention back to the household, by contrast, unavoidably brings economics more into contact with values, since the household is the site of care, love, and trust, as well as their most extreme opposites of abuse, hatred, and manipulation.

This new economy is not inherently incompatible with capitalism. Very familiar tools of market design can be used to encourage the spread of new business models: for example, the removal of regulatory barriers, break-up of monopolies, or dismantling of professional restrictions on trade. These may help the spread of familiar ideas of scale, concentration, and standardization into new service fields. Sweden, for example, already outperforms the United States in terms of retail productivity thanks to firms like IKEA. Everyday services such as plumbing and building, childcare and eldercare, look ripe for the rise of commercial brands, and some areas of manufacturing are being remade as services: selling "safe mileage" rather than tires (as Michelin is doing); leasing rather than selling carpeting (as Interface has done); or leasing rather than selling aerospace (as Rolls Royce has done with its "power by the hour" model for aircraft engines).

But parts of this emerging economy may be at odds with a disconnected capitalism in which owners feel no commitment to customers, and "spot" trades predominate. Market forces can undermine the subtle ecologies of systems: the wrong kinds of competition for schools can widen social divisions; too much competition for healthcare can erode incentives to share knowledge and information. The new platforms that enable people to use each other's spare capacity make great sense in terms of lived value, but little sense in terms of monetary value. Buzzcar, which allows people to rent other citizens' cars, is a good example, as is Etsy, which provides a marketplace for homemade crafts. Both involve much lower monetary exchanges than their traditional equivalents, like Avis and Hertz. A major shift from buying beds in international hotel chains to booking beds on sites like Couch surfing could look like a contraction of global GDP.[13] But for the individual these alternatives offer more value at lower cost, and they use some of the capitalist logic of seeking out, and then mobilizing, underused resources.

It should be no surprise that these parts of the economy link value to values. Modern capitalism took on the language of religion in the latter decades of the twentieth century, almost carelessly. Mission statements, speeches about vision and visions, and close attention to values all became corporate clichés. Firms wanting to make a living in environmental industries found that they had to demonstrate their bona fides as well as their commercial acumen. In healthcare, relatively few overtly commercial firms have prospered, largely because of the difficulties involved in trusting them. In the most open markets, such as U.S. healthcare, for-profit firms tend to perform poorly against mutuals and foundations, or public organizations: they generally find it harder to mobilize trust, the sharing of knowledge and information, and the ethos of care that customers seek. According to the Rand Corporation, veterans treated in veterans' hospitals—which are the ones furthest removed from the profit motive—"received consistently better care across the board, including screening, diagnosis, treatment and follow-up." Kaiser Permanente, a foundation, is often reckoned the benchmark provider for the general population. Medicare spends perhaps a sixth as much on administration as private insurers. Education, too, has proven difficult for for-profits. Just as commercially motivated doctors will tend to provide unnecessary treatments, commercially motivated educators will be tempted to provide paper qualifications insufficiently supported by content.[14]

CIVIL-IZATION

The relational economy appears more in harmony with the economy of cooperatives, charities, social enterprises, and mutuals than with cutthroat profit maximization. These social organizations can bind their users and consumers into governance structures, as members or partners, and they can prioritize values more easily than for-profit firms. Where there are big asymmetries of knowledge, and so a big risk of predation—as in most healthcare and education—they provide some assurance that users' interests won't be subordinated to the need for profit. They can also tap into the "other invisible hand" of generosity. This makes very different service models possible: for example, bus services that combine paid staff and volunteers, so that remote towns and villages can stay connected; or schools that combine paid teachers and volunteer learning mentors.

Although volunteer labor has been a blind spot for economics, it matters greatly in the creation of lived value. In any one month, 20 percent of the world's population say that they have volunteered time, 30 percent that they have given money, and 45 percent that they have helped a stranger.[15] It's not only the recipients of help who benefit: there is evidence of the effects of giving on well-being, and at a national level a healthy link between giving money and reported happiness (a coefficient of 0.69 compared to 0.58 for the link between GDP and happiness).

The civil economy, which combines monetary and non-monetary motives and outputs, has very old roots but also renewed relevance. The first mutual insurer set up in Italy in the thirteenth century, and several of the religious orders invented new financial services for the poor, as well as forms of "social investment" that remain relevant today in the various banks that are offshoots of the Catholic Church. In some countries civil society grew out of crises: England's charity laws, for example, first legislated in 1601, were a response to widespread destitution and crumbling public infrastructures, and later the modern civil economy grew up as the counterpart to commercial capitalism, a response to the inequalities, ill health, and human misery it brought, mobilizing altruism as well as self-interest, mutual care and love as well as material interests. In the nineteenth century, the citizens of the first industrializing nations depended on the social sector for financial services like insurance, savings schemes, and money for buying homes, as well as cooperatives providing everything from food shops to funerals. A strong and proud independent civil economy grew up, including what came a century later to be called microcredit, and today it includes very large cooperatives in Spain and Italy,[16] building societies in the UK, and charities tied to the churches in Germany and funded by tithes on income. But during the twentieth century, big government and big business often displaced socially owned organizations, with governments providing welfare and pensions, and business providing commodity financial products, on a larger scale and sometimes at lower cost than the not-for-profit predecessors.

By the end of the twentieth century, a study in twenty-six countries for which data were available showed nonprofit organizations accounted for only 6.8 percent of the non-agricultural workforce.[17] Their relatively small scale reflects their inability to thrive in an economic environment based on oil, large-scale manufacturing, and globalized finance. It also reflects their own inherent weaknesses. Civil organizations can be paternalistic as well as inefficient. When small they can be amateurish, when big they can become bureaucratic. The British building society movement is a good example: founded by Richard Ketley, the landlord of the Golden Cross Inn in Birmingham in 1775, it encouraged members to pay a monthly subscription to a central pool of funds which was used to finance building houses for members, which then in turn served as collateral for further funding. By the early twentieth century there were nearly two thousand societies in existence with 620,000 members. But by the later decades of the century there was little to distinguish the bigger societies from for-profit banks which offered similar products, and little resistance when many (unwisely) privatized themselves.[18]

All civic organizations find scale difficult—and although there are some very large NGOs, like the Red Cross, Grameen, or Caritas in Germany which employs some 400,000 people, the great majority are small, mainly because greater scale can corrode values, commitment, and intimacy. When organizations do grow large, they tend to do so in ways that maintain small units of activity: with federal structures linking hundreds of local branches, or cellular structures like Alcoholics Anonymous, or many churches.

Scale is also inhibited by diverse values. One of the first charities in England was set up to raise funds to buy wood with which to burn witches; a century ago another distributed cigarettes to wounded soldiers. Associations representing car drivers have views almost diametrically opposite to green groups, and all healthy civil societies are as much a cacophony of mutual disagreement as they are a harmony of shared beliefs. Yet for all that, the more organized parts of civil society have consistent biases that go with the grain of twenty-first-century culture: they usually believe in equity, acting with rather than to or for. They value activism rather than passivity; mutuality rather than hierarchy, and the spirit of Ibsen's comment that "a community is like a ship; everyone ought to be prepared to take the helm." They draw on secular ideas of equity and liberty but everywhere are also interwoven with faith, and the persistence of religion as a social and economic force. A good metaphor is that of "granite" from Guatemala: the idea that everyone can contribute their tiny grain of sand to making social change.

Pope Benedict's encyclical *Caritas in Veritate* provided a recent theological account of why a strong civil economy is needed to balance pure commerce. It argued for the role of love, truth, and giving in human development, and that "the primary capital to be safeguarded is man." Stopping unemployment had to be a priority for any society, and any healthy economy needed to nurture a bigger role for giving as well as selling: "the more we strive to secure a common good corresponding to the real needs of our neighbours, the more effectively we love them."

No trend guarantees that the world's charities, mutuals, and social enterprises will grow rather than shrink as a proportion of the overall economy. The fact that civil society is strong in sectors that are likely to grow for other reasons leads many to expect its share of GDP to rise. In the UK, for example, well over 30,000 NGOs are already contracted to provide services by the National Health Service. Some governments have encouraged this growth by contracting out a growing share of public services.[19] Business schools report a high proportion of their MBA students wanting to learn about social entrepreneurship and to find career paths that combine making money with doing good. There has been a healthy growth in global NGOs, providing humanitarian aid, campaigns or specialist expertise. A plausible future sees a continued expansion of the social economy helped by rising invest-ment.[20] Yet it's just as possible that for-profit businesses will continue to take over new markets that NGOs and social enterprises pioneered, as has already happened in fields as varied as organic food and social networks.

But even if the share of the civil economy in GDP doesn't rise to 20 percent or 30 percent of GDP, it is likely to shape other sec-tors. Much of business now tries to organize itself with some of the skills of voluntary organizations, with a greater emphasis on com-mitment, mutuality, and values; some at least are more at home with relational contracts, and with organisztional models that give their more valued employees greater trust and autonomy. Some expect a growth in the "project economy" with more temporary organiza-tional structures, bringing together collaborators, and using some of the habits of civil society but for commercial goals. In this economy, authority depends less on status and more on reputation, with ac-countability passing sideways and downward as well as upward.[21] Businesses are already competing to engage users more directly in the design of services and the shaping of knowledge around services and systems: for example, diabetics, or pioneers of energy efficiency, food enthusiasts or sports fanatics, and when they do so they try to look like NGOs.

In energy, utilities, and finance, businesses face acute pressures to demonstrate their social credentials, and most recognize that the regu-lation of markets is now being driven as much by civil society as it is by states and legislators. That has long been true in relation to health and safety or employment law. But civil society is also acting more directly as an investor and an influence on investment, using its very substantial assets. It is acting to orchestrate consumption, influencing consumers to adopt environmentally friendly products, locally sourced food, and fair trade goods. And it is trying to change the climate within which corporate governance takes place, pressing arguments through the me-dia and politics, as well as annual general meetings and lobbying other shareholders.

Civil society is active, in other words, as provider, campaigner, influencer, and orchestrator. It is part of an economy that is both precapitalist, echoing the work of the monastery or village crafts, and post-capitalist, pointing forward to complex collaborations across networks. What we should anticipate is not so much a quantitative growth but rather a broader process of "civil-ization": making business more civil in character, in terms of values, methods, and organizational forms, and a parallel "civil-ization" of states, integrating some of the tools and habits of civil society.

Social innovation has yet to find its equivalent to Vannevar Bush, who framed much of the modern U.S. innovation system for hardware and technology. But there are modest exceptions which could be the pointers to better funded and more powerful institutions in the 2020s and 2030s: public investment funds like Sitra and Tekes in Finland, Fundacion Chile, and the i3 Education Innovation Fund in the United States. There are specialized banks like Banca Etica and Banca Prossima in Italy, and Big Society Capital in the UK. A new generation of political leaders committed to systematic innovation has also appeared—including Michael Bloomberg in New York and Won-Soon Park in Seoul. Their support is feeding a growing field of intermediaries worldwide, which are becoming more adept at spotting and growing the most promising social innovations, and using the many techniques of open innovation.[22] They include publicly funded centers such as several hundred "living labs"; groups situated within governments like Mindlab (part of the Danish government, and serving four different departments), or Kaiser Permanente's team using design methods for innovation in health. Innovation agencies include Nesta in the UK, Vinnova in Sweden, and the Harvard-based Institute for Healthcare Improvement, and there are also emerging innovation universities, such as Finland's Aalto University, launched in 2009 from the merger of the Technical University, the Business School, and the School of Arts and Design. MaRS in Toronto links a university, hospital and business incubator, alongside a social innovation investment fund. At the more radical end, new online platforms are attempting to combine open co-design of the problems that need innovation, as well as open co-design of possible solutions: "many to many" methods of innovation.[23]

All of these are quite small in scale. But they are being helped by changes in thinking. Within business, social innovation is ceasing to be a marginal aspect of corporate social responsibility, there to help protect corporate reputations. Instead, in the words of a recent OECD report, companies now "realize that global challenges such as climate change, the supply of clean water, epidemics and social needs constitute a huge new market. By creating new and more responsible and sustainable solutions, companies can cultivate new business opportunities."[24] New measures of innovation are being developed to capture the scale of nontechnological innovation: one example, the Innovation Index, measures not just traditional research and development but also complementary investments to commercialize ideas, as well as design, training in new skills, and copyright. Finland was shown to have the largest share of GDP in innovation, with 14.6 percent of market gross value added compared to 2.7 percent of GDP invested in research and development according to traditional measures.[25] A 2009 Business Panel on Future Innovation Policy, for the president of the European Commission, recommended "to base EU action around compelling social challenges, to finance venture and social innovation funds, to incentivize large scale community innovations . . . ," and many of their recommendations went on to be adopted.

This drive to transform the nature of innovation is being mirrored by innovations in finance. Some have tried to strengthen relationships between providers and users of finance in a direct challenge to the tendency to multiply the degrees of separation. For example, Kiva links individual investors with socially useful projects around the world and has, since its establishment, raised capital from more than 700,000 lenders (individuals from around the world investing $25 or more toward a specific project). By the end of the 2000s, 240,000 social entrepreneurs had been supported with around $100 million in microloans.[26] A very different example—which is also one of commercial involvement in social innovation—is M-PESA, which uses mobile phones to provide banking services. It now has over 12 million Kenyan subscribers and 11,000 agents countrywide, and has also spread back into the first world.

MEASURING SOCIAL VALUE

The rise of the social economy has made it necessary to adapt capitalism's tools for measurement and investment to very different environments, where value is as much bound into relationships as it is disembodied in money and commodities. Innovative ideas can be thought of as occupying a continuum: at one end they produce only private, monetary value, that is easy to capture through property rights. At the other extreme, innovations produce only lived value, which is very hard to capture, and the socially recognized forms of lived value which are sometimes termed "social value." In between are many ideas and ventures which produce both.

In principle, public resources should subsidize social returns on investment, but not private returns; and where projects create both social and private value, hybrid funding models are needed, which make explicit the potential returns to be achieved, the levels of risk entailed, and the potential for different players to capture future returns. Yet traditionally finance has been divided between grant funding on the one hand, and equity and loan finance on the other. Looking to the future, new investment markets, institutions, and even asset classes may arise to finance these fields of activity, offering a mix of financial and social returns to investors, with public resources provided either through direct subsidies or through tax credits.

A barrier to making them work, however, is the absence of reliable measures of social value, or reliable information about what works: the likely impact of models for training ex-prisoners, teaching bored teenagers, or caring for vulnerable older people. Without data and analysis bankers struggle to assess risk, and potential purchasers of services have insufficient reason to adopt new ones. The Cochrane and Campbell collaborations (which collate global evidence), and projects like the OECD's Wikiprogess on well-being, provide one part of the answer, bringing together the global evidence of formal trials and pilots in easily accessible formats. The UK's National Institute for Clinical Excellence is another, a powerful public body that rules on the cost-effectiveness of everything from smoking cessation programs to cancer drugs. Generally, however, this kind of orchestration of knowledge remains rare, and, where it does exist, tends to be biased to formalized research evidence.[27]

Unlike the twentieth-century innovations that were scaled literally, through manufacturing plants and global brands, most social innovations spread through more organic growth: through inspiration and emulation, alongside the rarer use of franchises or licensing. They grow by building new relationships and meanings as well as by being useful. Urban bicycle hiring schemes; volunteer schemes for palliative care; urban microcredit; banking services provided over mobile phones—all can be quite easily copied without having to pay a license fee. Each adaptation can then improve the model, in the way that Asa improved on some elements of the famous Grameen Bank in microcredit in Bangladesh by simplifying paperwork to the bare essentials, providing detailed prescriptive guides for managers, and avoiding the requirement for groups of borrowers to guarantee the loans made to each member. Pratham in India is another good example that has spread on a large scale. It was originally backed by UNICEF and the City of Mumbai, providing education to very young children in slums, using a simple model, which works at very low cost, and with no assets, and has spread by mobilizing corporate, community, and philanthropic support (including organizations in the Indian diaspora worldwide). It now operates in twenty-one states with well over 20 million learners, and combines some of the feel of a social movement with effective access to wealth and power.[28]

These examples grew outside the state, and even in competition with it. Others have been driven from within parts of it, like the North Karelia Project, implemented in a region of Finland that suffered very high levels of heart disease. Between 1972 and 1995, death rates from heart disease fell by 68 percent. The project encouraged people to change their diets, exercise more, and cut smoking. Specifically, increased exercise helped reduce blood pressure levels, and the use of vegetable oil products, rather than butter, contributed to a 17 percent reduction of cholesterol levels between 1972 and 1997. These were only possible because of the systematic involvement of primary healthcare bodies and nurses, as well as collaboration with the food industry. It helped that the project was directed at the whole community rather than just a few "high-risk" individuals. Its aim was to change the whole environment for healthcare, confirming other experiences that the best way to make people healthy is to change the context within which they live, rather than trying to change them on their own. Examples of this kind of systemic change are rare: they are hard to design, hard to implement, and even harder to sustain. But the salience of problems such as obesity or climate change means that interest in more holistic strategies of this kind is unlikely to abate.[29]

Very similar lessons have been learned in the environmental field. For all the popularity of individually targeted behavior change programs that try to "nudge" people toward better behaviors, the lesson of research and experience is that these are weak tools, effective only for marginal changes of behavior. More fundamental shifts, for example toward low carbon living or radically different approaches to diet and lifestyle, depend on a combination of changing environments and shifting the rewards and penalties individuals face.[30] What works and what doesn't is never easy to deduce. The closer we get to human behavior, the more the details matter. One study in the late 2000s conducted by researchers at California and Arizona State universities illustrates the point. Their study was designed to explore what influenced household energy use. The researchers monitored how much power was used by several hundred households and then sent them each a note comparing their consumption with the average of the neighborhood where they lived. After a week the households that used significantly more power than the average had cut their use significantly; but those who used less than average had increased theirs, perhaps afraid that they might be thought to be too mean, or just out of step with their peers. Here we see the power of social influences, but also why subtlety is needed in influencing it, and why the thousands of innovative projects worldwide that are trying to cut carbon emissions are such a fascinating and unpredictable process of discovery, trial, and error.

Most of the social innovations that have been developed to improve environments or healthcare were made by many people and contributed benefits to many people too. Their stories are sometimes told as if they had a single author (just as scientific invention is). More often, though, they are better understood as coming from teams and networks, less like a novel than like the Japanese traditions of "linked verse" in which each poet contributed part of long poems, or the Talmudic tradition of interpretation, and interpretations of interpretations. For their creators value came from contribution, not consumption, from being part of a chain, not the end of it, and technologies now greatly assist in efforts to mobilize many minds to contribute solutions.

The knowledge that is used by successful innovators generally has not come from basic science or even primarily from social science (though more may be in the future).[31] Instead, much of the knowledge is made by doing. The field of social innovation, which is set to be so important to an economy founded on relationships, may as a result be closer in spirit to this description of the philosophical stance of pragmatism, the philosophy of Charles Peirce, William James, and John Dewey, than to traditional science:

> Pragmatists believed that ideas are not out there waiting to be discovered but are tools that people devise to cope with the world in which they find themselves . . . ideas are produced not by individuals—that ideas are social . . . ideas do not develop according to some inner logic of their own but are entirely dependent, like germs, on human careers and environment . . . and that since ideas are provisional responses to particular situations their survival depends on not on their immutability but on their adaptability.[32]

Chapter 10

· · · · · · · · · · ·

Capitalism's Generative Ideas

CAPITALISM spread as an idea, a form of life, and a way of seeing. Its more ardent advocates could only imagine a future in which that idea simply extended and deepened. Its strident critics could only imagine mirror opposites. In this chapter I suggest how some of the defining ideas of capitalism could shape an evolution beyond it. These are ideas that make capitalism the ally of life, and which, if extended, help rein in its predatory and destructive tendencies. The capitalist imaginary is both liberating and destructive; both beautiful and ugly. We need to amplify the beauty and the insight, and rein in the ugliness.

GROWTH

Growth is the great promise of capitalism: growth of income, growth of opportunities, growth in physical terms, with larger homes, more stuff, and more to consume. Economies are judged by how much they grow, and if growth falters, governments falter too. Larry Summers, an academic economist who served as secretary of the U.S. Treasury, said that the government "cannot and will not accept any 'speed limit' on American economic growth. It is the task of economic policy to grow the economy as rapidly, sustainably, and inclusively as possible." At one point growth was also to be the tool with which capitalism would be overthrown: Nikita Khruschev proclaimed, "growth of industrial and agricultural production is the battering ram with which we shall smash the capitalist system." Growth is indeed the most remarkable feature of the modern world, and economic growth has been strongly associated with growth in life expectancy, education, and in access to the essentials of life, from food to energy.[1]

Against the dominance of growth, a counterview argues that growth is bad: the pursuit of growth necessarily means the despoiling of the environment, running down scarce resources, sacrificing life, and imprisoning people on a treadmill of hope and dissatisfaction. Better to be satisfied with enough. Better to encourage a steady-state economy.

Sustainability is sometimes taken to mean an economy without growth. Some celebrated when Japan moved into a long period of stagnation in the 1990s and 2000s. Here perhaps was a new model of sustainability. But this is not quite right. Growth is not just a peculiar fetish of capitalism. It is what nature does too—the growth of plants, creatures, and ecosystems makes the natural world what it is. Where there is no growth there is no life. The problem is not growth, but what kinds of growth an economy produces, and how it copes with the corollaries of growth, which are decay, shedding, and dying. An alternative view argues that any economy should grow but in different ways. We should want our economy to "crowd in" good business and "crowd out" bad business. It should grow qualitatively but not necessarily quantitatively: grow in terms of the value of products and services, their usefulness and meaning, not through using more matter or energy or more stuff. Indeed, this might be the definition of a truly successful economy: that all of its growth is qualitative and achieved from the creation and absorption of new knowledge, with knowledge replacing matter wherever possible (for example by reducing waste). It should grow in the sense of complexity, offering richer and more fulfilling ways to be and to live, and not just in things. In this view there is no inherent reason why an economy should not grow 2–3 percent or more a year, without breaching any principles of sustainability (meeting the needs of the present without compromising the ability of future generations to meet their own needs, to use the simple and clear definition proposed by Gro Harlem Brundtland, in her classic report from the late 1980s). The rate of growth would be set mainly by the economy's ability to create and absorb new knowledge, the ability to do things better, in all areas of life. Inputs of matter, energy, and time could decline.

It's not implausible to imagine an economy growing over very long periods of time primarily due to its superior ability to create and use new knowledge. In such a scenario those parts of the economy most dependent on energy and matter (which bring with them physical limits to exponential growth) would steadily shrink as a proportion of GDP—while other parts would tend to grow.

In this view, the growth of economies should also take on other lessons of growth in the natural world. It should include and even encourage cycles of birth and death; encourage systems in which the waste from one form of life becomes the fuel for another; encourage kinds of growth which are not just about becoming bigger, but are about deepening (like the roots of a plant).

Economics grew up as a discipline without tools for judging the quality as opposed to the quantity of growth. But now we need to be more precise about which kinds of growth are productive, providing us with value, and which kinds of growth destroy value. Classical and neoclassical economics tend to see all goods as providing utility. But a more rigorous view judges all goods according to their balance of positive and negative effects on value (or positive and negative externalities in the language of economics). At least four very different types of good are aggregated together in current measures of GDP.

The first category includes goods that become more valuable if others are also consuming them—like telephones and other network technologies. Because of their "positive externalities," there is a case for judging growth in consumption of these as more valuable to an economy than growth of other kinds of consumption. Health can be of this kind; it's valuable for me if other people don't carry dangerous infectious diseases, or if they are brought up to avoid impulsive violence. Many communications technologies create a lot of indirect value, and their dynamic impact on growth during some periods reflects this special quality. In the United States, for example, although the whole information technology sector made up only around 8 percent of GDP, it contributed a third of the growth of GDP between 1995 and 2000.

Telecommunications accounted for only 3 percent, but by the peak of the dotcom boom was contributing a quarter of the whole economy's growth of investment in equipment and software. Publicly available knowledge, Marx's "general intellect," also provides positive externalities of this kind. Again, it's valuable for me or you to be surrounded by other knowledgeable people. Precisely how this additional value should be measured is not straightforward; but it's striking to see the imbalance between how stock markets value the great network companies (like Google and eBay), and how their activities are valued in GDP.

A second category encompasses more normal commodities like clothing or tins of baked beans. Whether or not I consume these doesn't have much impact for better or worse on other people. These are the types of good around which most economics is shaped. Their profitability can be improved by reducing inputs or increasing the extent to which they are reused or recycled. But their external effects are modest.

In a third category are goods that destroy value for some while creating it for others. These include cars (which create pollution, noise, and dislocation for those who don't own them), airlines (which disproportionately worsen climate change) and many other industries. Economics recognizes that they produce "negative externalities." It measures these when doing exercises in cost-benefit analysis, and policy makers try to internalize them through taxes or regulations. But only the most obvious, and material, externalities are recognized in economics; and even the ones that are recognized aren't measured in GDP or company accounts.

Finally, there are goods whose very value comes from the negative externalities created for others. At the extreme are weapons: teenagers buy knives and nations build nuclear missiles to frighten others. Their negative impact on lived value is not an unfortunate by-product but rather integral. Somewhere between the third and fourth categories lie what the economist Fred Hirsch called "positional goods," whose value comes from their exclusivity; stately homes and tropical islands developed for luxury tourism are classic examples as is getting on the guest list for the best parties or membership of the most exclusive golf clubs. Their scarcity can be physical—meaning that a good is scarce in some absolute or socially imposed sense (such as land used for pleasure and personal enjoyment), or the scarcity can be social—meaning that it can be subject to congestion or crowding through more extensive use (as in the case of a privileged education). In the past, these goods were often governed by rules. Only high-ranking Hawaiian chiefs could wear feather cloaks and palaoa or carved whale teeth. In China before the establishment of the republic, only the emperor could wear yellow. Now these exclusive and excluding goods can be bought in markets, but with prices to maintain their exclusivity. Their value is a matter of relative position. Unless others envy them, and feel dissatisfied because they can't have them, they lose their monetary value. As a result, greater spending on positional goods is unlikely to increase overall well-being, and may actually diminish it.[2] As Fred Hirsch wrote, "it is a case of everyone in the crowd standing on tip toe and no one getting a better view"; "if all do follow . . . everyone expends more resources and ends up with the same position."[3]

These four types of good run in a continuum from ones, like network technologies, that create lived value greater than their apparent value in the market, to those that tend to destroy lived value. It should be self-evident that these very different kinds of good cannot simply be aggregated into a single thing to be called "growth." Yet traditional measures of GDP make no distinctions between them. They conflate quality and quantity; they ignore both positive and negative externalities; and they take no account of the running down of natural assets or of non-monetized work.

GDP was developed as a tool to help governments manage economies. It provided a way of adding up production, and became the critical tool for macroeconomic policy after World War II. It provided aggregate numbers, and had to because macroeconomics was a craft of aggregates. Any government seeking to manage its economy will need some measures similar to GDP that measure the volume of economic activity and allow it to be related to measures of investment, trade, or borrowing. There is much to be done to improve GDP measures and help them better account for the nature of modern production (for example, treating public sector production in terms of its value, not just the cost of its inputs, or distinguishing those financial activities that are genuine outputs from those that aren't). But we also need tools that can disaggregate rather than aggregate, to help us distinguish growth we want from growth we don't want. Measures of growth that is monetized need to be complemented by other ideas of growth and wealth. Over the last few years the world's statisticians have been working hard to better measure societal social progress.[4] In France, the Sen-Fittousi-Stiglitz report, commissioned by President Sarkozy, proposed adapting GDP to better reflect the true value of economic and other activities, with a changed approach to financial services. It aknowledged, for example, the need for much better measures of public sector productivity to feed into the GDP numbers. For U.S. GDP to better represent the welfare of U.S. citizens, its health sector shouldn't be measured by its very high cost (around 17 percent of GDP) but rather its impact on health (about the same as many societies spending less than half as much).[5] It also advocated new measures of wealth to sit alongside measures of economic wealth. Ecological wealth is measurable in terms of the appreciation or running down of natural capital, such as metals dug from the ground or rain forests. Social wealth refers to the quantity and quality of social relationships, trust, and support. This kind of social wealth has turned out to be just as important for human happiness as economic wealth—indeed, evidence shows that the quality of relationships matters more than income or consumption.[6] All of us know in our own lives that the wealth of our social relationships—whether there are friends and family there for us when things go wrong, as well as in the good times—matters as much as how much we own or how much we earn. These new measures form part of a larger shift of attention and understanding: to see growth as something with many dimensions not just one, in which we may often have to choose.

COLLECTIVE INTELLIGENCE, COOPERATION, AND EMPATHY

Earlier I described the associations between capitalism and freedom. But capitalism is also strongly associated with cumulative interdependence, and what I've called "connexity": the old English word meaning connectedness. It thrives when the conditions are propitious for extended cooperation—and shrinks when competition is too fierce. Those favorable conditions include the various commitments described in chapter 2: laws, habits of trust, and expectations of continuity, and they allow a modern capitalist economy to be made up of large corporations, some employing hundreds of thousands of people. Legally, corporations are defined as persons; yet they are better understood as tools for large-scale cooperation that work hard to create a sense of shared identity and commitment. When Britain's Companies Act of 1862 made it possible for seven people to sign a memorandum of association to register a company with limited liability, the great Victorian jurist A. C. Dicey quite reasonably feared that this was the slippery slope to collectivism (just as, earlier, Adam Smith had warned that any alternative to owners also being managers would lead to "negligence and profusion"). But history was against them, and the individualist model of ownership and responsibility was largely displaced by big organizations.

As a historical phenomenon, capitalism is associated not just with much greater movement of goods and money but also with the growth of cities, of dense populations, and intensive communications between both friends and strangers.[7] Cities provide clusters of specialized skills; they breed ideas; they allow producers to reap economies of scale; and local demand allows firms to price above marginal cost, providing them with the profits for growth. But the close links between capitalism and urbanization are also to do with culture. The places where people come together are highly social, and this sociability is an asset that makes both enterprise and innovation possible and breaks down the barriers between people.

This was apparent to some of the greatest thinkers at capitalism's birth. John Stuart Mill presented the market economy as a great assimilator:

> formerly different ranks, different neighbourhoods, different trades and professions, lived in what might be called different worlds; at present to a great degree . . . they now read the same things, listen to the same things, see the same things, go to the same places have their hopes and fears directed to the same objects, have the same rights and liberties, and the same means of asserting them.[8]

A few decades earlier Adam Ferguson, one of the founders of the Scottish Enlightenment, in his *Essay on the History of Civil Society* had written of the larger story of progress within which the market economy was unfolding: "not only the individual advances from infancy to manhood, but the species itself from rudeness to civilization," and he and Adam Smith presented the market economy as dependent for its workings on mutual trust being strangers and as a means of teaching people how to engage with strangers. In Smith's words, "To feel much for others and little for ourselves, to restrain our selfish affections and to indulge our benevolent affections, constitutes perfection of human nature."[9] And so, in the ideal society, the rich would be rewarded with money for their work and enterprise, but their greed would be held in check by their hunger for respect and civic pride.

Norbert Elias described one part of this story of how new habits were learned in his great book *The Civilising Process*,[10] which showed how people learned to rein in the impulse to violence, as the old aristocratic idea of "courtesy" was replaced with the notion of civility, better suited for "a denser social life and a closer interdependence."[11] Civility wasn't just essential for day-to-day life in packed city streets; it was also needed for commerce and trade, which depended on dealing with strangers on an equitable basis, so that a shop would sell products at the same price regardless of whether the customer came from the same background as the shopkeeper.[12]

The most capitalistic cities have usually had a high tolerance for the strange and the weird, and on the edge of every mass market there have been experimental markets for every human vice or hope. They have also typically been welcoming to migrants, from Renaissance Florence to nineteenth-century London, and good at cooperating across boundaries. Most of Silicon Valley's recent start-ups were founded or at least cofounded by immigrants—Sergey Brin at Google, Pierre Omidyar at Ebay, and Vinod Khosla at Sun (and, between 1990 and 2005, 40 percent of high-technology public companies in the United States were[13]). But as Peter Hall, the master interpreter of creativity in cities and economies, has shown, it was not enough to tolerate or ignore the migrants and eccentrics: the critical question was whether the existing structures could integrate newcomers, and give them access to capital and power. The ideal was a mixture of benign neglect and benign embrace. The innovators themselves needed to be "loosely coupled," "intimate enough to learn from nuance, but detached enough to break with convention and the habits of the group."[14]

The positive result of interdependence is that it has enhanced humanity's capacity to get things done, and our ability to think and work together, which is the only meaningful sense of the word development.[15] Collective cognitive capacities have been greatly amplified—the ability to see (from outer space to atoms), to reflect, to judge, and to imagine—as have our physical abilities to recast the environment or to make stuff.[16] Seen at close range, what is apparent is the competition and the chaos of dynamic market economies. Seen from afar, what's apparent is the order and cooperation that have made capitalism one of the decisive forces for socialization in human history, for understanding the needs of others as well as their trustworthiness, and for reining in impulses and aggression.

That surprising truth can be seen at every level. A recent study of the collective nature of capitalism looked at the performance of Wall Street analysts, and asked whether the team or the individual contributed most to success. The study compared the careers of over a thousand top analysts in seventy-eight investment banks, looking in particular at the performance of stars and non-stars. The star analysts who moved from one firm to another generally saw their performance fall sharply, and for at least five years. What appeared to be their own unique skills were in fact the skills of the team

> and the practiced, seamless fit between their own skills and the re-
> sources of the company . . . an analyst who left a firm where he or
> she achieved stardom lost access to colleagues, team-mates and internal
> networks that can take years to develop . . . new and unfamiliar ways of
> doing things took the place of routines and procedures and systems that
> over time had become second nature.[17]

If this is true in the ultra-individualistic world of Wall Street, it is even more true in other parts of the economy: successful capitalism succeeds because it socializes.

Recognizing that capitalism rests as much on civility and equality, tolerance and sociability, as it does on laws and money, opens up different ways of thinking about its future. We can see it more clearly as combining cooperation as well as competition; and we can see it as a creator of civility as well as a beneficiary of it. In time we may be able to judge any economy not just by its traditional resources (such as financial or human capital) but also by the complexity of its cooperative capacities: how well people are able to cooperate with strangers; how well established are the norms that prevent predation or abuse; and how skilled people are in forming and sustaining extensive networks.

PERFECT MARKETS AND PERFECT COMMUNITIES

The next set of ideas that can help us imagine a world beyond today's capitalism involves perfection. We have seen how important utopias have been to recent human history: a means to think through what might be, to take ideas and ideals to a logical conclusion and determine if they still add up. Throughout modern history, new communities have tried to start from scratch and to leave behind the corruption and failure of the societies from which they came, inspired by visions of what might be. The medieval monasteries, the Pilgrim Fathers traveling to the United States, the communes, cooperatives, and garden cities of the nineteenth century, are examples that stretch from the grand to the modest.

Capitalism too has had its own utopias. Adam Smith sought a perfection in markets that clear, and where buyers' desires meet sellers' incentives to make money. Later economics burnished his ideas until they became a more perfectly formed vision of completeness. Their best exponent was arguably Leon Walras, who provided the ultimate expression of classical theory when he introduced the idea of equilibrium from physics into economics, and proposed, as a tool to think with, the idea of a perfect equilibrium in which no one could make any choices that would leave them happier.

This perfect equilibrium was founded on perfect competition and helped by perfect information. In it, everyone's wants are expressed, and then refracted through the market. Then, through the market, they are connected to an economy's productive potential. This was the vision in which money became the currency for all desires, from the mundane to the exotic, and made them all commensurable, manageable, and tangible. It's a vision compelling in its simplicity (however complex the mathematics) that seemed to go with the grain of human nature, and to offer the prospect of an automatic mechanism endowed with perpetual motion.

At the heart of the appeal of this vision is the ideal of reciprocity— that for every take there is a give; for every want, a capacity to meet it; the idea that every deal is ultimately fair. This is an ancient idea. These are the words of Louis XIV, the Sun King, exemplar of monarchical power, but here even he presents himself as part of a reciprocal exchange: "the deference and respect we receive from our subjects," he said, "are not a free gift but payment for the justice and protection they expect to receive from us."

We have seen the consistency of the critiques that argued that capitalism's claims to reciprocity obscured the patterns of predatory relationships, the inequalities that lay one layer below the apparent equality, and the blindness to other kinds of value or to unintended consequences. But a century on from Leon Walras, it is possible to imagine a very different kind of perfection, a possible endpoint, or at least an ideal against which to judge any reality. Seen in this light, capitalism is not so much an aberration as a step on an evolutionary path, and one that contains embedded within it some of the answers to its own contradictions. I want to suggest, in other words, that in ideals of perfection we can find some of the power to change our world for the better, and some of the fuel that can shape new settlements and new solutions.

Let us imagine not just a market that is perfect, but a community or a society. It has perfect information—accurate knowledge of its facts and its circumstances. It has perfect communication, the ability to share information, views, hopes, and fears, with its members. Each can communicate with every other, as twos, threes, tens, or millions. It has perfect judgment, the ability to make use of knowledge and information to advance its most important needs and wants. And let us assume that it can exchange many things, from money and things to services and even love. Let us also assume that this perfection involves equality and true reciprocity. It has no predation, violence, or bullying—and embodies the golden rule: that we should only do to others what we would have them do to us. This we could call perfect power, where any inequalities in power are consciously desired and chosen by the people who give up power, because they believe the result is likely to be more well-being for them.

This picture is stylized, and abstract.[18] But all of us will have experienced situations not so far from this ideal. Small groups of friends who are open, who share tasks and take turns experience a rough approximation of perfect community. With people we know very well we can communicate through our words, and through what we don't say. Perhaps this is what we aspire to in love as well. It is also not so far from what can be found in the happiest and healthiest families—taking turns, sharing the good and the bad, and being helped by mutual empathy.

This picture has many common features with the picture of perfect markets. But it will already be clear that it differs in important ways.

It has many currencies, not just money, to express wants and needs. It communicates through many mediums, not just the decision to buy or not to buy. And it is reflexive, able to think about itself rather than being able to think only within the rules of the system.

What methods of decision making, and what heuristics, would such a community use? Look at a group of people around you and it's not hard to imagine what it would need. It would need to be able to cope with multiple cognitive styles, and many abilities (of analysis, observation, and judgment). We could imagine that it would gravitate neither to equality of voice, nor to fixed hierarchy, but rather to contingent inequality—giving greater voice to those with the greatest reputation, the most admired, and the most reliable. We can already see this in the world of the web: the strength of your voice depends on how many others want to listen to you. They may want to listen to you because of your authority or your learning, but this isn't guaranteed. We might also expect the perfect community to recognize strength of feeling: how much you care about something affects how others respond to your hopes or your concerns.

Seen in this light, the market turns out to be just one special case of collective decision making. It uses binary decisions (whether or not to buy) and a single currency, money. But richer human communities transcend binary messaging and can cope with multiple currencies— from money to friendship or love.

Variants of this perfect community can be found in many modern utopias. They may be philosophically rigorous, like Jürgen Habermas's account of perfect communicative action, or fictional like the many science fiction fantasies of telepathy and global brains. But they are all imaginings of an enhanced ability to communicate and exchange on scales far beyond the family or local community, and beyond the narrow constraints of a money economy.

We can imagine that this community would confirm the findings of late twentieth-century researchers that humans are at root conditional co-operators who have dispositions both to cooperate and to punish anyone who violates the norms or rules, or fails to contribute, with moral pressure. We could also present this as an example of a Nash equilibrium. John Nash is one of the theorists who has done the most to make sense of the dynamics of groups. In his account, a group of players is in a Nash equilibrium if each one is making the best decision that he or she can, taking into account the decisions of the others. However, the Nash equilibrium does not necessarily mean the best cumulative payoff for all the players involved; in many cases all the players might improve their payoffs if they could somehow agree on strategies different from the Nash equilibrium (e.g., competing businesses forming a cartel in order to increase their profits). The simple insight underlying Nash's idea is that we cannot predict the result of the choices of multiple decision makers if we analyze those decisions in isolation. Instead, we must ask what each player would do, taking into account the decision making of the others.[19] And so his argument draws us to wanting to know what kind of communication they would need to make decisions that constantly took account of others (including ultimately what others feel but can't express).

These ideas may also have a bearing on how we think about ownership. During the last decades of the twentieth century powerful arguments were leveled against common ownership. Diffused ownership meant diffused responsibility. The story of the "tragedy of the commons" suggested that self-interest would be likely to destroy common lands since everyone has an incentive to overgraze or overfish. The implication appeared to be that property rights would do better, and great efforts were made to introduce them into fields as diverse as electromagnetic spectrum and fishing. In some cases this undoubtedly led to more efficient use of these scarce resources. But the empirical study of commons has shown how well many communities manage their common resources (rendering it a drama rather than always a tragedy). Most users of shared resources live in villages, and often over many generations have learned how to manage forest lands or fisheries. Strong social structures and relationships turn out to be capable of managing complex rules and constraints: they are closer perhaps to the perfect community, with subtle communication about patterns and actions. This more subtle research has also shown how vulnerable commons are to the intrusion of both markets and distant government bureaucracies, that don't understand these local arrangements.

The usefulness of the idea of a perfect community is very similar to that of the idea of a perfect market. It provides a tool for thinking with. We can look at any real institution and ask how far it deviates from the ideal: the quantity and quality of the communication, the degrees of equality of power. And we can innovate new devices to bring us closer to it, like crowd-sourcing, crowd-funding, and continuous feedback; a city that sees its own choices reflected back to it.

This is the implicit ideal of a modern culture—continuously reflexive and self-aware. Capitalism made this possible. Yet its imaginary stopped short, promoting mindlessness not mindfulness, a narrow view of human interaction not a rich one, a perfect market but not a perfect world.

MAXIMIZING FRIENDS AND RELATIONSHIPS

The fourth area where the capitalist imaginary is ready to be stretched is the relationship. From the moment we are born, we seek out friends who will help us and avoid enemies who will harm us. As dependent and social creatures this behavior is inseparable from our search for food or shelter. We live and survive because of others. This fundamental fact dominates childhood—where we learn how to read the patterns of support and enmity in those around us, how to shift alliances, how to replace one group of friends with another. And it continues through life with love, spouses, and friends. With any kind of attachment comes risk—the risk of betrayal and the risk of predators who will take advantage of us.

We can judge the extent of love or friendship by how much we would give, and how much we would sacrifice. The ultimate expression of love is to value another's life more than our own. This is the love that we aspire to in romance, and that nations aspire to claim from their citizens. But for anyone else who matters we will also be willing to make some sacrifices—whether of our time, our money, or our reputation. George Vaillant, the Harvard professor of psychiatry who conducted some of the most interesting recent studies of life patterns, found that one of the most important determinants of life expectancy is having someone you could call at 4 a.m. to share your troubles with (and the most important strength, he suggested, is the capacity to be loved).

At the opposite extreme there is hatred and enmity, as much a part of daily life as love. Its expressions include violence and war, as well as discrimination and disgust. Again we can be more precise. The extent of our hatred can be judged by how much we would sacrifice to harm someone else. There may be good reasons for this—what's called altruistic punishment, the willingness to accept a sacrifice to see a wrongdoer punished. Or the reasons may be bad: petty malice, vindictiveness, or prejudice.

The market sits squarely between these two poles. It is the world of calculated indifference, of commodities, prices, and facts. Its practitioners take pride in not caring too much, avoiding sentiment and emotion, or attachment. The market (or rather those most intimately involved in market transactions) presents itself as morally superior to war and hatred because it involves no strong emotions and no violence, and sees these as archaic. And it sometimes presents itself as more honest, and more reliable than the world of love and friendship. Here the capitalist imaginary is confident in its coolness. Investment bankers and traders take pride in calculation rather than care. They appear the opposite of love, treating everything with equal detachment whereas love treats its objects as utterly unique, with "infinitely particular distinctness," to use Hegel's phrase. By being loved we are reminded of who we really are, beneath our social roles.[20] In the marketplace by contrast we are treated only for our surface qualities—our qualifications, our wealth, and our creditworthiness.

It's conventional to see money and markets as the enemy of love and friendship. Robert Ellickson, author of *The Household*, correctly points out that "intimates typically have a strong aversion to engaging in monetised transactions with one another."[21] Most scholars assume that markets corrode intimacy, and vice versa. That anything can be bought or sold means that nothing is really valued, or sacred, anymore: all we're left with is a cold instrumental rationality. Conversely, too much passion threatens business. Sex is a threat to the orderly functioning of the workplace, and kept at bay with a host of prohibitions and norms.

Yet for all that, the market depends on both poles, on care as well as calculation. We've already seen the complex interrelationship with war (and in every real business there burns a fierce competitive drive to do down the enemy). And at the same time every business tries to make itself like a circle of friends, to kindle the warmth and commitment of a community. Every seller too tries to persuade buyers that they are his friend. This is the explicit message of much advertising, sending signals of warmth, reliability, and care.

The critics of capitalism have tended to see this as pure cynicism, the cooption of the best in human nature for something close to the worst. But this misreads. For one of the great achievements of a market economy is that thousands more people behave as if you are their friend, with smiles, providing you things, looking out for your needs. The smiles and warmth may be synthetic, and fall far short of true friendship, but they are preferable to hostility and indifference. Capitalism may often be associated with anomic detachment, and markets do indeed treat people as numbers, human resources to be bought, sold, and disposed of. But markets also meet some of our needs for other people.

The workplace certainly does this. A large proportion of people now meet their primary partner through work. Stefana Broadbent suggested that modern communication is re-establishing family and friendship connections during working hours, which is the way things used to be before industrialization.[22] Goods and consumption also unlock the world of people. Consumption is not an alternative to sociability, but often the route into it. This was the insight of the anthropologist Mary Douglas's work on the "world of goods." We consume to send messages that connect us to others and provide us networks of friends. Money can't buy you love, but perhaps it can buy you companions. At the very least it can open the door to a network of acquaintances who over time may then become true friends.

This connection between consumption and friendship can be seen in a surprising place: the patterns of alcohol consumption. It's not the poor who drink most, to drown their sorrows. Generally the richer you are the more you drink. Partly that's because you have more money. But it's also that you are able to be more sociable—to host more parties, dinners, and receptions—all fueled by alcohol. It's through money as well as love that we find and keep friends; consumption lubricates our dealings with others, and the goods we buy serve to communicate who we are and what we care about. And it's through consumption that we send signals to others about what kind of person we are, how generous and trustworthy.

Nonhuman primates live, like us, in a world where friendship and kinship are all-important, magnets in a web of commitments and relationships. Consolation has been studied extensively based on hundreds of cases—it's a common behavior among apes—and apes share food specifically with those who have recently groomed them or supported them in power struggles.[23] Human children, too, learn early who is with them and against them. The school playground is a world starkly divided between friends and foes. It's easier to keep your friends if you have a bit of spare money, and children learn that it makes you friends (they also learn that having too much will make others resent you). Within democracy the same applies. Around the formal structures of parliaments and parties there is a civil society that merges imperceptibly into daily life. Our circles of friendship are at its root, but layer upon layer of association extend the principles of friendship to religion, nation, and beliefs.

Anthropologists and sociologists have always recognized that the material economy rests on a relational economy. This relational economy is not so different from the material economy, which sees itself as a place to maximize utility. But seen through this alternative lens it becomes clear that we seek to maximize not so much our utility as the balance of effective friendships over effective enmities. This is not quite the same as maximizing your friends relative to your enemies, as if having a thousand friends on Facebook will insulate you from harm. What matters is the effectiveness of the friendship or enmity: whether it is close at hand, available at different times, and sufficiently attuned to who you really are. This is what I earlier described as social wealth: the value of the social ties that we have, that is every bit as important to well-being as economic wealth.

To get by, we need extensive networks of friends (and to understand the friendship paradox—that the simple mathematics of human networks means that your friends are likely to have more friends than you do on average). And we need intensive friendships as well, the small number of people we can expect to be loyal to us even if we behave badly, shout at them, and abuse their trust.

Everyone learns how to cultivate friendship, or at least how to attempt to maximize the balance of effective friendship over effective enmity. We learn this before we learn about how to consume or how to handle money. Moreover, we learn early that many moral dilemmas come from this aspect of daily life: the meaning of loyalty (who should you be loyal to, and what justifies you breaching their loyalty); the meaning of honesty (and when is it reasonable to lie); and whose secrets are kept and whose are shared.

Much of history has involved the creation of ever larger scale, and more widely spread, networks of friendship: the bonds of a religion that allow you to trust strangers, those of a multinational enterprise that allow people to work together and share their knowledge, those of the nation that encourage soldiers to sacrifice for each other, all bound up with fear and force but effective only because they tap the fundamental human need to be rich in friends rather than foes.

The importance of the human drive to maximize effective friendship explains much about the limits of capitalism and its dynamics. It explains both the successes in creating new spaces for civility and mutual trust, and the resentful reactions against the ways in which it can destroy them. It also explains much about the appeal of capitalism, which has never just been the appeal of more things, but has also offered the prospect of enhanced freedom and sociability, whether the promise of new lovers for young men and women, or new comrades in the workplace.

What would a future economy look like that maximized friendship rather than consumption? Its businesses would be concerned with whether they were good places to work, places that encouraged people to collaborate and cooperate. It might reward them according to their peers' feedback. Its industries would encourage and organize friendship: dating, interaction, and meeting up. And it would measure social wealth, social capital, and social connectedness as well as the volume of production or investment in the economy.

This is of course a partial picture of the twenty-first-century economy that is evolving even amidst an imaginary that denies its social nature. Google pays its staff according to finely calibrated 360-degree feedback. Businesses offer customers the chance to meet others. And social technologies make it possible to formally orchestrate friendships, their relative status and degrees of access.

That friendship matters is not news. But how it matters is. The best protection against a child developing a cold after exposure to the virus is being able to answer "yes" to questions such as "Do you have someone to talk to about your problems?"[24] The experiments of David Sloan Wilson in Binghamton, New York, leaving addressed envelopes in streets and seeing how many were delivered to the right door, found that the key factor was whether people believed themselves to be receiving many sources of social support. Another recent study analyzed data from 148 previously published longitudinal studies that measured frequency of human interaction and tracked health outcomes for a period of seven and a half years on average. It found that the extent of friendships contributed up to 50 percent increased odds of survival (and because information on the quality, as opposed to the quantity, of these relationships was not available, this is almost certainly an underestimate).[25] The reasons for this powerful impact are in some ways obvious—the effect of a calming touch, of support when things are hard, or people to share meaning with are immense. Yet they have been absent from the imagination of capitalism and from conventional thinking about economics.

The underlying message is one of interdependence. Our happiness is not easily separated from that of others around us: spouses, friends, children, and parents. George Akerlof was surely right in his comment that "a great deal of what makes people happy is living up to what they think they should be doing,"[26] and much of what they think they should be doing comes from what others think they should be doing. Large-scale regressions show a very striking correlation between national levels of happiness and levels of sociability—the proportion of the population who are members of one or more social organization. These correlations are much stronger than those between GDP and happiness.[27] By focusing solely on individual attributes we miss the crucial factor, which is that how happy you are depends on the way you live, and that in turn depends on the kind of society you live in. A good one cultivates friendships and relationships and treats these as paramount, not a marginal concern of private life.

VALUE, MEASUREMENT, AND WASTE

The next field we need to consider is waste and value. Capitalism prides itself on efficiency. The pursuit of profit drives out waste, whether of materials, energy, or time. But a common critique has been that in the name of efficiency other kinds of value are destroyed. Nature is sacrificed for production, families for profit. If one response is to go on the attack, denouncing the iniquities of the system, the other has been to use the tools of capitalism to measure and map where value is being destroyed and where waste is being generated. In the 1960s, the preferred tool was cost-benefit analysis which purported to deal with any kind of cost and any kind of benefit and continues to be widely used, particularly in transport (where it's often linked to environmental appraisals) and for big capital projects (where it's notorious for underestimating costs).[28] Economics has developed many methods to monetize social value by asking people what they would pay for a service or outcome ("stated preference methods"),[29] or by looking at the choices people have actually made in related fields ("revealed preference").[30] The burgeoning field of environmental economics has spawned methods for measuring everything from wetlands to emissions, combining these revealed and stated preference methods. Social Impact Assessment methods have been in use since the 1960s, trying to capture all the dimensions of value that are produced by a new policy or program. These attempt to estimate the direct costs of such things as a drug treatment program, the probability of it working, and the likely impact on future crime rates, hospital admissions, or welfare payments. Civil society has toyed with the idea of measuring "Social Return on Investment." In healthcare there are measures of QALYS and DALYs (quality and disability adjusted life years), making life rather than money a common currency. Australia's statistics office estimates unpaid work now at around 48 percent of GDP.[31]

This explosion of measurement can be seen as an odd pathology, using the language of value and money in places where it is inappropriate. Many of the measures are easy to criticize for lumping together very different things in a single number, or offering spurious exactness where it's impossible. But we can also see these as crude, early attempts to extend some of the virtues of capitalism into other fields. Those are the virtues of precision, the virtue of using data to see where waste is occurring, and making visible and explicit what is otherwise obscure. These various methods can change how we think about waste and value. Already measures of carbon footprints and emissions have provided a very different way of seeing economic life. Making flows of material waste visible transforms how we think about industries, and what counts as efficiency. The measures of wasted humanity are much less developed but potentially can shape a different economic imagination, where, as a matter of course, measurement captures the effects of economic activity on psychological stress and well-being, and the knock-on effects on family life. It's not hard to imagine every government Treasury using social impact assessments alongside its assessments of economic and environmental impacts (and some already do). Nor is it hard to imagine stock markets and large investors responding to public pressure to do the same, publishing more extensive accounts that capture not just money values but other values as well.

Thinking in more rounded ways about waste will also open up new perspectives on consumption. Economics has concerned itself with the productivity of making things, analyzing in great detail how inputs of energy, capital, and matter turn into things that can be sold. Capitalism prides itself on being good at raising productivity, and with good reason. But once money is in the hands of the consumer, the analysis stops. Yet the efficiency of consumption matters as much as efficiency in production. Some consumers spend their money in ways that deliver a big impact in terms of well-being, others hardly at all. Generally the rich consume much less efficiently than the poor: it's long been assumed that the marginal benefit of each extra dollar of spending diminishes as income goes up. But this surely understates the inefficiency of high end up consumption, such as the possession of many homes, many cars, or many hundreds of shoes. An economics fit for a world with more awareness of material and ecological limits needs to be as rigorous in its understanding of productivity in consumption (or "consumptivity") as it is of productivity in making things.

ENTREPRENEURSHIP BEYOND BUSINESS

Another field where we can see the ideas of capitalism in motion is entrepreneurship. In the 1897 *Oxford English Dictionary* an entrepreneur was still defined as the director of a public musical institution. Only in a later edition was the word used in its more modern sense, as the editors acknowledged that the control and direction of capital and labor in a modern economy might be so difficult and different from past experience that a new class of person was needed and with it a new word, adopted from the French (it was only a century later that George W. Bush commented that the problem with the French was that they didn't even have a word for entrepreneur).[32]

Joseph Schumpeter's view of how economies work has become much more widely accepted in recent decades. In his account the entrepreneur is the decisive actor, seeking out opportunities, spotting under-served markets or unused assets, taking risks, and reaping rewards. Schumpeter's approach is very different in spirit to most of mainstream economics. It emphasizes the search for what's not known, what's uncertain, and what's unmeasurable. In perfect markets with perfect information there is no room for entrepreneurs. Instead, entrepreneurship highlights the difficultness of the world, its resistance to predictable plans, and how we learn by bumping into things, and then navigating around them.

An opposite view of entrepreneurship (associated with the work of Israel Kirzner)[33] sees it not as the upsetter of equilibrium but as the force that creates it, using information to take advantage of disequilibria and thus push the economy back into balance. In either light, entrepreneurship is not peculiar to business. There are few fields of human activity where entrepreneurship isn't part of how change happens. Schumpeter wrote of entrepreneurship in politics as well as business (and was for a brief period a minister), and saw entrepreneurship as a universal phenomenon albeit one that was particularly dynamic in capitalist economies. Ludwig von Mises wrote that entrepreneurship "is not the particular feature of a special group or class of men; it is inherent in every action and burdens every actor."[34]

This is Schumpeter's description of the essential quality of the entrepreneur in any field:

> In the breast of one who wishes to do something new, the forces of habit rise up and bear witness against the embryonic project. A new and another kind of effort of will is therefore necessary in order to wrest, amidst the work and care of the daily round, scope and time for conceiving and working out the new combination. . . . This mental freedom presupposes a great surplus force over the everyday demand and is something peculiar and by nature rare.[35]

Rare it may be, but it is not unique to business. Within universities, some academics act as entrepreneurs, assembling teams, spotting gaps, promoting the superiority of their ideas, and bringing together whatever resources they can find to win allegiance. The founders and builders of great religions did all of these things too, and often combined business entrepreneurship with faith.

The idea of business entrepreneurship led in time to the idea that states should support it, and many governments provide tax incentives, training courses, and celebrations to encourage entrepreneurship. Social entrepreneurship is a younger idea but it too has encouraged various kinds of support, from governments and foundations: prizes, funds, networks, and celebrations. Can it be learned? Does it deserve subsidies or tax incentives? Does it warrant celebration? Are the founders of new enterprises the right people to grow them? Here again we see an idea taken from capitalism being generalized, and to creative effect.

In Adam Smith's classic account, *The Wealth of Nations*, the combination of markets, legal frameworks, and property rights translates the self-interest and greed of millions of individuals into a force that promotes the prosperity of all. The brilliance of the market mechanism is that it is automatic: by harnessing motives and energies that are already there, it avoids the need for a king or a commander to "run" the economy. Instead, the economy runs itself and rewards both performance and innovation.

In the eighteenth century Adam Smith was equally famous for *Theory of Moral Sentiments*, a very different set of writings that looked at the "moral sentiments" of sympathy and compassion that hold societies together. Although he didn't put it in these terms, the two strands of his work can be brought together in the idea that all modern societies depend not only on the invisible hand of the market but also on another invisible hand: the legal and fiscal arrangements that serve to channel moral sentiments, the motivations of care, civic energy, and social commitment, into practical form and thus into the service of the common good.[36]

In many societies these arrangements are weak or nonexistent. Most countries lack adequate legal forms for independent nonprofit organizations; fair, let alone favorable tax rules for donations, or for trading; laws and a political environment that make it possible to argue, criticize, and campaign; and protections from violence, or the arbitrary caprice of bureaucrats. This is why so many social entrepreneurs in much of the world live embattled lives, constantly struggling to survive, and having to appease powerful interest groups and suspicious states.

In other countries these basic conditions are well-established. Citizens' rights to demonstrate and advocate, to organize trade unions and political parties, sit alongside laws that make it easy to create new organizations, to employ staff, to trade, to fund-raise, and innovate. Just as markets draw on the energies and creativity of entrepreneurs willing to risk money and prestige, so does social change draw on the often invisible fecundity of tens of thousands of individuals and small groups who spot needs and innovate solutions. So social entrepreneurship in its widest sense turns out to have been part of modernity as well as part of its future, bringing with it a different imaginary, part capitalist, part social worker, part individual hero, part servant. With it comes a necessary restlessness that was perhaps captured best by Georg Simmel in his writings about the nature of life and its processes.[37] Life, he wrote, involves flux, freedom and the creative exploration of new combinations,[38] yet it constantly creates forms and it is through forms that action is organized. So genetic mutations lead to the form of the body and the cell; musical experiment leads to forms like the symphony or the three-minute pop song; and social action leads to the creation of new institutions. Yet it is the nature of forms that they run counter to the creative spirit of life: they are fixed, permanent, limited by rules. And so forms both express life and also stand against it. For the innovator or entrepreneur this means that the very moment of greatest success and pride, when their idea becomes a venture or a policy, is also a moment of anxiety, because at that very moment it is no longer theirs.

TIME, RATHER THAN MONEY, AS THE GOAL OF ECONOMIC LIFE

Capitalism's defining idea is the search for value that can be exchanged and monetized. It makes money the common currency of life, and sees anything and everything through that lens. Yet money can only ever be a means, even if the miser takes it as an end. The end for which it is a means is to enhance life in some way, through better places to live, better food to eat, or better clothes to wear. When capitalism is a means to these ends, it thrives. But when it appears to lose sight of this, to make life subservient to money, its legitimacy is called into question.

For anyone living rationally and wisely, the quality of life will always be a higher value than money or consumption. We live only once, and every step of life is a step toward death. As consumers we may occasionally be drawn to the modern equivalent of grave goods, but compared to our ancestors we are less likely to be fooled by their significance.

If capitalism is at heart a system for the realization of exchangeable value, its successors may be systems for the realization of meaningful time, including both the time of lived experience and the much longer cycles of biographical and ecological time. Capitalism showed the world as controllable, amenable to manipulation, and adaptable to human desires. This may have often led to hubris. But it was also liberating, at one with life, in that it sought out the things and places that were dormant, dead, and unrecognized, and tried to animate them and render them productive. The same mentality can be applied to time: seeking out where and when it is wasted, dormant, unsatisfied, and unrecognized, and then finding ways to bring it to life.

If time becomes the primary, and most visible currency of life, what follows? Money is frozen time; capital is frozen work. All of the numbers of a capitalist economy are numbers in time: discounted, forecast, or hedged. Capitalism provided new tools for thinking about time and managing in time, beyond astronomy, and observation of the heavens, and it showed time to be not given or determined by fate. So how might its techniques and methods be spread to encompass the quality of lived time? There are some simple implications, many of which are already visible. If as much attention is paid to time as is now paid to money we can expect proliferations of time accounts, time banks, time exchanges, time rights, and time credits, which allow people to store time or to swap it with others. We might expect ever more rights linked to time—including rights to paid and unpaid leave, rights to training time, rights to adjust the fixed hours of the working week. We might expect educational institutions devoted to helping people use time more effectively, schools of life as well as schools to prepare for work, and coaches skilled in pointing out to people how they might use their time more effectively. None of these are fantasies or utopian. All exist already, though on nothing like the scale of their equivalents in and around money.

We should also expect an economy in which more attention is paid to happiness and fulfillment in time: not just the happiness experienced in the moment (which researchers track by asking people to tell a monitoring machine how they feel), but also the happiness or satisfaction we experience retrospectively, for example our appreciation of an unusual holiday or friendship. We can already see new industries growing up around pleasure and experience: they encompass everything from carefully constructed experiences of exhilarating danger to drugs and therapies or stimuli to parts of the brain.[39] Education systems can teach us to better understand happiness in time, remedying our poor track records in judging our own experiences and what will make us happiest.[40]

We might also expect more attention to be paid to the productivity of life beyond work. The data show that only a minority of our time—about 23 percent of our time spent awake—is now devoted to paid work. In contrast, we spend more than three-quarters of our adult lives engaged either in "unpaid work"—cleaning, washing, looking after our kids, building flat-pack Ikea furniture, and mowing the garden lawn—or in leisure—playing sport, shopping, reading, watching TV, etc. Two generations of labor-saving inventions have still left the home as a place where we have no choice but to spend large slices of time on essential care and maintenance, whether for ourselves, our children, our pets, or our homes and gardens. The richest people will contract most of these roles out, and many even on middle incomes pay others to clean their homes or look after their children. But seen in the long view, what's remarkable is how little these figures have changed, and if the data are to be believed, parents spend more time with their children now than forty years ago. Having children doesn't make people either happier or less happy overall. But the combination of genetic impulse and the search for love and fulfillment clearly animate people to devote time and energy to family life as much as ever before.

Various attempts have shown that as much as half of the GDP of developed countries is accounted for by unpaid labor (though all such attempts to put a monetary value on time are fraught with theoretical and technical challenges), providing fuel for the feminist argument that it should be recognized in welfare systems. The economist Gary Becker took a very different approach, going further than any other economists in applying the economic method to other fields, from marriage to housework, and used wage rates as the "shadow price" of leisure. The home was portrayed as just like a firm, a place where resources are combined to produce outputs such as meals. The oddity of this view is that it assumes that cooking only makes you happy insofar as the meal does. Family life is never a good in itself, only a means to an end.

Similarly instrumental types of analysis have struggled to make sense of the dynamics of time. Time and motion studies sought out waste in the factory (though with little or no concern for the well-being of the worker). More recently the understanding of flows has been applied to many other fields of life. Firms like Toyota mastered the flow of products through their factories, and then applied similar thinking to hospitals and their patients, and to airports and their travelers. In every case the aim was to reduce unnecessary actions, and also to save people time. The dream has been to make life frictionless, an effortless flow through transport networks, shops, schools, and hospitals, without bottlenecks or queues. Yet oddly most people dream of something almost opposite to this—the meaningful friction of real-life relationships, where others care enough to argue, to be difficult, and sometimes to stop us doing what we want.

Some have used monetary equivalents to assess how much it's worth spending to save time. Cost-benefit analyses put a value on the time that might be saved by a new road bypass, and use examples of how people trade off time and money to generate estimates. An interesting comparison of travel choices tried to add up the time spent earning money for different modes of transport and came up with what they called "effective speeds" of kilometers per hour. The luxury car came out at 14.6, economy cars at 23.1, public transport at 21.3, and the bicycle at 18.1.[41]

There have been some attempts to calibrate not just the time spent traveling but also the nature of the experience—how relaxing or stressful it is to sit on a coach, or stand in a line. Clearly the accounts needed for time are different from those for manufacturing, if only because our experiences are so radically different. But the quality of lived time can be measured, and can be compared.

Seen through these lenses, the choices facing any society start to look very different. If we move an activity from being paid to unpaid it looks like a decline of GDP. But it might lead to more happiness (imagine two neighbors who take it in turns to cook each other meals instead of going separately to a restaurant). If a new service allows people to visit their doctor over a video clinic rather than a physical one, this saves them time, but has no effect on GDP (and could mean less pay for the doctor). So time accounts can map in more detail how much time people have, what they use it for, and what fulfillment they achieve from it. And they can surface different choices than measures of money.

Another good example of this is the use of a measure of quality-adjusted life years, QALYs, in healthcare, which predicts the number of extra years of life achieved by a new drug or treatment, adjusted to whether those years are likely to be disability-free. QALYs per pound spent (or DALYs per dollar) are becoming the most important measures of the effectiveness of healthcare, and the test that any new drug or service has to pass. The important point here is that time and money are being brought together, on an even footing, and with surprising results, including a strong encouragement for simpler and cheaper therapies like smoking cessation programs, or exercise as a treatment for moderate depressives.

National Time Accounting is a recently devised set of methods for "measuring, comparing and analyzing how people spend and experience their time—across countries, over historical time, or between groups of people within a country at a given time." These are not yet complete or wholly settled, or ready to displace national money accounts and output accounts. But the data arising from time accounts brings new insights which have obvious implications for how we live our lives and how public policy should be run. Detailed work on how people use their time in the United States has suggested that many people would be better off if they commuted less and spent more time with their friends and family, or if they shifted their leisure from passive to more active pursuits. In analyses of this kind we see the outlines of a new way of looking at the world, in which the qualities of time would matter as much as the quantities of income and money.

A society that was more attentive to time would reverse the relationship between time and money that is found in contemporary economies, where time is the servant of money, there to be carved up, measured, and managed in order to increase monetary profit. So what would happen if the relationship was inverted, and money became the servant of our aspiration for more and better time?

Within markets the future is valued less than the present, and interest rates, usually set by central banks, effectively tell us by how much. These become widely used—for housing, borrowing, and as a guide to public investment as well. They treat time and its uncertainties as uniform and universal.

Yet if we look instead at how real individuals and institutions treat the relationship between time and value, very different patterns become apparent. Parents invest in their children without much expectation of a financial return (or if they do expect one, they are likely to be disappointed). Anyone who feels part of a community will feel duty-bound to contribute to shared capital projects, like building a new church roof, even though they may experience few of the benefits. Within governments, too, very different treatments of time can be seen: education systems invest in children regardless of discount rates, and governments invest in defense projects with a very long horizon. In health, many countries apply a very low or zero discount rate to their decisions, on the grounds that today's young people shouldn't be disadvantaged relative to the old. In climate change a furious debate has raged about what discount rates should apply—again in part a moral argument about what weight we should give to the needs and choices of future generations (an argument that is colored by the observation that, if economic growth continues, future generations will be much richer than us, raising the question of what sacrifices we should make for our richer descendants). Often governments—and foundations—behave more like a guardian or steward, who is charged with sustaining or growing capital, rather than like the strictly rational consumers of economic theory who always value present consumption more than future consumption.

Our relationship to time reflects our relationships with others. The stronger our bonds of connection to others, the lower our effective discount rates, and the greater our valuation of the future. Money becomes a servant of time and the future, and of our commitments, rather than governing them. This is a subtle, and profound, aspect of the working of the world that is missing from economics, and from capitalism's understanding of itself, but becomes more visible as time takes center stage.[42]

All of the clusters of ideas described during the course of this chapter—from new ideas about growth and cooperation to friendship, value, and entrepreneurship, remain young. They have not had the decades or centuries that it took for capitalism's ideas to move from broad brush strokes to precise diagrams, honed down into theories and data sets, competing schools of thought and practice. But add them together and it's possible to see how capitalism may evolve in the realm of ideas and imagination as well as in reality.

Chapter 11

. . . .

New Accommodations

or How Societies (Occasionally) Jump

> At first it was to have been different
> luminous circles choirs and degrees of abstraction
> but they were not able to separate exactly
> the soul from the flesh and so it would come here
> with a drop of fat a thread of muscle
> it was necessary to face the consequences
> to mix a grain of the absolute with a grain of clay
>
> **ZBIGNIEW HERBERT, "REPORT FROM PARADISE"**

IN 1938, a group of men gathered in the small town of Saltsjöbaden near Stockholm. Sweden was reaching a new accommodation, which turned out to be one of the most successful ever, laying the foundations for many decades of healthy growth and social success, and the global triumphs of firms like Volvo, Ikea, and Ericsson. At Saltsjöbaden, the representatives of business, government, and unions agreed to create a society with "no rich individuals but rich concerns." The agreement hadn't come easily. In the 1920s, Sweden had been beset by strikes and high unemployment. Pervasive class war threatened the nation's very future. No one had to look far to see what could happen if the conflict worsened—just over the Baltic Sea was Nazi Germany, and, a short distance to the east, the USSR was in the midst of murderous purges. The people gathered there had grasped a common lesson of modernity: shocks are much worse in societies riven with deep social conflicts and weak institutions to manage those conflicts. Having institutions that can quickly create a consensus about what needs to be done when a shock hits, whether it's a financial crisis or a war, creates great value. Saltsjöbaden kept government out of industrial conflicts—but its spirit was integral to the welfare state that then took shape, and "the spirit of Saltsjöbaden" came to stand for consensus, pragmatic compromise, and trust. In some respects the details of the agreement mattered less than how they had been achieved. As President Eisenhower is reputed to have said, "plans are nothing, planning is everything," and the agreement had forced the partners to plan together.

Other countries have had similar moments of definition. The Netherlands after World War II adopted what came to be called the "Polder model," giving to each religious and social group a share of power and, like Sweden, committing to a model of consensus. Its legitimacy came from memories of what had happened to the Netherlands in earlier periods when divisions had been allowed to fester. Germany at roughly the same time had a new settlement forced on it by the occupying powers, with a constitution that divided power among the regions and an economy that institutionalized a substantial role for free trade unions. Those parts of big business that had cooperated too readily with the Nazis were cut down to size. A few years earlier in the United States, Franklin Roosevelt had introduced the New Deal in a similar spirit of compromise and cooperation: "Better the occasional faults of a government that lives in a spirit of charity," he said in his second acceptance speech, "than the consistent omissions of a government frozen in the ice of its own indifference." And after World War II, Britain introduced its own version, with the welfare state, a national health service, and a reformed education system. As the architect of many of these reforms, Sir William Beveridge, put it, "a revolutionary moment in the world's history is a time for revolutions, not for patching."[1]

The words used for these moments are telling. They are described as accommodations, or settlements, suggesting that societies were trying to create new homes for themselves to live in, arrangements within which they could belong more comfortably. They came out of crisis but turned the problems into opportunities. Each accommodation transformed what capitalism was and how it was experienced. Each transferred more power and more protection to the people, both as workers and as consumers, and created new common goods. Each was an accommodation in the sense that all sides compromised. And each settled not only new rules and formal roles, but also a new spirit.

New Zealand is a particularly striking example. After a prosperous 1920s, the country was hit hard by the Great Depression. As export prices collapsed, income fell by 40 percent in three years. Farmers struggled to pay their mortgages, and urban unemployment soared. Discontent erupted in riots (my cousin, John Mulgan, wrote one of the country's most famous novels, *Man Alone*, about the unrest and misery that unsettled the country in the early 1930s). Out of the misery a new, Labour government was then swept into power in 1935 with the promise that every New Zealand citizen should have a right to a reasonable standard of living. Its guiding principle was that the community was responsible for ensuring that people were safeguarded against economic conditions from which they could not protect themselves. It went on to introduce a welfare state, and to provide healthcare free at the point of use, pensions, as well as extended benefits for families, the disabled, and the unemployed. The legislation was described as "the greatest political achievement in the country's history," confirming the country's status as the "social laboratory of the world" (decades earlier it had been the first country to introduce universal suffrage).[2] The first welfare system designed to protect New Zealanders from the "cradle to the grave" was popular enough to keep Labour in power for fourteen years.

Like the other accommodations, New Zealand's created a new social contract that strengthened bonds of mutual commitment. In part this was a response to risk. Before the Great Depression the middle classes of many countries had been able to buy insurance against some of the biggest threats they faced. But insurance markets collapsed alongside the markets for stocks, shares, and commodities, and the middle classes were forced by necessity to join coalitions for common welfare.

Each accommodation also represented the triumph of new methods. In the 1920s, many of the most eminent economists thought that the solution to economic crisis was rather like the eighteenth-century doctor's solution to illness: to draw blood from the body, or in this case to cut spending. By the time of these accommodations an almost opposite lesson had been learned, about the need to create demand and increase spending rather than cutting it. Each of these deals and accommodations also recognized a wider circle of claims—claims for attention and respect from the poor, from children, and from the elderly. In the natural world predators are often resisted by "mobbing," when groups of smaller and weaker animals or birds band together to fend them off. These accommodations are our large-scale human equivalent.

The deals that crystallized on each of these occasions lasted for many decades. But each in different ways frayed over time. The accommodations that widened the role for the state suffered when states became overly eager predators themselves, or free riders trying to get something for nothing. This happens most often through debt when governments succumb to value illusion—hoping that they can create value by printing money rather than things of true value. The Soviet Union's debt tripled in the first three years that Mikhail Gorbachev was in power. China's acute foreign exchange crisis in 1978 prepared the way for the reforms led by Deng Xiaoping. Shortly afterward, India's reserves almost ran out, forcing it into a parallel series of reforms. Britain in the mid-1970s had to ask for help from the IMF, and soon adopted the ideas of Margaret Thatcher for a radical extension of markets.

These settlements can look like cycles, with expansions of government followed by contractions. But there are also cumulative patterns when seen in a longer historical perspective. In Dani Rodrik's words,

> the last two centuries of economic history can be interpreted as an ongoing process of learning how to render capitalism more productive by supplying the institutional ingredients of a self-sustaining market

economy: meritocratic public bureaucracies; independent judiciaries; central banking stabilizing fiscal policy, antitrust and regulation, financial supervision, social insurance, political democracy.[3]

Since 1945 most developed economies, from Europe to east Asia, have added on universal education, universal healthcare, and public health as well as ever more rigorous environmental policies, not solely to make capitalism more productive, but also to make it more useful and fair. Most developing economies judge their success not just by their levels of GDP but by the things they buy with it: Thailand, for example, committed to universal healthcare in 2001, and China is rapidly introducing a welfare state and healthcare. Indonesia, like Mexico and Brazil, has extensive conditional transfers; India guarantees its rural population a right to work (up to 100 days a year) on infrastructure projects.

The more far-reaching accommodations are rare and difficult. More often one is willed but not achieved. For example, Japan has fumbled its recent attempts to find a new model. The Meiji restoration, and the postwar miracle that succeeded its defeat in World War II, both proved Japan's ability to reinvent itself to spectacular effect. But later efforts to remake the Japanese economy and society, and define a new stage of capitalism, largely failed, like the Maekawa report under Prime Minister Nakasone, which sought to justify an easier, less stiff and hierarchical model for the country, which it hoped would lead the world in enjoying the fruits of growth, not just creating them. Russia after 1989 adopted a succession of new economic strategies which on paper described a radically transformed market economy, but which were largely ignored in practice. Each time oil prices rose, and money surged into the state, the pressure for reform abated.

The conditions for change are unusual and even unnatural; they depend on crisis and on a shared reading of crisis. But they also depend on preparation. Each of the successful examples described previously succeeded in part because hard work had been done over many years to define the elements that would go into a new accommodation. These may have appeared at first to be utopian fantasies, and all good ideas begin their life half-baked. But they prepared the way, and usually at their heart was an insight into what will bring successful order—an idea of rights or freedoms or of the most compelling risks that need to be avoided. If human history is a drunkard's walk where people learn by successes and failure, bumping into walls and then lurching forward, and rarely walking for long in a straight line, these are the moments when for a time a clear view ahead becomes possible.

As John Dewey put it, every political project then needs to create the public who can be its author. That brings with it contradictions, and the paradox identified by Jean-Jacques Rousseau in any truly democratic change: that we want a power that will eliminate its own power and transfer it to the people.[4] Every accommodation in this sense ultimately disappoints, in that power doesn't wither away. But huge strides forward are made along the way.

So what can we reasonably hope for? Let's imagine the crises of our times might pave the way for new accommodations, perhaps not next year or even in ten years' time. What would they look like? What preparations would they need? What new common institutions and common goods would be created? And what questions would they try to solve?

History breeds many possibilities, and today many kinds of capitalism are possible. They include new mutations of state capitalism, with resources captured in sovereign wealth funds, as well as the counterculture capitalism of green jobs, capitalisms of multiple monies as well as capitalisms offering markets for psychological states. There are as many malign possibilities as benign ones, from revived militarism and autarchy to stigmatization of minorities and accelerated ecological collapse. But within what's present it is possible to see some of the more positive elements that could come together out of the slump. Seeds of the future can always be found in the soil of the present. The same was true in the 1900s and the 1940s when ideas that were in the ether, or implemented on a small scale, were picked up and melded into programs for action by creative political leaders.

My interest here is in what can reinforce the productive, life-enhancing qualities of capitalism and rein in its predatory, life-constraining side, strengthening the makers relative to the takers. The answers to the crisis of the 1930s turned out to be about much more than monetary and fiscal policy, and the same is true today. Dealing with the overhangs of debt, and the unsustainable imbalances between different parts of the world, is a necessary condition for recovery, but not sufficient. So too is the creation of stronger transnational institutions to govern an interdependent world, whether in relation to money, carbon, or information. But once again we also need to amplify and accelerate creativity—in production, work, and consumption—while reining in predation. Amplifying creativity involves a mix of investment, pressures, and freedoms. Reining in predators involves rules, laws, and norms; the power of shame as much as formal penalties, countervailing forces as well as restraints.

Every real accommodation will be different, colored by history, culture, and circumstance, emerging from practice as much as from blueprints. As Roberto Unger puts it, we rethink and redesign our productive tasks in the course of executing them, using "the smaller variations that are at hand to produce the bigger variations that do not yet exist."[5] This is as true for whole societies as it is for small projects. But the lesson of past moments of accommodation is that evolution is often convergent; relatively similar arrangements can come into being in very different societies, partly thanks to the natural affinities of types of economy, technology, ideas, and values, and partly thanks to suggestion. In what follows I therefore sketch some potentially convergent changes—a changed view of what wealth is; of how wealth is created; and of how wealth is used.

1. Mobilizing Collective Intelligence and Creativity

In chapter 10 I explained why zero growth has as little inherent attraction as growth that involves ever higher costs and ever greater damage to environments. The alternative view of growth, I suggested, sees it as an expansion of productive potential, of the ability to do and make things, driven by the accumulation of knowledge, and the capacity of society and economy to absorb knowledge. So the first priority is to raise the economy's capacity to grow without deteriorating the stock of natural capital or cutting into family life. That requires a sharp increase in investment in new knowledge and its diffusion and uses, with attention to the realization of ideas, and their absorption, as well as their invention. Material things—fuels, foods, and objects—will continue to be vital to our experience of value. But our wealth will increasingly come from what is immaterial and intangible: the knowledge embodied in things, in systems, practices, and people.

It's not a new insight that knowledge and its uses are decisive for economic growth. For fifty years, work has been under way to map, measure, and understand the dynamics of a knowledge-based economy. But institutions have only partially adjusted to this shift. So what should be done? A society dedicated to cultivating collective intelligence needs to advance on many fronts in tandem. Earlier I suggested that the mark of a mature innovation system is that it provides free resources for creative exploration, whether by scientists or artists, but also goes further, aligning awareness of the most compelling needs for innovation, the capacities of its most creative people, and systems for turning ideas into effect. That alignment is all too rare. But it has to start with devoting a greater share of resources to new knowledge. Many countries are already committed to growing investment in research and development, alongside policies to encourage spin-offs from universities and growing industrial clusters. For reasons discussed earlier, many of these plans will disappoint. But the key is to extend this work, not to narrow it: investing in new ideas in design and knowledge as well as science; mobilizing citizens as well as experts; and creating new kinds of university that are more directly engaged in creative problem solving. There's truth in the cliché that although research is expensive, ignorance costs even more. The rhythms of discovery are bound to vary. Digital technologies are continuing to produce a flood of new technologies. By contrast life sciences, genomics, and biotechnology have so far largely failed to deliver on their promise. But that's mainly because the underlying knowledge remains insufficiently mature. Looking two or more decades to the future it's as likely as ever that new understandings of life, and of fields such as brain science, will be transforming not just economies but also how we see the world.

But more research isn't enough on its own (rising research spending has actually coincided with declining productivity). Just as important is investment in translation from research into useful products and services, and investment in the skills needed to adopt innovations.[6] Germany's Fraunhofer Institutes are one model for doing this; others have suggested new professions of innovation advocates and champions, charged with scanning for promising ideas and helping nurture them into life. The critical point is that without deliberate support, many potentially very valuable ideas go to waste.

A society committed to collective intelligence also has to both expand and transform its institutions of education. Universities have greatly grown in scale, but they have been slow to innovate. There are some exceptions, including Aalto University in Finland, the Open University in the UK and its equivalents around the world, or new platforms like iTunes University and the Peer2Peer University, as well as smaller innovations within older universities.[7] What is needed is both the unavoidable elitism of the most advanced science, and the open democracy of other kinds of innovation (it's no coincidence that a high proportion of the most successful firms of recent years were started by university dropouts). Only a very few can innovate at the leading edge of software or biology, but many are capable of innovation in such fields as service design and work organization. The very uneven patterns of patent creation and start-ups in countries like the United States and the UK, are pointers to just how much creative talent is being wasted.

Schools still reflect their nineteenth-century roles in providing malleable workers for industrial organizations, rather than cultivating habits of discovery. As Roberto Mangabeira Unger put it, children need to be provided from an early age with the "means to resist the present" and not to see it as fixed, law-like, and immutable. Just as they need to learn to write as well as to read, they also need to learn how to code and program as well as to use software designed by others. The tools needed to innovate aren't inherently strange or inaccessible.

Very little innovation is truly "out of the box," except when seen from a distance. Seen from close up it's much more often made up of combinations of incremental steps,[8] which are not hard to pick up through practical projects in the classroom.[9]

Economic policy also needs to adapt. Most of the departments and agencies that support innovation are products of the relatively distant past—the 1940s or 1960s. Innovation is thought of in terms of inputs (with targets to grow the share of GDP spent on research) rather than outcomes or capacities. Most public spending on industry goes to old industries: to subsidies for agriculture or cars, banks, and steel, fixing the problems of the past rather than the future.[10] Singapore is almost unique in having reshaped its tax credits to support the full range of investments in innovation—from research to design and human capital. Elsewhere, little of the tax system has been adapted to reward investment in knowledge, though there are some exceptions: Canada, for example, offers a broad-based R&D tax credit of up to 35 percent, while the Netherlands lowers the corporate tax rate for innovation-related profits, such as from royalties or the sale of patents. All of these policy tools are hampered by the absence of reliable measures of intangible investment, let alone incentives to encourage it, and many investment incentive schemes do little to distinguish predatory from productive investments.

Innovation systems are bound to vary greatly in different fields, from substantially science-driven fields like new materials or pharmaceuticals, to fields like design, fashion, retailing, or finance where knowledge is much more like a craft.[11] As Friedrich Hayek pointed out half a century ago, highly educated policy experts invariably exaggerate the importance of formal knowledge relative to less formal knowledge; systematic science relative to craft skills. But all have their place, and at their best, innovation systems achieve a clear line of sight between a new idea and its full realization: a line of sight that may include research projects, seed funding, angel or venture investment, and organizations with the capacity to take the idea to scale. In most fields that line of sight is blocked and messy, and the majority of resources are captured by the most powerful sectors and institutions.

As we've seen, finance has become distant from innovation—with barely 2 percent of investment in technological innovation coming from venture capital in countries like the United States and the UK. The lesson of recent decades is that innovation is most likely to find investment when investors with a deep knowledge of the field get involved. This is not surprising: whether to back a promising new material or software program requires subtle judgments that can't easily be mimicked by a standardized assessment tool. The more investment is aggregated into global investment banks or funds, the less is likely to end up with risk-taking innovators. The same is true of public funds. Large national funds tend to become risk-averse, or captured by large corporate interests. DARPA is one good model, and is rare for giving entrepreneurial individuals space, and money, to follow their instincts. More often public innovation agencies are set up according to the bureaucratic norm of defining tasks, budgets, and roles first and finding people to fill the roles second, an approach that tends to lead them to follow lines of least resistance. It's better to have a messy but dynamic landscape of competing, entrepreneurial innovation funds than to have neat boxes that fit logically into an organogram. Funds need a minimum scale to pool risk and support new ideas through to production. But it's better to have competing funds rather than monopolies; better to support ones with some specialism and depth of knowledge; and it's vital that funds are small enough to be allowed to fail. All of these are precisely opposite to the inclinations of big finance and big government, which tend to create funds that are too bureaucratic and too big to fail, but also too big to succeed in interesting ways.

In fiscally constrained environments it's a brave political leader who will argue for a jump-in investment in knowledge and innovation. Many see innovation as the destroyer of jobs, not their savior. Hence the need to show that innovation is as much about new fields of service—like care for the elderly, or management of waste—that are likely to remain quite labor-intensive, as it is about automation.

Embedding innovation also matters vitally for government itself: indeed, with intensive pressures on public spending, and given the lack of competitive market forces in public services, the amateur approach to innovation carries a high cost in the form of stagnating public sector productivity. Very few governments devote significant funds, talent, or energy to creativity and the selection and spread of new ideas. The nature of their innovation systems is bound to differ radically in fields where professions and formal knowledge dominate (like medicine), from ones that are organized much more as fields of practice (like traffic management). But all benefit from more attention to evidence, more structured experimentation, and more investment in rapid learning in a culture where every public servant assumes a responsibility to know their impact.

In some of the most important fields, a higher level of complexity will also need to be addressed. Major public research initiatives like the Manhattan project, the mapping of the human genome, and CERN (the European Organization for Nuclear Research, which gave birth to the World Wide Web) were hugely complex in themselves. But some of the most important challenges require sophisticated natural science to be allied to social science, and to the engagement of users. This is true of challenges like dementia or obesity, and it's even more true of environmental issues. The complex project to reverse erosion on China's Loess plateau is a good example. Affecting the livelihoods of some 90 million people, it had to combine multiple disciplines from agriculture to water management, along with sociology and economics, and active involvement by farmers. In other cases the collaborations have to cross national boundaries. It's widely acknowledged that individual firms will tend to under-invest in basic research because it's so hard for them to capture the resulting knowledge. But the same is true of national governments. From a purely economic point of view, they probably achieve the best returns from investing in adoption of technologies, near-to-market innovation, or scientific skills, since the results of basic research become available to others too.[12] For the world to cope adequately with its really big challenges, such as aging or climate change, we will need global collaborations and global pressure to overcome the pull of self-interest.

Just as innovation systems are becoming more diverse, so is the treatment of knowledge. Economics redefined knowledge as a kind of property, bounded by clearly defined rights that were policed by governments and courts. It was thought of as wealth in just the same way that land or machinery is. In the late twentieth century, some promoted a radical "propertization" of knowledge in universities and elsewhere, turning previously open research into private contracts. Yet knowledge too is bifurcating between traditional capitalist models and radical alternatives. A decade ago, every government's industrial policy put a premium on the creation and protection of intellectual property. Intense pressure was put on China and other countries to respect intellectual property laws. Universities were forced to hide and commercialize their ideas, on the grounds that without financial incentives there would be no way to galvanize biotechnology or the next generation of artificial intelligence. Yet against expectations, only a handful of universities have actually made a profit on these activities.[13] The intellectual case for hard IP looks weaker than it did as we learn more about how much of innovation creates value through spill-overs. And the dominant models of intellectual property look much shallower than their equivalents in other fields, like land, where ownership has multiple forms, and multiple responsibilities as well as rights.

Meanwhile very different models have thrived as well. A high proportion of the software used in the Internet is open source.[14] India has run an imaginative Open Source Drug Discovery project funded by government that is creating an online repository of information about the tuberculosis bacterium. Tiered pricing is being used for pharmaceuticals for poor countries—a creative solution to the lack of incentives for commercial firms to invest. The creative commons is rapidly gaining ground in culture as an alternative to traditional copyright, and Wikipedia has become an unlikely symbol of post-capitalism. Intellectual property law remains vitally important—and a significant share of innovation is protected. Clever schemes are often proposed for getting the right balance of private reward and public benefit.[15] But it looks increasingly as if the right answers change over time, and according to the sector and the state of technology. Sometimes there may be a public interest in overriding property rights—as with technologies to address climate change. And often property rights need to coexist with radically different methods that reward through recognition as much as money.

The next accommodations also need to be able to buttress truth, which should be the highest value in societies organized around information and knowledge. We are each entitled to our opinions. But we are not entitled to our own facts. Functioning modern societies require institutions that can sort truth from falsehood, better knowledge from worse, and we can't rely on faith that the crowd, or the cloud, will do it for us. Some of these institutions exist in and around governments—like the national institute for health and clinical excellence in the UK[16] which publicly rules on which treatments are effective and cost-effective, a model that looks set to be copied in other fields such as education and criminal justice. Others are rooted in civil society, like the specialist think-tanks providing a running commentary on the claims of governments and bloggers criticizing claims in the media or cyberspace. So far the Internet has empowered distorters as well as clarifiers (as the old saying put it, a lie may be halfway round the world before the truth has put its boots on). But strengthening the ecology of truth matters as much for markets as for any other field of human activity: without constant scrutiny, skepticism, and corrections, false representations can cause havoc: dramatic overvaluations of firms, and a pattern of incentives in which it is more sensible for a firm to invest in spurious marketing, lobbying, and public relations, than to create useful products. Our hope should be that a small slice of the resources circulating in the knowledge economy provide a countervailing force on the side of truth and against falsehoods.[17]

At least some of that new knowledge will come from data, and ubiquitous data also have the virtue of making predatory behaviors harder. In industry and commerce, the capacity to collect and analyze large quantities of data has supported dramatic changes in manufacturing and retailing, over the last few decades. In Japanese factories data is collected by front line workers, and then discussed in quality circles that include technicians. Statistical production techniques reveal patterns that are not evident to those directly involved; similar methods have been transferred with remarkable results to the medical treatment of patients in the United States.[18] But despite the explosion of data collection, intelligent usage has lagged behind.[19] During an earlier phase, data were primarily collected and analyzed for commercial purposes: customer relationship management systems collected information about buying patterns and preferences, and tried to target the right offers. But the tables are potentially turned in new models of "vendor relationship management" which allow citizens themselves to control their own personal data and lend it out to private firms or public agencies when that suits the individual. These models are the mirror of the great databases held by big firms and big public agencies. Currently they exist in small-scale projects which put citizens in control of the personal data held by big firms and public agencies and allow them to monitor their conditions and chart their own behavior and actions.[20] They point to a future where personal records can be instantly linked to other databases, so that a CV is automatically validated (for example by the databases of a university, confirming a degree), or a health record is validated by a hospital or medical practice. The principle they embody is that data about us should be controlled by us: a simple idea but one that radically overturns many of the business models of the late twentieth century. The parallel principle is that any data about the public should be open to the public to use and recombine.

It may not be long before we see digital constitutional conventions to establish new rules to govern a very novel landscape of power and knowledge. In the meantime, energetic experiments are under way to apply some sounder principles in practice, showing how citizens can both control and shape the data that matter most to their lives.[21]

We should also hope for rapid advance in systems to orchestrate collective thinking, combining elements that are open and elements that are closed. There are many pointers, from the elaborate systems now in place for handling corporate data and knowledge to examples like Intellipedia, the U.S. intelligence community's wiki for sharing information. It provides one of many possible models for a future where whole fields naturally share data, information, and judgments in relatively open sites. Within science the use of "big data" is already transforming how theories emerge and get to be tested: hypotheses may be prompted by patterns in the data, and can then be tested using existing data sets rather than new experiments. Health is a step further advanced, combining clinical data and guidance, with patient-run systems, and edging toward more transparency on the status of different kinds of knowledge: from the scientifically validated, to experiential knowledge and the advice of peers. These new public platforms will become as decisive for the twenty-first century as electricity and railways were to the nineteenth,[22] as they advance from the aggregation of data, through information and knowledge to the much more complex tasks of supporting judgment and wisdom.

At present the orchestrators of intelligence, data, and knowledge remain much less visible and powerful within governments, firms, and agencies, than the orchestrators of laws or money. In part that reflects the slow progress in developing this as a field of practice. But any accommodation that does not involve a fundamental shift of power and prestige in their direction will be doomed to fail. And any accommodation that does not make more explicit the state's role as a discomforter, disrupter, and challenger, directing resources and energies to new ideas and possibilities, will condemn societies to stagnation.

2. Make Capital a Servant, Not Master, and Spread Both Ownership and Control

The second priority is to channel more capital into creativity and useful activity. Innovation should matter more than circulation, genuine value more than paper value. Capital is a kind of power but it breaks many of the rules that make power good. We've learned through the painful experiments of history that power is more likely to be good when it is bound by rules: when it is kept divided rather than being too concentrated; when it is subject to external laws; when it is required to answer for itself; when it's easy to remove; and when it's transparent. The principles that are so essential to political power are equally applicable to concentrations of economic power. We need concentrations of capital just as we need concentrations of power in the hands of states. But we need capital, like governments, to be a servant, not a master.

Most advanced economies provide special favors that serve particular capitalists but do not serve capitalism: subsidies, tax breaks, and special insurance schemes are all common, and all favor well-connected incumbents over outsiders. Many are justified as supporting innovation: but most in the long-run work against it. Replacing them with simpler, fairer rules and tax codes must be part of any credible program for economic reform.

Equally important will be new models of regulation that recognize the arms race between predation and creation in financial markets; it was once thought that regulations could be simple and unchanging. But in dynamically competitive contexts, regulation has to constantly adapt to shifting strategies of predation. Raghuram Rajan comments on the damaging effects of the financial modeling done in the 1990s and 2000s which governed both firm strategies and the behavior of regulators: "modelling that took the plumbing for granted ensured the breakdown of the plumbing"; but the point is a wider one. In information-rich, reflexive systems, no plumbing can be taken for granted.[23]

But the biggest challenge in very unequal societies is simply to spread ownership and control of capital and achieve a fairer spread of financial capital and savings; housing; and human capital. Liberalism traditionally recognized the virtues of a wide spread of ownership. We feel more of a stake in society if, objectively, we have more of a stake, and the more people are guardians of things and other people, the more likely we are to act responsibly. Yet that is missing for large groups in most wealthy countries. Capitalism doesn't produce many capitalists. Later in this chapter I address what can be done about the greatest concentrations of wealth. For everyone else the challenge is to find ways to make ownership both meaningful and visible. Personal accounts for learning, personal budgets, and entitlements are all likely to be part of the answer. So are savings devices that are simple, flexible, and in some cases linked to local services. One of the oddities of the recent wave of financial innovation is how few of the innovations met the needs of relatively poor people: for example through devices to help people understand their finances and their risks, or through financial products fitted to their needs, like mortgages allowing for periods of nonpayment.

Capital is also bound to be part of new settlements in a very different sense. One of the oddities of the contemporary economy is that systems of capital allocation have become divorced from the real economy, and from the norms of openness and accountability that we expect in other fields. The obligations on holders of capital to explain their actions are modest, whether at global, national, or local levels. A global investment bank has no need to justify its actions to the millions of people whose money it allocates any more than a supermarket enjoying a monopoly in a small town has any obligation to explain its choices to the people it serves. The larger challenge for any new accommodations is to find the right ways for capital to be brought into a richer conversation about choices: about the virtues and vices of particular technologies, investment strategies, or employment practices. Too much oversight can lead to paralysis; too little leads to abuse. Here there is no avoiding the need for balance (and there's little virtue in wild swings, like the former head of General Electric Jack Welch, who moved from being the prime advocate of shareholder value to describing it as the "dumbest idea in the world").

The share of the one thousand largest firms in OECD GDP has risen from 31 to 72 percent since 1980, so how they're held to account is bound to matter more than ever before. Environmental, social, and governance reporting (ESG) is providing some of the tools for doing this, reversing the trends that have shifted finance from attention to the real long-term value of particular mines, manufacturing, or ideas, and toward taking positions against real value—into hedging and betting with instruments of ever greater opacity. Johannesburg's Stock Exchange, for example, already requires listed firms to report on their ESG performance, as do some pension funds.

Even before the crisis there were many moves underway to reestablish capital as a servant of the real economy. They had practical justifications in that market risk is amplified the more degrees of separation there are between the prices of financial assets and their underlying sources of value. But there were also moral ones, in that the more degrees of separation there are, the less possible it is for markets to act with moral responsibility. The many moves in this direction can be understood as attempts to strengthen the moral voice and the moral sense within capitalism. They include the still tentative steps to make pension fund investments more accountable not just for their profits but also for their social and environmental effects (for example through big U.S. funds like Calpers, the California pension fund, or adviser managers like Calvert). Some have argued that stock exchanges should police the transparency and integrity of their investors, so that they don't become money laundering tools for Russian oligarchs or Latin American crime barons. The same motive, combined with governments' wish not to lose out on revenue, has prompted moves to outlaw offshore tax havens. There has been a slow but steady rise of a "social investment" industry formally linking social, environmental, and commercial goals. There has been an equally slow but steady rise of shareholder activism, as it dawns on members of the public that they own the firms they watch on TV. Among policy makers, one of the effects of the crisis has been to revive interest in policy options once considered too radical, like equivalents of the U.S. Community Reinvestment Act, which required banks to publish where they lent their money, and to serve all communities,[24] the creation of new publicly owned banks to finance housing, infrastructure, or innovation, or Tobin taxes to dampen down very short-term capital movements.

Another intriguing part of this story is the growth of capital in the hands of trusts and charities, which now face the dilemma of whether to use their very substantial assets not just to deliver an annual dividend but also to reflect their values. Bill Gates found himself at the sharp end of this dilemma when critics pointed out that the vast assets of his foundation were often invested in ways that ran directly counter to what it was trying to achieve through its spending.

Simple principles could achieve a lot: principles of clearer accountability and transparency, so that the key decision makers are held to account right along the investment chain; principles of good incentives, so that funders and investors share in losses as well as gains, implying no risk-taking without risk-bearing, and no incentives without mirror disincentives (a remarkable proportion of investment organizations managed to persuade their funders to let them gain the gains but not suffer losses). Simple rules, such as requirements that stock options should be held for at least five years, with any exercise made public, would help to change behavior. At a macro level, there is a strong case for greater pluralism to make systems more resilient, so that alongside private and quoted companies there are more mutual and cooperative financial institutions organized on radically different principles. Peer to peer lending; crowd-funding; and other devices (such as CrowdCube, Kickstarter, or Zopa) that link people who have money to people who need it are already showing that they can be much more efficient, and engaging, than traditional banks.[25]

Exemplars today show what mainstream finance might look like in the future. The Norwegian Government Pension Fund follows ethical guidelines blocking investments that "may contribute to unethical acts of omissions, such as violations of fundamental humanitarian principles, serious violations of human rights, gross corruption or severe environmental damages." There are many ethical banks including Triodos Bank and the Co-operative bank in the UK, RSF Social Finance in the United States, GLS Bank in Germany, the Alternative Bank in Switzerland, the Banco Popolare Etica in Italy, and the Citizens Bank in Canada, some based on genuinely radical principles.[26] India has considered legislation to influence all companies to spend 2 percent of profits on community activities, with a scarcely veiled threat that any firms that fail to do so will be treated as ineligible for government contracts.

To guide these investors, new numbers and measures are being devised. Again the exemplars exist at least in an early form such as the various measures being developed by the Global Impact Investing Initiative (GIIN). These remain relatively marginal, but are growing in scale and power, each an expression of values into value.

A parallel shift may be under way in public capital. The numbers that dominate discussions about public debt are at best misleading;

at worst they encourage bad decisions that shrink investment relative to current spending. We need governments to be able to distinguish between spending and investment (with this interpreted beyond the narrow confines of physical things). Debt that is used to cover current spending should be treated very differently from debt that is used to finance investments that will in the long-run raise GDP and tax revenues. Governments need to be oriented to the future just as much as markets.

One of the more radical options that could accompany new accommodations is a wholesale shift in how money is organized. There are fascinating efforts now under way to create common languages for financial industries—with a shared classification of organizations, products, and patterns of risk. The promise is that these may achieve similar gains to common standards in fields such as retailing and networks, lowering barriers to entry, and improving efficiency. More radical options suggest a bigger role for governments. Governments retain their role as guarantors of money, and they have become guarantors of banks. But they could do much more, creating underlying infrastructures both for payments and for simple financial transactions. Every citizen could have a personal financial account with government to be used for paying taxes, fines, and receiving benefits. With such an infrastructure in place it becomes straightforward to use it for payments from one citizen to another. It also becomes straightforward to offer citizens loans, secured on lifetime income streams, potentially opening up radically new options for welfare. Governments already have to monitor their citizens' income for tax purposes, and most already manage personal identifiers for their citizens; huge savings could be achieved by removing the need for parallel bureaucracies in banks and other institutions, and the paraphernalia of marketing that creates so little value for customers. The rates charged for financial services could also be sharply reduced.

Denmark already provides personal accounts. India's Universal Identifier Programme could be one of the pioneers—a project that aims to provide every citizen with a secure identifier, and that could in time provide the backbone for a twenty-first-century welfare state of insurance payments, loans for microenterprises, and pensions.

Financial intermediation would potentially become much more efficient. But just as important, financial institutions would be pushed into seeking profit from genuinely productive activities, rather than making excessive margins off the relatively passive and simple transactions of mortgages and bank accounts.

Few governments now have the confidence even to contemplate options of this kind, such is the intellectual and political grip of the banking industry. But monetary systems are by many measures a public good, and governments are already implicated as guarantors of banking systems. They should have to compete to create value, not to extract it.

3. Encourage the Shift to Sustainable, Collaborative Consumption, and Declare War on Waste in All Its Forms

The third place we should look for change is around consumption, its regulation, governance, and cultures. Consumption is set to be as important a field for innovation and creativity as production. Adam Smith wrote of consumption as "the sole end and purpose of all production."[27] But what if consumption of commodities turns out to be just one of many kinds of economic use, and perhaps not even a dominant one in the long term? After all, consumption has in the past been contentious and contended. Savonarola's "bonfire of vanities" was an extreme reaction to the vice of consumption, when his followers burned paintings and costly tunics that undermined piety and faith. When the first cooperative society shop was opened in Rochdale in England in 1834, the display of any "bobby dazzlers" in the window was forbidden for fear they would tempt the members to want more than they could afford, and many past societies have sought to rein in what they saw as the wrong kinds of consumption.

In the high-debt countries (including the United States and Britain) harsh economic realities may simply force less consumption, and more saving. Both followed a growth model that depended on credit to sustain production at the cost of running up unsustainable levels of debt. But necessity can combine with virtue and choice. Savings rates have already shot up across the world and there are strong movements to restrain the unbridled excess of mass consumerism: slow food, voluntary simplicity, the many measures to arrest rising obesity, are all symptoms of a swing toward seeing consumerism less as a harmless boon and more as a villain that sometimes stands against human welfare. In São Paolo, Brazil, the Mayor Gilberto Kassab banned all billboards in 2006. Some politicians of both the left and right (such as Britain's David Cameron) have warned against "toxic capitalism" corrupting young children, and described the behavior of firms pushing toys or unhealthy foods as a kind of predation.

New questions inevitably follow. One is whether choice is always good. It's usually better for consumers to be able to choose between suppliers, and we associate choice with freedom. But too much choice can be disabling, and in complex fields such as choosing a pension, or even a mobile phone, it can disempower as much as it empowers (one study suggested that it would take many years of study to understand the various options for mobile phone service). The implication of psychological research is that in some markets people should be able to choose how much choice they want, with easier options to take up regulated default options, as well as freedom to assemble more complex personal choices if that's wanted.

The other issue that is being recast is the question of sufficiency: what counts as enough? Twentieth-century models of growth assumed continuously rising consumption. But having too much of anything can be disabling too, which is why all wealthy societies generate movements for restraint, and aesthetics of simplicity and minimalism.[28] Collaborative consumption platforms offer ways to adjust consumption so that standards of living are maintained but at lower cost, and with less damage to the environment. A good example is the household drill: typically used for only ten to twenty minutes during its life, it can just as easily be shared with others through borrowing or rental websites. Cars are another example, again used for only a relatively small proportion of the week. Why not use the web to enable people to rent and hire out their cars, as organizations like Liftshare and Buzzcar are doing, to rent out bed and breakfast rooms (AirBnB), or to invite strangers to use a bed for the night (Couchsurfing)?[29]

Many of the arguments about consumption are fought out in daily life and culture. But they impinge on public policy too. Tax and regulatory structures have already been adapted to cut down on wasteful packaging and to require ever higher proportions of recycling. One of the most powerful potential levers for changing attitudes to consumption would give each citizen a personal carbon account, an entitlement to emissions reflecting the capacity of the biosphere to cope with the weight of population. These might start off at generous levels (and would be politically impossible otherwise). But in time they could rein in excessive air travel and high-carbon lifestyles, and at the very least they would bring to attention some of the effects of consumption that are otherwise invisible.

The shifting balance of the economy away from products and classic services, toward a more relational economy based on maintenance and care, has been shaped by multiple influences: from consumers and public opinion; from regulators (for example, reducing salt and sugar content in food); from legislators (for example, shaping rights to care). Looking to the future some pressures will come top down: for example, to promote vitamin-enriched foods and improve children's diets. Other pressures will continue to be exerted bottom up, as consumers are aggregated to assert their views, and in some cases to become owners (on the edge of the market there is a growing subculture of clubs that aggregate consumers to buy their own producers). Groupon became a huge, if very imperfect, commercial success by allowing consumers to pool their purchasing power. Other examples include Ebbsfleet United in England and Hapoel Kiryat Shalom in Israel, where fans came together on the web to buy their teams (and even to advise on which players to put on the field), mirroring other fan-owned clubs like Atletico Bilbao and Barcelona, the world's second richest club. The new platforms for collaboration merge into parallel roles around civic action, or production, like the "Fever Friend" Networks in China, an online community engaged in discussions of controversial and contemporary issues from mining regulations to urban migration, or Ohmynews in South Korea, which provides an online publishing platform for tens of thousands of citizen reporters, encouraging readers to be writers as well.

There are good reasons for governments to promote mutual forms of business organization: they can be more resilient and they can encourage consumers to be more responsible. For example, a mutually owned energy company is likely to find it easier to encourage reductions in energy use, just as a mutually owned healthcare company is less likely to face conflicts between its interest in selling goods and services and the interests of its patients. Such conflicts are ever more visible, as social movements all over the world turn their attention from the toxic contents of products to the toxic ways in which they are promoted. Protecting consumers from harm now also means protecting children, and sometimes adults, from harmful, or stressful images and messages. The Internet is already a major battleground, with an array of controls to contain the flood of pornography, violence, as well as the risks of individual predators feeding off the young and innocent.

Businesses need ways to communicate new messages, so as to inform the public about new products and services. But they struggle to justify doing so in ways that are damaging to viewers and readers, the great majority of whom will not choose to purchase the product. The right to free speech may be sacrosanct: the right to impose messages and clutter the mental landscape of people who have not chosen them, is not.

Nowhere is the consumption of commodities set to stop. Nor is the glamour and appeal of stuff likely to diminish. But everywhere the balance between consumption and maintenance is set to change along with casual attitudes to waste.

4. Make Production More Circular—and Grow the Economy of Maintenance

These shifts in how things are sold need to be matched by more radical shifts in the world of production. Stricter rules and constraints on production can, paradoxically, accelerate creativity and advances in productivity.

Capitalism is tentatively moving away from ways of making things that carelessly damage nature. These shifts have mainly responded to pressure from laws and regulations, though a few firms have pioneered circularity as ultimately more profitable.

The classic model of production took inputs of materials, labor, and energy, and produced a physical product that, when discarded, was buried underground. Staggering volumes of waste, many times the weight of the final product, were generated during the production process.

The alternative is a more closed loop of production, where the elements of a television set or a car are collected together once it has reached the end of its useful life, and recycled. Nearly twenty years after pioneers advocated "factor four"—a fourfold increase in the energy and material efficiency of products—the language of a "circular economy" and clean technology have become commonplace, as have regulations to force different behaviors from firms, though volumes of waste have not declined. Patents for renewables, hybrid cars, and energy-efficient lighting and building, biochemical fuel cells, and green plastics have multiplied two to three times as fast as patents in general.

The shift to these new models of production involves the combination of pressure from taxes and regulations, creative innovation on the part of firms themselves, and pressure from consumers. There are many examples of where this is working: more stringent building regulations to accelerate innovation in low carbon design; more demanding regulations for cars to improve engine performance; and higher standards for safety to improve systems design. Regulatory tools such as feed-in tariffs for energy can create new industries, without the risks associated with backing particular technologies.[30] In principle, long-term certainty should greatly help investment in new kinds of infrastructure.

Within business new organizational models are spreading which raise incentives for more closed, efficient production models. Energy services companies; chemical services companies; design, build, finance, and operate companies, each in different ways takes responsibility for the lifecycle of a service, with a stronger incentive to cut the inputs required for each unit of output. Public funding can go into fundamental research (such as applications of nanotechnology for environmental goals) or into prizes. ARPA-E in the United States, for example, funds prize-like grants for renewable energy, while General Electric has committed $200 million to prizes for a smarter electric grid.[31]

In principle they should contribute to the goal of "decoupling"—so that economic growth can continue without worsening effects on the environment. But in practice decoupling has proven much harder to achieve—partly because of rebound effects, as every gain in efficiency frees up consumer spending for more stuff. Similarly moving activity from the physical world to the virtual world should reduce environmental impacts (though servers and data centers already account for around 1 percent of global electricity consumption and this is expected to rise).

But the funding of new ideas and technologies is likely to be the easy bit. Much harder is the job of forcing change on established systems with heavy sunk investments in older, carbon-intensive technologies. More successful systemic change will usually involve close collaboration between very different kinds of organization. Even the recycling of something as simple as paper rests on elaborate reinforcing elements: rules and regulations imposed by governments; new infrastructures to collect paper, and keep it separate from other waste products, as well as new everyday habits on the part of the public; businesses to recycle it; and tax systems that encourage use of recycled paper rather than its alternatives.

Other examples such as the shift to electric cars are much more complicated. They require infrastructures across cities—so that people can recharge their cars quickly and easily; they require new organizational models, for example, so that people can rent a car for a short journey of twenty minutes or an hour; manufacturers who can produce on a sufficient scale and at low cost; variegated taxation and license systems and, potentially, parking rules that give precedence to electric cars over their petrol-based competitors.

We know some of the characteristics of the next generation of infra-structures, growing alongside the roads, railways, and electricity grids that so defined the last century. They are likely to be more distributed, more intelligent and more interlinked. Smart energy grids should be able to take energy from homes and cars as well as supplying them, for example through thermal ground sources, or solar power, as well as a lattice of high-capacity communication routes. They can both support and rest on the "Internet of things," the jungle of sensor links and data that is growing in and around cities. But smart grids too face the challenge of overcoming the accumulated efficiency of old models, and they often require political agreements as well as investment: agreements on precedence, on prices, and on fair access.

It remains unclear which parts of the world will adopt circularity first. The language of circularity may have spread even faster in Asia than in the West, and Asia now accounts for more than 40 percent of global mobile phone sales and 35 percent of car sales. It's possible that Asian societies will move through commodity enthusiasm and out the other side more quickly than the west did. Japan led the world in energy efficiency a generation ago and has produced many of the best recent patents. But in other parts of Asia the economic growth imperative may hinder new policies. Even more than elsewhere, governments will be reluctant to reset prices so that they reward conservation. Economists generally agree that taxes should weigh more heavily on materials, energy, and land, than on income or profits. Yet the politics of shifting the balance of a whole economy isn't easy—and the very industries whose behavior needs to change most will have the most resources, and the best-connected networks, to lobby against change.

5. Promote Work as an End as Well as a Means (and Play as Part of Life)

The next place we should look for new accommodations is the world of work, where the priority is to widen access to work, to grow its quality, and to make work contracts less predatory.

The varieties of work experience are vast, with huge disparities of pay, fulfillment, and power. For many, work remains insecure, unfulfilling, and often unfair. Yet work remains as much as ever a primary source of recognition and identity. Unemployment damages happiness much more than a pay freeze for psychological as much as economic reasons. Being inactive, and unrecognized, is rarely healthy. A striking indication of its importance can be found in the measures of happiness collected by the Canadian statistical office: looking at activities for people over sixty-five they found that the one they enjoyed most, more than spending time with friends, eating at restaurants, or seeing films, was paid work. More leisure and less work isn't the utopia it was once thought to be. Recent UK data on well-being confirm the point. Those working more than 46 hours a week had almost identical levels of life satisfaction to those working 31–45 hours, scoring a fraction higher on both satisfaction and anxiety.

Many societies have moved further toward enforcing obligations to work as the condition for receipt of welfare benefits. The corollary of this is that governments are pulled more into having to guarantee some rights to work, particularly if aggregate demand remains weak. Simple rules like Germany's legal prescription for firms to share work out during downturns can have a large impact, as can tax and regulatory arrangements that make it easier for firms to retrain staff, or invest in innovation during downturns (as happened in Korea after 2008). These are certainly preferable to large, government-run work programs. Some of the parallel currencies mentioned later in this chapter also help people to stay useful.

The importance of work, and useful work for all, is likely to be a theme for future accommodations just as it was for previous ones. We may see extensions of existing policies— like requirements for larger employers to employ a proportion of staff with disabilities (or pay someone else to do so). Innovations will also play a role—with new platforms linking the supply and demand for labor (such as Slivers of Time in the UK, Kickstarter or TaskRabbit in the United States, each reducing frictions in the labor market),[32] new halfway houses such as adult internships and apprenticeships that help the unemployed re-skill, or measures to radically simplify job creation by microenterprises.[33]

For several decades, policies have emphasized better matching of people looking for jobs and employers looking for staff. But if the people are insufficiently skilled, and the jobs are of poor quality, better matching isn't a panacea. Instead we need to pay more attention to the very nature of jobs. More work needs to be matched by better work. Modern capitalism has repeatedly seen radical experiments to change the terms of the work contract. Very wealthy companies like Google have given their staff time (a day a week) to pursue projects. The company Whole Foods operated an "open book" policy, meaning that anyone could know anyone else's salary (contrary to the claims of many social scientists that the best way to fuel employee dissatisfaction is to make others' pay visible). The company also attempted to keep a narrow margin between top and bottom, with team decisions on hiring. In Brazil, Ricardo Semler won fame for his businesses in which staff could collectively set their own remuneration. Gore Associates, producers of the Gore-tex material, are famous for keeping all their plants no bigger than 150 employees, with a minimum of job titles and hierarchy and collectively agreed salaries. Cooperatives like the Mondragon group in Spain (which has some 100,000 employees and has doubled in size each decade) and employee-owned firms like John Lewis in the UK, have thrived. In other sectors, too, there has been a long-term trend toward more people wanting work to be an end as well as a means, a source of fulfillment as well as earnings for consumption, and there has been a slow but steady rise in the proportion of firms with some element of employee ownership, encouraged by some evidence that they perform better in terms of market values.

Ownership at work brings with it tensions, including the question of whether it's healthy to have too much of your savings bound up in your workplace. There are also tensions to be navigated around the meaning of democracy in the workplace: is it representative or participatory, and how should the conflicting interests of different groups (consumers, families) be balanced? An economy founded around the relentless pursuit of higher productivity requires that any firm has to periodically kill jobs, which is bound to be hard in a context of democracy. But there is an evident appetite for new rules to govern the employment contract, and to find a better balance between the need for flexibility and peoples' desire for work to be meaningful. Rights to voice generally advance when jobs are plentiful; but although they then retreat when times are harder, they don't retreat as far. Two steps forward, one step backward is the pattern we might expect in democracies, as the idea that the employees should give up their freedom and voice when they enter the hierarchy of the firm comes to look ever more anachronistic. Work that takes up such a significant proportion of our waking hours, and that is such a central part of many peoples' identity, cannot simply be a means to consumption.

One intriguing aspect of this is that the more work becomes an end and not just a means, the closer it comes to play. The great cultural contradiction of capitalism was that it encouraged people to be dutiful and puritanical in work, but hedonistic in consumption. The rise of creative industries encouraged the idea that work could be fun. Paradoxically, the best consumption was often more like work too, in the form of hobbies and pursuits that involved exertion, skill, and challenge.

The apparent contradiction may be resolved by making play ubiquitous. This is the compelling case made by theorists such as Pat Kane in his book, *The Play Ethic*. It is encouraged in many firms in computing, design, and consumer services which try to make play both a means and an end, the means to more profitable business and an end for consumers willing to pay. For children we now know that play is a vital part of learning. Collaborative games such as scratch.edu teach many things, from confidence and communication to logic and strategy. Brian Sutton-Smith, the dean of Play Studies at the University of Pennsylvania, put it well: "The opposite of play isn't work. It's depression. To play is to act out and be willful, exultant and committed, as if one is assured of one's prospects."[34]

Of course, play is also the opposite of consumption: it has to be active and engaged. It usually doesn't consume things—it's renewable. And it connects us back to life. That is surely why the re-imagination of old age now places such a stress on play. The more that you play in old age, the more that you re-enliven yourself through such things as brain gyms, mind games, as well as sports like golf. We see a mounting body of evidence on how the right kinds of play can arrest dementia.

Societies that celebrate play may be less likely to destroy themselves. Lightness and humility protect against hubris. Serious attention to play has followed in part the rise of vast industries organized around play. Some celebrate violence, fast cars, and warfare. Others celebrate the dynamics of creating a city or a community. The computer-games analyst Sebastian Deterding suggests that the test of a great game experience is that it allows "meaning, mastery and autonomy," and points to the importance of social games like FrontierVille, Mafia Wars, or Millionaire City. They have also created new kinds of economy. Second Life pioneered some of these with payments for property in cyberspace. Others have taken further the scope for micropayments and sales of virtual property.

It may seem strange to mention play in the context of societal accommodations. But there are important links. Play depends on security: we compete in play because we're not competing for survival. Play teaches both autonomy and collaboration. And play, like good work, makes us more fully alive.

6. Reshape Education, Health, and Welfare Around Relational as well as Instrumental Ends

In a typical developed economy health, education, and welfare together make up between a quarter and a third of GDP. Each sector still bears the imprint of the era when they first took shape as crucial parts of a material industrial economy. Here I suggest that each may radically change to better support active engagement rather than passivity, and to give more weight to the relational aspects of lived value.

The strongest critique of existing welfare systems is that, in the name of meeting needs, they dampen the drive to make and create and so lock in a disempowering dependence. The critique echoes an idea that first took shape forty years ago in the research of the sociologist Aaron Antonovsky, who showed that Israeli women who had survived the concentration camps developed unusual degrees of resilience that kept them healthier than their peers. He suggested that the stress of the camps had strengthened their capacities to be healthy and resist disease. The "salutogenic" approach he then developed shifted attention from the causes of disease to the causes of health, and from seeing stress as a source of difficulty to seeing it as a source of growth.[35] Having a "sense of coherence"—a meaningful account of your place in the world—he argued was valuable for both physical and mental health, and often that involved feeling useful.

The salutogenic idea is one with much wider implications than health. It points the way to a welfare state that is as much about reinforcing strengths as it is about making up for weaknesses; and as much about helping people create useful narratives about themselves and their lives, as it is about therapy or coercion. In the short term, welfare states may be shrunk and shriveled by public spending cuts. But in the long term they may evolve better to support active, creative lives—to promote health in its widest sense rather than only protecting people from risks.

Education for Collaboration and Creativity

The industrial economy rested on vocational skills, such as how to work a lathe or a computer, and on professions such as law, accountancy, and medicine. The test of any educational system was whether it prepared people adequately for work, and researchers avidly analyzed the causal relationships between primary, secondary, and tertiary education and economic growth. Education was conceived as a capital, and at least for university education, young people were encouraged to think of participation as an investment with a cost now and returns later.

The variety of skills that make up a modern education system have evolved in subtle ways to fit the demands of a complex economy, with a tendency to specialization in fields like intellectual property law or forensic accounting, marine biology or neuroscience. But with the rise of an economy based more on working with people than with things, a very different perspective on skills has become necessary.

What matters as much as knowledge or specialist competence is the ability to work with others: to empathize, understand, persuade, or cooperate. Character, a prime concern of pre-industrial education systems, has again come to the fore partly thanks to research pointing to the ability to defer gratification as key to future success.[36] Self-regulation turns out to be the most valuable gift that family influences and schools can provide, while for the future adult's well-being, the cultivation of mindfulness as well as functional skills, character as well as competence, matter greatly. Nobel Prize–winning economist James Heckman's work has shown just how much noncognitive skills explain success in the workplace and in life. The best schools have always attended to these as well as skills in math or physics; so have elite leadership programs. But industrial-era education systems tended to push these to the margins—and left them out of measurement and analysis.

If the ideal education system for a traditional capitalist economy promoted competition between children, and the skills needed to work with things, perhaps a post-capitalist economy will place as much emphasis on cooperation and working with people. We're all born with the ability to cooperate, just as we're all (or nearly all) born with the ability to sing or to run. But as with singing and running, our innate abilities also need to be cultivated and trained if we are to become good collaborators. Schooling for collaboration would shift more of the curriculum onto projects where pupils work with each other, solving problems and creating things. Getting teenagers to work together to plant an allotment, to raise fish, to fix a car, or to program a computer game, teaches several things in one go: math, literacy, and science as well as the skills of human interaction. For skills of this kind, apprenticeships are a better model of learning than the classroom (and it is striking that more than half of all American Nobel Prize winners had worked as graduate students, postdocs, or junior colleagues of other Nobel laureates).[37] Studio Schools embody this approach in the UK, with most of the curriculum learned through practical projects; and on a more limited basis Citizen Schools do so in the United States, bringing in volunteer teachers outside school hours. Much of this teaching has to happen face to face. But technology can also help here: the Internet has often fostered a passive individualism, and even sometimes narcissism. But at their best, social networks encourage people to collaborate together, for example in multiuser games, and some expect that it won't be long before schools systematically measure how good pupils are at collaborating with their peers over networks. Some of these skills can be measured, including collaborative problem-solving, and a plausible future sees these being measured and compared across nations, with scores for collaborative problem solving ranked alongside the more familiar data for math and science.

Welfare

Parallel considerations apply to welfare. When the last great accommodations were made in the 1930s and 1940s, the overwhelming priority was to meet peoples' material needs. Housing, healthcare, and income support for unemployment and old age were what mattered most. These were the greatest risks that the capitalist economy exposed people to. After the traumas of the Great Depression and then war, security was all-important. Policy makers could assume that many people who were materially poor lived in close-knit families and communities that could provide emotional as well as practical support in hard times. The state's job was to insure people against material risks; society's job was to meet the psychological and psycho-social ones. The solidarity that underpinned the welfare state was based on a shared understanding of risk: that for a majority of the population there was a serious risk of becoming unemployed, or sick and in need of hospital care, or old without adequate savings.

More than sixty years later the picture is very different. Some people are still homeless, and classic poverty has not disappeared. We depend as much as ever on the state to protect us if we lose our job or become sick. But few in the wealthier countries go seriously hungry; and few have literally nowhere to sleep. Decades of economic growth have created societies which by past standards enjoy material abundance; indeed that are as concerned with excess consumption as under-consumption (whether in the form of obesity, smoking, alcohol abuse, or gambling).

Yet during this same period many societies' ability to meet people's psychological and psycho-social needs appears to have declined. The buffers of religion and family that helped people cope with setbacks have been corroded. The rise of individualism, and of more overtly meritocratic societies, has encouraged people to be more ambitious for themselves, but also made them more vulnerable to failures—and more likely to blame themselves rather than fate if things go wrong.

It's possible that a new basis of solidarity is slowly coming into view in which we are bound together by a new set of shared risks: the risk of loneliness and isolation; the risk of mental illness; the risk of being left behind. These risks are not yet reflected in political settlements or policies, and are inherently harder to reach through the standard tools of public provision. They depend less on professional provision and services and more on finding ways to mobilize support from friends and neighbors as well as professionals.

In the United States, the proportion of people who say that they have no one to talk to about important issues rose from 10 percent to 25 percent in twenty years (between 1985 and 2004).[38] Loneliness and isolation are endemic, and are coming to be seen not just as matters of luck, but as having an impact on health comparable to high blood pressure or smoking. Contemporary biology and social science have confirmed just how much we are social animals—dependent on others for our happiness, our self-respect, our worth, and even our life. There is no inherent contradiction between capitalism and community. But the connections are not automatic: they have to be cultivated and rewarded.[39]

Resilience

If economic policy tries to embed a capacity for innovation and change, welfare policy needs to attend to people's ability to cope with change, promoting "salutogenic" institutions and environments. A Japanese proverb describes resilience as the capacity to "fall down seven times and stand up eight," and it is becoming a primary goal in fields as varied as the management of water supplies, community development, and counterterrorism. Economics too has moved away from seeing optimization as a sensible goal, because optimization at one point in time may lead an organization or system to be less prepared for a change of circumstances. The question then becomes how to enhance resilience in firms, individuals, and communities: what may help them to cope better with uncertain future shocks?

Resilience has become a much more common object of study partly because of empirical observation of the huge variations in peoples' and communities' capacity to cope with threats. One of the earliest attempts to empirically measure resilience was prompted by observation of the resilience, fortitude, and bravery shown by Ernest Shackleton and his crew in the Antarctic one hundred years ago.[40] More recently a huge literature has developed, much of it concerned with ecosystems, and with the practical purpose of encouraging the ability to anticipate, mitigate, and cope with threats. A parallel literature has grown up around personal resilience.[41]

This research shows that resilience depends on[42] individuals' capacities, assets, and confidence; their relationships, the people who can be turned to when things go wrong; and structural conditions, for example whether the economy is creating jobs in their town.[43] Resilience isn't just a personal attribute; it's also a social one. But it's more like a muscle that has to be exercised than like a stock of money in the bank.

For communities as for individuals, traumas can be debilitating, yet many quickly bounce back. A good example is widowhood and divorce, which cause a serious dip in psychological well-being, but usually, despite grief, that dip lasts only a year or two before well-being recovers to its previous levels. Some people are "steeled" by their experiences, and become stronger thanks to adversity (which is why protecting children from threats can be counterproductive).[44] But others crumble.

How could an accommodation be concerned with resilience? My suggestion here is that we will look to governments and communities not just to provide for needs but also to help people to be resilient, and responsible for themselves and those around them. That may mean new approaches to schooling (many programs successfully teach psychological fitness and resilience to young children, and the U.S. Army has introduced a comprehensive program for all of its troops). It also has implications for healthcare (for example training people recovering from a heart attack to manage their thoughts and emotions, in the light of evidence that this may be as important for recovery as clinical treatments).[45]

Welfare states typically see people as bundles of needs and problems that have to be neatly categorized and then administered to. What we need are agencies that more often ask things of people; that make them feel useful; and that see the possibilities in them rather than the limitations.

But the details are all-important. The ability to recover and bounce back after adversity is not always healthy. Some people cope with shocks by hardening themselves: strengthening what can be called survival resilience that comes from thickening the skin.[46] Being too preoccupied with eliminating risks can be damaging too: excessive fear is disabling, as is being too neurotic, or having too much self-esteem without having earned it.[47] Some actions that appear likely to support resilience can backfire, like giving teenagers too much responsibility too early, or providing special help to children of drug users that, through labeling them, reinforces their sense of otherness.[48] But across a range of fields we should now direct attention not just to static rights and static provision, but also to dynamic capacities to adapt: to grit, bounce, and the resilient skill of growing through adversity.

Raising the Status of Care

During the twentieth century, care moved from the household and family into the public sphere, as it became the responsibility of welfare states, healthcare systems, and residential homes. In the rapidly aging twenty-first century care is growing fast as a share of GDP. These new demands are being met in the market economy, by governments, and through the everyday support provided by partners and family members.

Yet in many countries formal care is provided by a low-status and low-paid, primarily female, workforce. Informal care within the family is being squeezed by the fact that mothers as well as fathers expect to go out to work. Everywhere there are signs of a painful divide between work and family as a rising proportion of employees, especially women, have to simultaneously care for young infants and aging parents.

Volumes of evidence now confirm the vital role that families play in nurturing the skills and attitudes of the future workforce. Capitalism remains much more tightly linked to families than is often appreciated: family-owned businesses account for 60 percent of world GDP.[49] Many of the areas of greatest prospective employment growth are on the periphery of the family, in health and care, children's services, and home maintenance. But care is currently undervalued, whether it's provided as a paid-for service or as an unpaid service within the home. The ubiquity of smart phones and email has allowed work to penetrate home and leisure time—but families have been largely kept out of the workplace.

Over several decades, a new architecture of rights and flexibilities has slowly taken shape—from career breaks and parental leave rights to reduced hours for periods of care—which could turn work from the enemy of the family to something more like a partner. But when it comes to care, the gap between lived value and monetary value is wide, and probably widening. At worst, too much care has turned out to be predatory, with chronic abuse in many institutions not just of children, but also of the vulnerable elderly. But even everyday, well-intentioned care sits uneasily within other institutions that seem ill-suited to it.

The questions that follow include ones about pay rates and status, as well as the tax treatment or validation of unpaid work. They include hugely complex tasks of designing fair ways of handling the lottery of the last years of life—how much should the risks be pooled? How much should people with enough money pay? How much should be expected of spouses, or of children? Any new accommodation will have to face up to these questions, with answers that are likely to involve both paid work and volunteer work in new hybrids that formalize the gift economy.[50] The net result will almost certainly be a larger share of GDP devoted to care: but what remains unclear is how this will be organized, and how societies will escape from the unease and guilt that so often surround care.

7. Multiply Systems of Exchange Alongside Money

These issues take us to the broader one of how different kinds of value can be exchanged. The labor market is a market in time: it buys and sells blocks of time, a forty-hour week, a forty-eight-week year, or a single shift. But it is not the only exchange system for time. Parallel monies have always coexisted with formal monies, and have repeatedly sprung up when the formal market shrinks, so that people can exchange their time for cleaning, sewing, or cooking. Cyberspace has the monies of Second Life and the credits of multiuser games. I've already mentioned some of the many existing currencies, such as the German Talent, Italian Misthos, Mexican Tlaloc, Argentine creditos, and Ithaca HOURS in the United States. Brooklyn, New York has its Member to Member Elderplan, which allows older people to pay 25 percent of premiums in Time Dollars. France has Systemes d'échange Locaux (SEL), Italy, the Banca del Tempo.

These twin economies exist amidst some of the most prosperous capitalist economies.[51] There are now an estimated 2,500 local currencies operating worldwide. Some are pegged to existing monies; some are barter systems; some use time as their currency. One of the largest schemes is the Japanese Health Care Currency, or Fureai Kippu, which was created by the Sawayaka Welfare Foundation in the mid-1990s as it became apparent that the growing elderly population could not be adequately cared for with government revenue. Work helping an old person with shopping or housework earns credit, and there is some variation: each hour worked outside the hours of 9 to 5 earns one and a half hours' credit, and each hour of body care work earns two hours. The time credits can then either be used for themselves or donated to

friends and relatives elsewhere. There are some 300 community currencies now operating in Japan, many using smart cards, and focusing
on the provision of care. A striking feature of the scheme is that the
participants tend to prefer the services paid in time credits to those
paid in yen. Indeed this is a common feature of most of these currencies: they create meaning as well as value, and have as a declared aim
the strengthening of commitments between people.

A very different example is the move by the French city of Nantes
(whose mayor became France's prime minister in 2012) to introduce
its own virtual currency, so that local businesses could pay or be paid in
currency units to be called the "Nanto." This aimed to stimulate trade
during a period when the euro-based, monetary economy was being
squeezed by tighter monetary policies. There are many other examples.
Just as cigarettes became a currency in Prisoner of War camps during
World War II, so mobile airtime has become a currency for mutual
and market exchange in Africa. People can send minutes of prepaid
airtime to each other by mobile phone using M-PESA or Me2U, or
use prepaid mobile cards for interpersonal transactions or to purchase
goods on the market. A very different example is Bitcoin, a web-based
currency founded on the mathematical properties of strings of numbers that are inherently limited, with around $100 million currently
in circulation.[52] The significance of these platforms for exchange is
that they suggest a quite different kind of economy sitting alongside,
and sometimes overlapping with, the money economy. Some may be
particularly important for relatively local services and relatively labor-
intensive tasks. Others may end up better suited for the most global
exchanges.

In the 1920s, Irving Fisher, the great American economist, was an
enthusiast for parallel currencies, particularly as the depression shrank
the money economy in so many towns and cities across America, and
he almost persuaded President Roosevelt to support them. It's intriguing to imagine how different things might look if he had succeeded.

Today's examples of parallel currencies are only modest pointers
to the possible future, and they have only begun to use the potential
of social network technologies to orchestrate time exchange. Most of

the local ones treat all time as equal in value, whereas labor markets pay unequal wages. For some this is an advantage, a democratic assertion of people's underlying equality.[53] But it has also been a constraint, since clearly not all peoples' time is valued equally. An hour of a great cook counts for more than that of a mediocre one; an hour of a competent surgeon counts dramatically more than an hour of an amateur.

Fully formed time accounts would extend the dimensions in which time could be exchanged, over time itself, over space, and across different types of labor. They might also allow rights of time for education, for parental leave, or for sabbaticals; rights of time for caregivers to look after themselves for a change. They might allow people to give or lend time to others: for example, lending their entitlements to leave to a friend or relative needing to care for a sick spouse.[54] Even if time accounts allow for differential payments, with more for some than others, time as a currency still has the interesting effect of being much more democratic than money; it can't be accumulated beyond individual need, unlike cars or jewels. Nor can you take your time with you beyond the grave.

8. Promote the Norm That Wealth Is a Means and Not an End

Capitalism's most ardent advocates claim that the incentive to become rich drives everything: hard work, inventiveness, creativity, and the willingness to take risks are all motivated by the universal desire to acquire wealth. This justifies inequalities and a panoply of odd incentives, from subsidies for venture capital to low tax rates for private equity investors. Without the prospect of very unequal rewards the system would grind to a halt, and the lazy majority would free-ride on the hard work and enterprise of others.

But is any of this true? And if it is true, how much is it true? The impact of incentives on willingness to work hard and invent remains surprisingly unclear and contested. Certainly economies without incentives to get rich aren't likely to grow much. If all your hard-earned money is grabbed by the state, or taken by your extended family, then you might as well enjoy a quiet life. As Ronald Reagan put it: "They say hard work never did anyone any harm, but why risk it?"

But even the strongest advocate of performance-related pay or rewards for entrepreneurs would admit that there is very little evidence of a correlation between entrepreneurship and inequality, whether within organizations or whole societies. There is no evidence of any link between inequality and innovation. Nor is there any evidence of a link between equality and innovation,[55] though this may simply reflect inadequate data. The share of women in U.S. patents was 2 percent in the early 1980s—a rough measure of massively underused potential.[56] And high levels of taxation can coincide with highly entrepreneurial economies. Sweden in 2010 was rated Europe's most innovative economy according to the most authoritative survey, yet it has some of the highest tax rates. The U.S. economy's golden age in the 1950s coincided with extraordinarily high marginal tax rates.

It's safe to say that getting rich does motivate people to work hard and take risks. But there is no evidence that the incentive of rising in wealth from a net worth of $10 million to $100 million or $1 billion has much meaning or useful incentive effect. The very rich may be spurred on to become even richer by other very rich people. But it's not clear that it is money rather than status that matters most. Worse, this sort of wealth is likely to lead to chronic waste. Any individual who owns five homes, or ten cars, for example, is bound to be engaged in profligacy, since their assets are likely to lie idle for much of the time. Economics has paid little if any attention to productivity in consumption as opposed to consumption; if it did, these would be examples of extremely low productivity.

Instead of being able to drive five cars simultaneously, the rich may spend on ever more elaborate kinds of consumption, or drive up prices for art or antiques. These are peculiarly negative activities, with important side effects for others, since they tend to drive up property prices, or lead to a hoarding of positional goods. Nor is it clear that what people most want after the first few million is a tenth home or a twentieth car. Usually what they want is recognition.

So how may future accommodations cope with extreme inequality, and the extreme wealth of a small minority? A solution that would greatly reduce waste might be to set thresholds on privately held wealth, while allowing freedom for privately directed wealth. In other words, over a set level wealth would be heavily taxed unless it was placed in a foundation for charitable investment. Recognition would be encouraged; profligacy would not. This is a kind of wealth that also better fits the golden rule. We will willingly see some accumulation of wealth and recognition for hard work, luck, or talent. But nobody likes to see waste. This is also a solution that better fits the productive spirit of capitalism, which favors putting money to work rather than letting it lie idle.

Such an approach—bringing wealth to life—might encourage a new era of patronage of the arts, of technological invention, and of social philanthropy. Donors would still benefit from recognition—and the status that comes from exuberant patronage. But the things they paid for would become a lived value for others.

This solution also has the virtue of retaining the great strength of capital markets, which is their ability to direct large sums of capital to the most productive needs. The capital held in trusts and foundations would still be invested in the productive economy. But it would reduce the damage associated with the kinds of capital accumulation most closely associated with inequality and waste. Any measures of this kind are inherently hard for nations to introduce in isolation without triggering the prompt departure of their wealthiest citizens. But the United States or the European Union could take steps in this direction with variable wealth taxes, as could China. It's easy to forget that there are successful precedents, like the 40 percent death duties introduced by Britain's Liberal government in the early twentieth century to break up the aristocratic estates. Weak and marginal economies may not be able to afford to alienate their wealthiest citizens; but strong economies have more room to maneuver than they imagine.

9. Measure What Matters

When Sir Thomas More wrote his book *Utopia*, coining a new word for the world, it came from the Greek words meaning "no place." But it was also deliberately a homonym for Eutopia, the place of happiness. Progress should mean more happiness in all its different meanings, from pleasure to satisfaction with life, fulfillment to meaning, and part of future accommodations should include new measures of societal progress that more accurately capture how well societies are becoming places of happiness. Some governments already use subjective measures as targets, part of a shift away from the materialist fallacy that only things can be measured. These subjective measures include: fear of crime as well as recorded crime; patient satisfaction as well as health outcomes. Use of these indicators encourages public agencies to behave quite differently. Hospitals have to pay attention to the fine grain of patient experience; police have to pay attention to the finer grain of social dynamics, and feelings of safety. Measuring connectedness (whether people feel that there are others they can turn to) and influence (whether people feel that they can influence the decisions that affect them) also shifts the gaze of governments and the ways in which they work.

The UK's Office of National Statistics from 2011 onward has asked 200,000 people to record their answers to four questions on how satisfied, anxious, or fulfilled they are with their lives,[57] which is providing a huge bank of knowledge on correlations and causes. This will enrich the many tools already in use, such as the HDI (Human Development Index), the Canadian Index of Wellbeing, People's Life Indicators in Japan, and the measures of Gross National Happiness in Bhutan.[58]

Greater attention to happiness will rapidly accelerate understanding of the often complex relationships between economic growth and well-being (discussed earlier). One important effect is to force attention to inequality. The strongest argument that economic growth does indeed influence happiness calls in aid data from the United States showing that although GDP rose in recent decades, typical household income didn't because of rapidly rising inequality. In other words, if wealth had been spread more equally, happiness would have improved. It also forces attention to the more granular details of daily life: the physical design of cities and housing; the provision of care; or how well children learn resilience. Numbers matter because they signal what we think is important. I've already suggested the value of a measure of social wealth alongside ecological and economic income and wealth. The greatest value of these types of indicator lies less in the aggregate numbers than in how they are disaggregated, and how they show the relative condition of different parts of society.

We should also expect new measures of GDP that cope better with the value of outputs (for example from the public sector, or finance); new measures that capture intangibles and knowledge) and, crucially too, new measures that capture the changing position of natural assets.

During the Great Depression governments lacked the data they needed to manage economies—realizing that prompted the successful design of new statistics, including GDP. Today governments are equally lacking in some of the right data to make good decisions. They have no statistical tools to distinguish productive from unproductive public spending; they have few tools for measuring investment in innovation and intangibles; and they lack good measures of resilience. Each of these deficiencies is soluble, and there are pioneers pointing to what would be possible in the future. But for the time being misleading numbers are all too likely to encourage misguided decisions.

10. Cultivate Mindfulness as Both a Public and Private Virtue

The last cluster of proposals may seem odd to include in the context of political settlements and accommodations. We usually think of these as being about money, rights, and institutions. But I want to suggest a subtler change that links the others described earlier.

The systems that support collective intelligence now provide greater feedback on almost every aspect of life (sometimes too much) and are set to provide vastly more in the future. Collaborative platforms for managing data, information, and knowledge may come to permeate every area of life. These are likely to evolve away from the simple aggregation devices of the contemporary web to more subtly structured tools for handling complex fields of knowledge, and ultimately toward tools to support fine-grained judgment and wisdom. The hope must be that they will also open up awareness of the meta-questions that lie behind flows of knowledge. Intelligence is not just about thought and processing, let alone automation. It also involves reflection on thoughts and goals, and this matters as much for societies as it does for individuals.

Earlier in this chapter I emphasized the importance of aligning means and ends when it comes to systems of innovation and knowledge. It's not very sensible just to be in favor of innovation, creativity, or entrepreneurship, since we know that these can lead to bads as well as goods, harm as well as progress. A mindful society has to be capable of reflecting on the ends of innovation as well as the means; on the ethical dimensions of new knowledge (however hard these may be to know in advance); and on the relative claims of different challenges and tasks (and judgments about which tasks warrant the attention of the brightest and most creative minds). A mindful society also has to be able to reflect on how it uses its time, and how it understands what contributes to well-being and fulfillment. If mindfulness of this kind matters, we should look at institutions and ask not just about which ones are profitable, or instrumentally effective, but also about which ones promote mindfulness. Spending time with which institutions leave individuals or communities stronger and better equipped, and which ones leave them weaker or more dependent? Which institutions see the world as it is, and help us see clearly? And which ones distort or "dumb down"?

These are radical questions to ask; they inevitably challenge powerful institutions in the media, politics, and business that in their daily practice act as enemies of mindfulness. They are also questions that have been pushed aside by the shrunken discourse of much modern capitalism, which has lost the richness that animated Adam Smith and his contemporaries. They have also been excluded by the narrow discourse of public policy that presents questions of this kind as irrelevant to public debate: matters of private life rather than public interest.

But it's not far-fetched to expect mindfulness to become a public as well as a private issue. There are already programs promoting meditation among school children, or teaching them to assess the media according to their accuracy. Health planners know how important it is to promote mindfulness of health, and to encourage the connections between mental and physical health. Urban designers once again assume that they should create spaces of tranquility and reflection as well as central business districts and buzzy neighborhoods. Nor is it far-fetched to hope for societies that promote buffers, silence, and reflection, to counter the risk of what Indians call "monkey mind," the inability to focus thanks to the incessant chatter of always-on machines. Ideas like the Digital Sabbath may be forerunners of new ways of thinking about the social construction of mindfulness.

A mindful society would also be more conscious of the horizons of its thinking. The immediate, compressed time of global cyberspace where everything is simultaneous and where our implicit discount rate tends to infinity, can be the enemy of mindfulness. By contrast we need more attention to the time horizons of ecology, or climatic shifts that may work themselves out over decades and even centuries—the "long now" that serves as a correction to the short now, and that sees as absurd the high discount rates of market capitalism, which effectively value at zero anything more than a generation or two off into the future. That requires institutions with a long horizon built in to their design and their accountabilities.

The long now is alien to much of capitalism. In his work, *A Tract on Monetary Reform* (1923), Keynes wrote that in the long run we're all dead, a single-generation view that now looks odd (and not just because of the anti-Keynesian monetarists who proclaimed that Keynes was dead, and that they were the long run). An economic system that cannot describe and manage very long-term projects stretching over many generations is inadequate. Even one that cannot connect the interests of a twenty-one-year-old putting away money for their savings, to pay a pension they might rely on eighty years later, looks partial and not fit for purpose.

HOW ACCOMMODATIONS HAPPEN

These are a few possible parts of new accommodations that will take different shapes in different countries but will share the twin goals of amplifying creativity and reining in predation. Precisely how, when, or where they will happen is impossible to predict. The chemistry that turns apparently stable, even frozen, societies into cauldrons of revolt is only dimly understood.

It will have been apparent that in each of the ten areas of change described above, I've painted more than just a program for government. Instead, change has to come from the interaction of the top-down work of states, the horizontal competition of businesses and markets, and the bottom-up push and pull of citizens. Decrees and programs can never be enough. Instead, transformative change depends on a shared sense of direction, and of moral necessity, that affects all institutions and not just the state. A useful model for the first steps in this direction may be provided by one of the countries that suffered the worst effects of the financial crisis of 2008. Soon after Iceland was hit by the dramatic collapse of its banking system, its currency, and its confidence, the population fell into a state of shock. Many went every Saturday afternoon to Austurvöllur Square in central Reykjavík to talk to one another, brought there by Twitter, Facebook, and word of mouth. They didn't know what to do, but they needed to do something. Ministers came to some of the meetings to hear the complaints and confusion of people who knew that for many years to come they would be bearing the cost of others' mistakes. Before long the anger of the "kitchenware revolution" was taken to the Althingi, the national parliament, where thousands came together, banging pots and pans to disrupt the business of parliament, succeeding before long in ejecting not just the government, but also the heads of the central bank and the financial regulator. After the election that followed, the new prime minister, Johanna Sigurdardottir, announced that "The people are calling for a change of ethics. That is why they have voted for us." What then followed was an attempt at a new kind of conversation to find a way out. The think tank, the Ministry of Ideas, organized the first National Assembly in Reykjavik with some 1,200 citizens randomly selected from the national register and 300 invited guests, including cabinet ministers and MPs, trade unions, representatives from the media and others. Making up 0.5 percent of the population, its task was to shape a new vision for the country and to imagine what kind of society Iceland could now become, perhaps the first attempt to crowd source a national settlement. It quickly established some consensus on the issues, with integrity considered the most important value, followed by equal rights, respect, and justice. The nation's new priorities—honesty, equality, and love—were projected on to a huge screen.[59] New initiatives emerged—like the Icelandic Modern Media Initiative, a parliamentary proposal unanimously approved in 2010 to make Iceland a safe haven for freedom of information and expression.

But there also followed a painful debate about the many causes of the crisis: not just a hugely inflated banking sector, but also a web of dubious practices surrounding Iceland's traditional economic base in fishing, encouraged by its once admired quota system. Iceland's return to values as the starting point seems to be a common pattern. Whenever a society loses its way in economics, it also feels that it has lost its way morally.[60] The converse is that any return to economic growth must also be accompanied by moral renewal too.

Chapter 12

· · · · · · · · · · ·

Outgrowing Capitalism

AN OLD STORY tells of a shaman who described himself as containing two bears, one a cruel, warlike, and violent hunter, the other caring and compassionate. A young boy asks him which will win out, and the shaman replies: whichever one I feed.

Capitalism has triumphed, crashed, adapted, triumphed, and crashed once again, and then bounced back: mainly because of choices made to feed it. Even when it runs into the sand, most want nothing more than that it should get moving again. The economic system that dominates the world economy has penetrated our culture, our politics, and perhaps even our souls, to such an extent that it now appears to be a fact of nature. Its main challengers have been outrun, and its critics have grown hoarse through frustrated repetition. So what comes next? And who will triumph, the predators or the creators?

The capitalist idea has dominated the history of modernity, both in its appeal, and in the revulsion it has elicited, and then in revulsion against the systems that were borne out of that revulsion. Its strongest appeal is the promise of plenty—making available to the many levels of wealth that were once only available to a very few. This was what attracted the people of eastern Europe in 1989—shops full of goods rather than empty shelves. The medieval era saw sanctity in poverty, but in a modern capitalist economy there is little love or respect for poverty, only pity or neglect.

The promise of plenty was mirrored in the promise of a world opened up: a widening scope for personal and geographical mobility. This had always been present in some trades, times, and cities, but was generally the exception in societies where children were born into castes, roles, or guilds. In most societies customary obligations mean that if you get rich you have to share your wealth with your relatives, a disincentive if ever there was one, not to mention the risk of your wealth being appropriated by an indebted king or baron. Capitalism by contrast promised a world where personal freedom included the freedom to ignore others.

Capitalism was not a political party or a program. But as it took shape it took on some of the characteristics of a program or manifesto. We can now see that these were a series of deals, perhaps appropriately for a system founded on trading. One promised that if a society gave power to capitalists in the workplace, the net gains in wealth would outweigh both the feelings of disempowerment and the fact that the capitalists would take a large share of the surplus. Even if all gained unequally, all would gain. Another was the promise that restless experiment and innovation, including widespread failure, would achieve such gains in productivity and wealth that they would more than make up for the waste of duplication and failure. And a third promised that the huge overheads associated with a market economy, the insurers, accountants, lawyers, and intermediaries who in some estimates make up over a third of all jobs, would also pay their way through the dramatic growth made possible in the whole economy.

These are very surprising claims, quite at odds with the medieval or renaissance mentality. No one could pretend that they are common sense. They were not self-evident to the people in the midst of them, the investors or traders. They were not evident to Adam Smith or David Ricardo, neither of whom had a feel for the vast coordination tasks of a modern economy, or its dependence on science and technology. But they were also dynamic deals—they promised a ride with no visible end point, no final utopia: instead, endless growth and an endless multiplication of desires and the means of meeting them.

In the previous chapters I've suggested that the very things that make a society great can destroy it, and that they need to be outgrown. All societies have suicidal tendencies: in monarchy the tendency to grossly excessive military spending and debt, and in religion the tendency to become so hypocritical that even supporters are disgusted. In capitalism the suicidal tendency is toward wild risk and debt, over-exuberant optimism, and untrammeled greed. As with predatory animals, too much success can be counterproductive. With animals the problem is that the prey disappears. In markets, the risk is that extracting too much profit leaves too little investment in the future, and the pillars connecting the foundations of lived value to the elaborate towers and turrets of monetary value crack.

The many criticisms made of capitalism didn't go away because they continued to hit home: they highlighted its weaknesses. Its predatory tendencies have been reined in again and again, but they have also repeatedly reemerged. Capitalism has some capacities for equilibrium within itself, but it lacks the capacity to equilibrate in a wider sense, to deal with its own dynamic imbalances. And so societies have been in a continuous dialog, and sometimes struggle, with capitalism—to contain its excesses, to cope with the costs, to channel its productive capacities usefully. They have been caught in what now looks like a dynamic struggle to grow what they want to grow and not grow what they don't want to grow.

The anti-capitalist revolutionaries dreamed of a mirror world, a world that would be opposite to what they saw around them: without property, without money, and without inequality and predators. We need these utopias to help us see the world as plastic—to protect us from the tendency to see what is merely temporary and contingent as permanent and natural. And we need radical ideas that challenge what is: to be able to imagine a world without waste, whether of matter or people; to be able to imagine a world that gives as much attention to relationships as to money; to imagine time and happiness as the universal currencies, the measures of things; to imagine walking lightly on the earth. But the mirror worlds have not materialized. Their impact has come through interaction with the worlds they critique—not through replacing one with the other.

The Italian politician and philosopher Antonio Gramsci wrote from his prison cell that the only way we can verify social predictions is through collective action to make them happen. Imaginary futures serve as prompts for action; they promise to open possibilities; but they cannot guarantee them, and any pretense at inevitability is simply pretense.[1] As Clint Eastwood's character put it, if you want a guarantee, buy a toaster.[2] But without mobilizing the future as a spur to the present, we risk being unnecessarily imprisoned by the past, and we can never know the limits of possibility.

The revolutionaries thought that a frontal assault could accelerate the switch from the present to the future, from black to white, from hell to heaven. The alternative is to approach problems at a tangent.[3] That is a poet's way, and perhaps now we prefer a poet's way, to find our way around problems, to seek hybrids, alliances of opposites, impure compromises, and to be wary of the human brain's love of coherence when impure compromises may serve us best.

The hope of progressives throughout the modern era has been that it would be possible to embed reciprocity and love at ever larger and more complex scales, and to channel selfish and predatory ambitions into the common good. Two centuries of modernity has made it possible to see intelligence and wisdom as the most important capacities that any individual, group, or society can have, and that these can be better organized to make the most of millions of brains. Democracy; markets; universities; the Internet and new semantic webs are all tools for orchestrating that intelligence with varying degrees of success. The later stages of modernity have made it possible to see well-being and happiness as the most important goals that intelligence can be directed toward. And they have confirmed that relationships are the source of most of what we value, rather than things or abstractions.

So what place is there for capitalism? Any advanced economy needs capital. It needs stores of value; it needs money to finance its great projects, the development of new technologies, and the growth of ventures. And it needs markets to help with these tasks since they are better mechanisms for allocating money to competing causes than the alternatives. But as we've seen, capitalism no longer serves these functions well. It has become detached from the real economy; capital has come to serve capital, not value; and financial systems have too often become predators. The result is not just a periodic crisis of economics and of excessive risk. It is also a crisis of sense and meaning. A system that promises productivity, service, and the elimination of waste too often delivers profligacy and contempt for customers. What we need are capital markets that can accumulate money, and can intelligently invest it. But to do that well the degrees of separation need to be kept few; the players need incentives that align their interests and those they are meant to serve; and every part of the system needs proportionality, the right balance of risk and assets. All of this then needs checks and balances: strong media, strong institutions in civil society to scrutinize, to warn, and sometimes to shame. Just as governments need all of these things to be kept honest, so do banks and investors.

Economies that are good at providing for the wants and needs of their people can still have plenty of room for ferocious competition, generous rewards for the successful risk-takers and entrepreneurs. But what they don't need are the overheads of predation, the costs of sectors and firms whose primary purpose is to extract value from others rather than to provide it.

The arguments set out here suggest a different future to the traditional accounts in which capitalism was to be overthrown and replaced by a wholly new order. They also challenge the common story accepted by most professional economic commentators and practitioners in which capitalism simply continues with business as usual long into the future.

Just as likely is a slow marginalization of capital and capitalist power in their current forms, as other forms grow: concentrations of capital guided by social and environmental goals as well as commercial ones; circular production systems; the civil and social economy; the ever-growing social industries, providing health, care, education, and support; the collaborations of cyberspace and new tools for collective intelligence; the household reasserting itself as a place of production; the worlds of parallel exchange systems, collaborative consumption, and time accounts.

During the 1990s and 2000s, around half of Harvard Business School's graduates pursued careers in finance, and in many other countries the best and brightest graduates in fields such as physics and engineering also went to finance, pulled by vastly higher rewards. Other industries and fields suffered an acute problem of "crowding out" as talent followed the money. One measure of the shift I describe above may be how many of the best and brightest go more directly into creating value for their fellow citizens, whether as inventors and producers, charity workers or public servants, rather than into the often predatory work of separating people from their money.

An analogy can be found in what happened to monarchies and empires. Two centuries ago the world was run by monarchies. There were occasional republics, like the great Italian cities or the young United States. But the wave of revolution that had begun in Paris in 1789, and reached its climax with the guillotining of the royal family, had run its course. Many leading thinkers had concluded that democracy was an aberration, an experiment that had been tried and failed. Monarchy by contrast was bound to succeed because it was rooted in human nature: human beings are designed to live in hierarchies, and societies are bound to be divided into the weak and the strong, with the strong in charge. Anything else was soft-headed wishful thinking. Worse, any attempts to empower the people would ultimately end in bloodshed. Only kings and emperors, in service to god, could guarantee order.

As we know, each element of this common sense was turned on its head. Although monarchy pervaded every sinew of social life, from the passing of laws to the award of honors, and from land ownership to warfare, its naturalness proved deceptive. Monarchies were soon relegated to the margins, surviving only as quaint anachronisms, limitless divine right replaced with limited and largely secular responsibilities.

Analogies are risky tools for reasoning with. But they can help us to imagine, and to avoid the tendency to see plastic, temporary social institutions as endowed with permanence. We can at the very least imagine a fate for the barons and monarchs of contemporary capitalism not so dissimilar to what befell the all-powerful rulers of a previous era: less deference, less respect, and in time less power. Few can confidently claim that capitalism is rooted in human nature in face of abundant evidence from psychology and social psychology that while acquisitiveness and greed are part of our nature, so are cooperation and care. Nor is the superiority of the private firm as self-evident as it once appeared: instead, in some very diverse sectors we are learning about the value of pluralism in economic life, the effectiveness and resilience of models that share ownership or that explicitly commit themselves to social or moral missions as well as profit. Economics for a time aspired to be a universal science. A more realistic and modest view sees it as a collection of regularities, but without any permanent laws; a sophisticated craft for making sense of money and value, but not a science capable of too many predictions.

My argument suggests that the dominant forms of contemporary capitalism will be displaced by new forms that reflect ideas latent in capitalism: changed conceptions of growth; changed conceptions of the role of human relationships; changed ways of thinking about value. From these we should expect to see radically different kinds of organization and service being born—more open, more relational, more rooted in life—as well as different ethics and aesthetics. Elements of these possible futures can be found in every advanced economy—they are the seeds waiting for conditions to change so that they can grow into the mainstream. Those conditions are as much conditions of success as failure, and the new forms of economic life are more likely to spread as the consequences of growth rather than of no growth, of material abundance rather than lack, even though crises of growth may precipitate their advance. As such, they may thrive in many possible future scenarios—from a future "pax Sinica" overseen by a hegemonic China, to a more fractured global apartheid, or a world where the older powers of Europe and North America revive like phoenixes.

The monarchies had their most glorious years just before they lost power. Some lost it suddenly. Others saw their power wane slowly, as parliaments chipped away at their prestige and functions, turning them from being paramount institutions in their society, the magnets of both love and hate, to becoming marginal. It is too soon to predict with confidence a similar fate for the dominant institutions of capitalism. But there are good reasons for doubting that they are at a high noon. They may be at a moment more analogous to that of the sun before it sets, shining gorgeously before it sinks toward the horizon. If that is the case, they may soon be replaced by changed views of what wealth is, of how wealth is created, and of how wealth should be used.

To discover what comes next, maybe we should look upward. Skylines provide the simplest test of what a society truly values, and where its surpluses are controlled. A few centuries ago the most prominent buildings in the world's cities were forts, churches, and temples, reflecting the priorities of societies ruled by warriors and priests. Then for a time they became palaces. Briefly, in the nineteenth century, civic buildings, railway stations, and museums overshadowed them. And then, in the late twentieth century, banks became the tallest buildings, with the most luxurious atriums and entrance halls. Central business districts towered over the other parts of cities, their glass towers oozing confident superiority. But what will come next? Great leisure palaces, casinos, and sports stadiums? Universities and art galleries? Water towers, hanging gardens, and vertical farms; or perhaps (as in many Hollywood films), biotech empires? No one knows the answers. But imagining what might fill the skies is one way we can rekindle our capacity to see the systems we live in as alive and in motion.

Notes

. . . . . .

CHAPTER 1
AFTER CAPITALISM

1. Civil movements, from Solidarity to the Civic Forum, played decisive roles in overthrowing the old communist governments, and more than a few eminent sociologists played their part too. But their role was often overshadowed by the role and appeal of the market, market mechanisms, market thinking, and market behaviors.

2. George Unwin, *Studies in Economic History: The Collected Papers of George Unwin* (London: Frank Cass, 1966).

3. William Baumol, who has consistently been one of the most thoughtful economists, wrote well about this in "Entrepreneurship: Productive, Unproductive and Destructive," *Journal of Business Venturing* 8, no. 3 (1990): 197–210. He particularly emphasizes the rewards from directing energies to such things as lobbying and lawsuits as opposed to productive creation.

4. A good recent example is Daron Acemoglu and James Robinson, *Why Nations Fail: The Origins of Power, Prosperity and Poverty* (London: Profile, 2012).

5. See for example the results of a BBC World Service survey of twenty-seven countries in 2009 which found majorities in all counties wanting more government intervention. Barely one in ten thought that the system was working well; twice as many thought it fatally flawed. (Globescan survey for BBC: http://www.globescan .com/news_archives/bbc2009_berlin_wall/).

6. To borrow the brilliant metaphor James Buchan used as the title for his book *Frozen Desire* (New York: Welcome Rain Publishers, 2001).

7. Walter Benjamin, "Theses on the philosophy of history," in *Illuminations* (London: Pimlico, 1999), 249.

8. Mainstream forecasters now expect the E7 emerging economies (Brazil, Russia, India, China, Turkey, Mexico, Indonesia) by 2050 to be around 50 percent larger than the current G7 (United States, Japan, Germany, UK, France, Italy, and Canada), with China expected to overtake the United States as the world's largest economy in the 2020s. PricewaterhouseCoopers, "The World in 2050: How big will the major

290 NOTES TO PAGES 15-22

emerging market economies get and how can the OECD compete?" March 2006. These figures have subsequently been revised substantially.

9. Typical forecasts suggest a share around 15 percent by 2050. "Global Europe 2030–2050, State of the Art of International Forward Looking Activities beyond 2030," paper drafted for the European Commission, DG Research and Innovation (Social Sciences and Humanities), Annette Braun, including inputs from several members of the "Global Europe 2030–2050" Expert Group, Dusseldorf, August 2010.

CHAPTER 2
BARREN AND PREGNANT CRISES

1. http://www.imf.org/external/pubs/ft/survey/so/2010/res042010a.htm.

2. As Warren Buffett put it, when the tide goes out you see who's swimming naked, but the implication is that what's happening is a predictable tide, not an unpredictable tsunami.

3. Joseph Schumpeter, *Economics and Sociology of Capitalism* (Princeton: Princeton University Press, 1951), 189.

4. Speech at West Point, December 9, 2009.

5. M. Guidolin and E. A. La Jeunesse, "The Decline in the U.S. Personal Saving Rate: Is It Real and Is It a Puzzle?" *Federal Reserve Bank of St. Louis Review*, 89 (2007) 6: 491–514.

6. G. A. Akerlof and R. J. Schiller, *Animal Spirits: How Human Psychology Drives the Economy and Why It Matters for Global Capitalism* (Princeton: Princeton University Press, 2009); S. Green, *Good Value: Reflections on Money, Morality and an Uncertain World* (London: Allen Lane, 2009).

7. LSE, *The Future of Finance: The LSE Report* (London: London School of Economics and Political Science, 2010), 29.

8. Global Footprint Network, *World Footprint: Do We Fit on the Planet* (GFN, 2010), http://www.footprintnetwork.org/en/index.php/GFN/page/world_footprint/.

9. *Business Cycles*, vol. 1 (Cambridge, MA: Harvard University Press, 1939), 1011.

10. Michael Bordo, Barry Eichengreen, Daniela Klingebiel, and Maria Soledad Martinez-Peria, *Is the Crisis Problem Growing More Severe?* NBER, 2000.

11. P. Cohan, "Big Risk: $1.2 Quadrillion Derivatives Market Dwarfs World GDP," *Daily Finance*, 2010, http://www.dailyfinance.com/story/investing-basics/risk-quadrillion-derivatives-market-gdp/19509184/.

12. B. Mandelbrot and R. Hudson, *The (Mis)Behaviour of Markets: A Fractal View of Risk, Ruin and Reward*, (London: Profile Books, 2008).

13. http://www.vanityfair.com/business/features/2010/11/financial-crisis-excerpt-201011?printable=true#ixzz16F7bRjcC.

14. "World Wealth Report," Merrill Lynch and Gemini Consulting, 2000.

15. For example, the Wharton Business School was founded 1881.

16. In a speech given at the Lord Mayor's Banquet for Bankers and Merchants of the City of London, June 20, 2007.

17. This was the crucial insight of Hyman Minsky in his book, *Stabilising an Unstable Economy* (New York: McGraw Hill, 1986/2008).

18. Opinion is divided over whether credit cards count as a de facto currency in their own right or only a tool for handling currencies.

19. Australia was an extreme example: a fiscal stimulus, and strong demand from China, helped the country avoid recession altogether. The crisis also helped to accelerate a longer-term shift in geopolitical power, forcing the IMF to include Brazil, Russia, India, and China among the top ten IMF members in terms of quota and voting rights.

20. See A. Beatty, "Chapter Closes on Vilified US Bank Bailout," *Economic Times*, 2010, http://economictimes.indiatimes.com/news/international-business/Chapter-closes-on-vilified-US-bank-bailout/articleshow/6675895.cms; A. Batson, "China's Vanishing Fiscal Stimulus," *Wall Street Journal*, 2010. http://blogs.wsj.com/chinarealtime/2010/02/08/chinas-vanishing-fiscal-stimulus/.

21. It is intriguing that they were much more willing to deal toughly with the car industry—and achieved remarkable success in a forced restructuring of what appeared to be a terminally ill industry.

22. Piergiorgio Alessandri and Andrew Haldane, "Banking on the State," Bank of England, presentation to the Federal Reserve Bank of Chicago conference, 2009.

23. These figures come from the work of William Lazonick in the 2012 FINNOV program supported by the European Commission. http://www.finnov-fp7.eu/people/william-lazonick.

24. In economic theory, share buybacks can be a good thing, since they free up capital for investment in other firms with potentially more productive and profitable ideas. That theory presumes that financial markets provide finance for innovation; unfortunately, that's not borne out by the evidence. The reality no longer fits the theory.

25. F. Berkes, J. Colding, and C. Folke, *Navigating Social-Ecological Systems: Building Resilience for Complexity and Change* (Cambridge: Cambridge University Press, 2003), provides one of the best definitions of resilience:

> the capacity of an individual organisation or system to absorb disturbances and reorganise itself while undergoing change in ways that retain or enhance its capacities to think and act.

CHAPTER 3
THE ESSENCE OF CAPITALISM

1. Long before the Roman Empire there were neutral offshore entrepots, like Gadir/Cadiz off southern Spain, or the isle of Ictis off Southwest Britain, supposed to be the place for buying tin according to Diodorus Sicolus, the Greek writer.

2. Foxxconn is notorious for many things, including a work regime that drove over 100 staff to threaten mass suicide in early 2012. But it's also a symptom of a new global division of labor in which "an increasing percentage of the economic growth generated by novel product technological innovation is reaped outside the locality in which it originated." Dan Breznitz and Michael Murphree, *Run of the Red Queen, Government, Innovation, Globalization and Economic Growth in China* (New Haven: Yale University Press, 2011), 9.

3. Entrepreneurship, in David Stark's words, "is the ability to keep multiple orders of worth in play and to exploit the resulting ambiguity." It depends on uncertainty—rather than just calculable risk. David Stark, *The Sense of Dissonance: Accounts of Worth in Economic Life* (Princeton: Princeton University Press, 2009).

4. Joseph Schumpeter, *The Theory of Economic Development: An Inquiry into Profits, Capital, Credit, Interest and the Business Cycle* (New Brunswick, NJ: Transaction Publishers, 1934).

5. C. Tilly and C. Tilly, *Work under Capitalism: New Perspectives in Sociology* (Boulder, CO: Westview Press, 1997), 24.

6. Still the greatest account of the rise of big firms is arguably Alfred Chandler, *Strategy and Structure: Chapters in the History of the American Industrial Enterprise* (Cambridge, MA: MIT Press, 1962).

7. Legal Newsline, "Tort System Costs Over Two Per Cent of GDP Yearly, Study Shows"; http://legalnewsline.com/news/192567-tort-system-costs-over-two-percent-of-gdp-yearly-study-finds.

8. M. Castells, *The Rise of the Network Society. The Information Age: Economy, Society and Culture*, vol. 1 (Oxford: Blackwell, 1996), 412.

9. Connectedness has become ever more the defining feature of daily life. But increasingly, we're also learning the need to restrain connectedness too so that we can be civil and social in more meaningful ways: unlike machines, human beings work best when they're not always connected.

10. Many forecasters expect that fossil fuels will still make up 80 percent of the energy mix in the 2030s. U.S. Joint Forces Command, Center for Joint Futures: The Joint Operating Environment (JOE) 2008: http://www.jfcom.mil/newslink/storyarchive/2008/JOE2008.pdf.

11. E. Bournayet et al., *Vital waste graphics 2*. The Basel Convention, UNEP (GRID-Arendal, 2006).

12. French MOD, Délégation aux affaires stratégiques: Geostrategic prospectives for the next thirty years, 2008; http://www.defense.gouv.fr/das/content/download/138857/1207078/file/SYN.pdf.

13. OECD, "The Future of the Family to 2030—A Scoping Report—OECD International Futures Programme," 2008; http://www.oecd.org/dataoecd/11/34/42551944.pdf.

14. Lefebvre described this as "rhythmanalysis." See Henri Lefebvre, *Rhythmanalysis* (London and New York: Continuum, 2004).

15. Quoted in Bruce Carruthers and Wendy Nelson, "Accounting for Rationality: Double-entry Bookkeeping and the Rhetoric of Economic Rationality," *American Journal of Sociology* 97, no. 1 (1991): 31–69.

16. See Adam Smith, *The Theory of Moral Sentiments*, part IV, chapter I. "Of the beauty which the appearance of Utility bestows upon all the productions of art, and of the extensive influence of this species of Beauty" (Cambridge: Cambridge University Press, 2002).

17. Claude Shannon, a twentieth-century American mathematician and engineer, is known as the father of the information age, mainly thanks to the paper he wrote in 1948: "A Mathematical Theory of Communication," published that year in the *Bell System Technical Journal.*

18. Max Weber, *The Protestant Ethic and the Spirit of Capitalism* (London: Routledge, 2005 [1930]), 108.

19. Lawrence James, *The Middle Class: A History* (London: Little, Brown, 2006), 75.

20. The philosopher Jon Elster calls this "self-binding," and has used the metaphor of Ulysses and the Sirens to illustrate what he means. Ulysses tied himself to the mast of his ship to help him resist the temptations of the sirens. Similar precommitments embody "a certain form of *rationality over time.*" Jon Elster, *Ulysses and the Sirens: Studies in Rationality and Irrationality* (Cambridge: Cambridge University Press, 1979), and Elster, *Ulysses Unbound: Studies in Rationality, Pre-commitment and Constraints* (Cambridge: Cambridge University Press, 2002).

21. Seen through this lens, capitalism goes awry when the bindings are loosened: when people shop too much, build up unaffordable debts, or stop working so as to maximize their fun now. This isn't always true: as Keynes showed, the "paradox of thrift" is that spending less and saving more can leave everyone poorer (and two centuries before, Bernard Mandeville made parallel, and scandalously received, arguments in his *Fable of the Bees* (London: Penguin, 1970), which showed how private vice could sustain public virtue). But it's rather hard to believe that if Keynes were alive today he would see too much thrift as the problem in the two countries he knew best, the UK and the United States.

22. Harrison C. White, *Markets from Networks: Socioeconomic Models of Production* (Princeton: Princeton University Press, 2001).

23. Fernand Braudel, *The Structures of Everyday Life: Civilization and Capitalism 15th–18th Century* (Berkeley: University of California Press, 1992).

24. These are the words of Walter Bagehot, a famous nineteenth-century English economist and journalist.

25. The evolution of capitalism is inseparable from the widening networks of loans and debts that simultaneously fueled growth and led so many into bankruptcy and the debtors' prison: one of the oddities of economic history is how many traders were unable to track their own debts and assets.

26. These fears are particularly acute given the "balance sheet weakness" of the United States and Europe, both heavy with debts.

27. The collapse caused Iceland's currency to plunge 60 percent in value. Forty percent of its home owners became insolvent. The gains from the period of expansion were mainly enjoyed by the top 1 percent of the population, while the costs of putting the crisis right were shared. Dramatic falls in the value of the currency combined with capital controls, sharp tax rises, high interest rates, and a robust refusal to pay off creditors, contained the crisis, and, just, retained confidence.

28. With rare exceptions such as Akerlof and Schiller, *Animal Spirits* on animal spirits, or Christian Marazzi, *Capital and Language* (Cambridge, MA: MIT Press, 2008).

29. See Ha-Joon Chang, *23 Things They Don't Tell You About Capitalism* (London: Allen Lane, 2010). Thing Number 7 is that very few rich countries got there by following the prescriptions of free market economics.

30. F. Block and M. Keller, "Where Do Innovations Come From? in *State of Innovation: The U.S. Government's Role in Technology Development*, ed. Block and Keller (Boulder, CO: Paradigm, 2010).

31. C. M. Reinhart and K. Rogoff, *This Time Is Different: Eight Centuries of Financial Folly* (Princeton: Princeton University Press, 2009).

32. Piergiorgio Alessandri and Andrew Haldane, "Banking on the State," Bank of England, presentation to the Federal Reserve Bank of Chicago conference, 2009.

33. Y. Huang, *Capitalism with Chinese Characteristics. Entrepreneurship and the State* (New York: Cambridge University Press, 2008).

34. Franklin Allen and Meijun Qian, *Building China's Financial System in the 21st Century* (Cambridge: Harvard University Press, 2003); Franklin Allen and Meijun Qian, "Will China's Financial System Stimulate or Impede the Growth of Its Economy?" in *China's Economy: Retrospect and Prospect*, Asia Program Special Report No. 129 (Washington, DC: Woodrow Wilson International Center for Scholars, 2005), 33–41.

35. W. Baumol, R. Litan, and C. Schramm, *Good Capitalism, Bad Capitalism: And the Economics of Growth and Prosperity* (New Haven: Yale University Press, 2007), argues that the best form of capitalism is a mix of big firms and entrepreneurial small ones, with the latter creating ideas and the former putting them into practice. Baumol is an impressive economist—yet his accounts are intriguing both for what they include and for what they leave out, for example, the huge U.S. public investment in science.

36. GPS came from the military NAVSTAR satellite program, multitouch displays from an interface funded by the NSF and CIA. Vernon Ruttan shows how the key technology complexes in the United States (the "mass production" system, aviation, space, information technology, the Internet, and nuclear power) were all critically dependent on government investment. V. Ruttan, *Is War Necessary for Economic Growth? Military Procurement and Technology Development* (New York: Oxford University Press, 2006).

37. Christopher Freeman, Working Paper, International Institute for Applied

Systems Analysis, WP 95-76, "History, Co-evolution and Economic Growth," 1995. Sometimes the imperative of industrialization meant states forging alliances with the merchants and makers; sometimes it meant overcoming their resistance, as in nineteenth-century Japan. Elsewhere the state simply got in the way: capitalism faltered in much of Africa not just because of the relative underdevelopment of its markets but also because of the rapaciousness first of colonial governments, and then of so many governments after independence, leaving markets dominated by informal networks of traders and customary leaders, stretching out across borders into diasporas, but with governments present only as costly predators to be bought off.

38. Individual terrorists, of course, more often turn out to be quite highly educated.

CHAPTER 4
TO MAKE OR TO TAKE

1. Andrew Bernstein, *The Capitalist Manifesto* (Lanham, MD: University Press of America, 2005).

2. Ian H. Birchall, *The Spectre of Babeuf* (Basingstoke: Palgrave Macmillan, 1997).

3. William Nordhaus, "*The Health of Nations* and *Irving Fisher and the Health of Nations*," *American Journal of Economics and Sociology* 64, no. 1 (January 2005): 367–392.

4. The economist Jeff Sachs ascribed the differences in economic development across the world to climatic impact and geography. See for example D. Bloom, J. Sachs, and C. Udry, "Geography, Demography and Economic Growth in Africa," *Brookings Papers on Economic Activity* 1998, no. 2, 207–295.

5. Siberia lacks the global firms and networks of the other countries of the north; but it does have a long tradition of excellent science (in places like Tomsk and Novo-Sibirsk), and ports such as Murmansk which are well placed to benefit from potential temperature rises around twice the global average.

6. Scott Shane, *Illusions of Entrepreneurship* (New Haven: Yale University Press, 2011), 16.

7. Quoted in Christopher Freeman, Working Paper, International Institute for Applied Systems Analysis, WP 95-76, "History, Co-evolution and Economic Growth," 1995.

8. William Nordhaus, *Invention, Growth and Welfare: A Theoretical Treatment of Technological Change* (Cambridge, MA: MIT Press, 1969).

9. Ricardo Hausman's "The Atlas of Economic Complexity" is a fascinating exercise, mapping products according to the complexity of their processes. MIT Media Lab and Harvard University, 2011.

10. "800 varsities, 35,000 colleges needed in next 10 years: Sibal." *The Hindu*, March 24, 2010.

11. There are clearer correlations between firms' investment in innovation and sales from innovative products, and many studies have found significant private and social returns from investments in R&D.

12. Ron Hira and Phillip Ross, "R&D Goes Global," *IEEE Spectrum On-Line*, November 2008.

13. We know that intangible investment in training, software, branding, and businesses' processes tends to exceed investment in classic research and development, and we know that innovation seems to work better in systems that cut across the boundaries of firms and nations. Yet the main statistics measure traditionally defined activity (such as R&D spending or patents), within boundaries. The Innovation Index, measuring the UK's Investment in innovation and its effects, NESTA, November 2009.

14. John Kay, "Intellectual Property Protection: What Role in 20th Century Innovation," in Technology and Poverty Reduction in Asia and the Pacific, OECD Development Centre. OECD, Asian Development Bank, June 2002.

15. A recent study shows just how unclear the evidence still is on the impact of copyright on growth and even on rewards to authors; see Ray Corrigan and Mark Rogers, "The Economics of Copyright," *World Economics* 6, no. 3 (2005): 153–174. IP clearly matters a great deal in some sectors. But it's not all-important. Of £140 billion invested by UK business in IP in 2008, for example, £65 billion was protected by intellectual property rights.

16. In Walter Isaacson, *Steve Jobs* (New York: Simon & Schuster, 2011).

17. Alan Hughes, "Innovation Policy as Cargo Cult: Myth and Reality in Knowledge-Led Productivity Growth," Centre for Business Research, University of Cambridge Working Paper No. 348, June 2007.

18. Another measure of the gap between rhetoric and reality can be seen in the numbers for investment in innovation in the United States: venture capital contributed about 2.3 percent, 47.2 percent was internally funded by business; 23.9 percent came from angels, 3.9 percent from universities and 22.7 percent from federal and state government. Alan Hughes, "Innovation Policy as Cargo Cult."

19. Breznitz and Murphree, *Run of the Red Queen*, p. 3.

20. Yann Moulier Boutang, 2007, *Le Capitalisme Cognitif: La Nouvelle Grande Transformation* (Editions Amsterdam, 2007). See also Y. Benkler, "Coase's Penguin: Or Linux and the Nature of the Firm," *Yale Law Journal*, 112 (2002): 69–446.

21. This is documented in a forthcoming study by Sandro Mendonça, based at the Science Policy Research Unit in Sussex University.

22. Google built on existing search technologies. The critical one—Hypersearch, on which PageRank tools were based—was developed by Massimo Marchiori; the business model was adopted from another company, Overture, and even its PageRank technology patent is held by Stanford University. Yet Google combined great skill, luck, and timing and then the extraordinary benefits of economies of scale. That the share of its revenue coming from a single source—advertising on the search engine—remained so high, around 96–98 percent, means that it is at best uncertain that it can sustain its dominance.

23. Some see it as remarkable that the Internet, a technology that grew with such ideals of cooperation, should end up dominated by a firm that discovered the secret for turning the Internet into a vast brain dedicated to advertising.

24. Both are worth around $170 billion. GE employs around 300,000; Google employs around 30,000.

25. Erik Brynjolfsson, Erik Saunders, and Adam Saunders, *Wired for Innovation: How Information Technology Is Reshaping the Economy* (Cambridge, MA: MIT Press, 2009) gathers many of the key statistics and arguments.

26. P. Aghion, E. Caroli, and C. Garcia-Penalosa, "Inequality and Economic Growth: The Perspective of the New Growth Theories," *Journal of Economic Literature* 37 (1999): 1615–1660.

27. http://articles.businessinsider.com/2009-11-09/ wall_street/30054567_1_blankfein-goldman-sachs-year-end-bonuses.

28. In April 2005, the German politician Franz Müntefering (from the social democratic (SPD) party) used the term locust to describe private investors, private equity funds, and investment banks. See *Time* magazine, May 15, 2005.

29. There has been a longstanding debate within economics between the logic of equilibrium—in which there should be no profits in perfectly competitive markets—and the more dynamic views of the Austrian school which see markets as constantly creating imbalances and disequilibria.

30. Jadgish N. Bhagwati, "Directly Unproductive Activities," *Journal of Political Economy* (1982): 988–1002.

31. For a fuller discussion see E. C. Pasour, "Rent Seeking: Some Conceptual Problems and Implications," *Review of Austrian Economics* (1987): 123–143.

32. Vito Tanzi, *Governments versus Markets: The Changing Economic Role of the State* (Cambridge: Cambridge University Press, 2011).

33. Mancur Olson also argued that long periods of stability would inevitably lead to stagnation, as powerful interests became ever more successful predators, monopolizing any surpluses. Mancur Olson, *The Rise and Decline of Nations* (New Haven: Yale University Press, 1982).

34. Mariana Mazzucato and Giovanni Dosi, eds., *Knowledge Accumulation and Industry Evolution: The Case of Pharma-Biotech* (Cambridge: Cambridge University Press, 2006).

35. W. Lazonick and M. Sakinç, "Do Financial Markets Support Innovation or Inequity in the Biotech Drug Development Process?" Paper presented at the DIME workshop, Innovation and Inequality: Pharma and Beyond.

36. Tony Blair, my former boss, and former prime minister of the UK, earned a reputed £3.5 million each year as an adviser to JP Morgan, £0.5 million advising Zurich Financial, £1 million advising Kuwait, and another undisclosed sum advising private equity firm Khosla Ventures. He's a man of very great talents. But we can be safe in assuming that they weren't paying for his expertise in designing financial products.

37. R. Sobel, "Testing Baumol: Institutional Quality and the Productivity of Entrepreneurship," *Journal of Business Venturing* 23/6 (2008): 641–655. This paper tests and confirms Baumol's theory.

38. And important work by Gordon Tullock, including "The Welfare Costs of Tariffs, Monopolies, and Theft," *Western Economic Journal* 5, no. 3 (1967): 224-232.

39. The CBO estimated that from 1979 to 2007, the top 1 percent saw real incomes rise by 275 percent, while middle-class incomes rose by only 40 percent.

40. Karl Polanyi, *The Great Transformation: The Political and Economic Origins of Our Time* (Boston: Beacon Press, 2001), 224.

41. This was a theme explored by Gerda Lerner, among other feminist historians.

42. James Boswell, *The Life of Samuel Johnson*, vol. 4 (London: Routledge, 1859), 133.

43. The intimate connections between economic power and military power were studied by Immanuel Wallerstein in his accounts of capitalism as a single world system, integrated and coherent albeit with many cultures and political units. The global system is divided between a core that's high tech, highly skilled, and capital intensive, and a periphery that's the opposite. In this model the core is militarily as well as economically strong and appropriates the bulk of the surplus of the whole economy, yet the dynamics of the system, absorbing ever more parts of the world into it, and itself becoming increasingly intensive, paving the way ultimately for world socialism. This conclusion may just confirm that this is one of many accounts that find too much coherence, too much pattern, and too much meaning in messy realities. See I. Wallerstein, *World Systems Analysis: An Introduction* (Durham, NC: Duke University Press, 2004) and his many other writings from the 1970s onward.

44. Fairfield Osborn, *Our Plundered Planet* (Boston: Little, Brown, 1948); William Vogt, *Road to Survival* (New York: William Sloan, 1948). A. Leopold, *A Sand County Almanac and Sketches from Here and There* (New York: Oxford University Press, 1949).

45. Kenneth Arrow, Partha Dasgupta et al., "China, the US, and Sustainability: Perspectives Based on Comprehensive Wealth," Stanford Center for Sustainable Development, Working Paper No. 313, 2007.

46. From the TEEB (the economics of ecosystems and biodiversity) project, run under the auspices of the United Nations; http://www.teebweb.org/.

47. Johan Rockström of the Stockholm Resilience Centre has defined nine planetary boundaries, stratospheric ozone, land use change, freshwater use, biological diversity, ocean acidification, nitrogen and phosphorus inputs to the biosphere and oceans, aerosol loading, and chemical pollution.

48. This predation on natural systems has encouraged some of the familiar patterns that have accompanied the period of capitalist ascendancy: the heavy involvement of Western powers (and their challengers) in the Middle East, and the willingness to fight wars to preserve access to oil; China's ever more assertive buying up of natural resources in Africa, Australia, and elsewhere, with a scarcely disguised goal of becoming a price-setter for "rare earth" in future decades (88% of platinum, a key resource for fuel cells, for example, comes from just two mines in South Africa).

49. http://www.stuxnet.net/. Stuxnet turned out to originate in the United States.

50. Millennium Ecosystem Assessment (MEA), *Ecosystems and Human Well-Being: Synthesis* (Washington, DC: Island Press, 2005).

51. This latter study looked at willingness to pay in Italy and the UK. This and other studies mentioned are drawn from UN-sponsored TEEB (the economics of ecosystems and biodiversity) project publications in 2010 and 2011.

CHAPTER 5
CAPITALISM'S CRITICS

1. The word capitalist is traced back to the seventeenth century, and was quite widely used in the eighteenth. David Ricardo used it extensively in the early nineteenth century. But Blanc was the first to write of capitalism as opposed to capitalists.

2. One of the most contentious questions of recent decades is whether global inequality has grown or shrunk. Inequality within nations has risen; but overall inequality has by some measures reduced, mainly because of the rapid economic growth in India and China, even though the gap between the richest countries and the poorest has grown. No reliable data exist to compare the experience of the whole of the world's population. What is certain, however, is that a small global elite has benefited disproportionately from growth, extracting a growing share of income.

3. http://www.newscientist.com/article/mg21228354.500-revealed-the-capitalist-network-that-runs-the-world.html.

4. T. Smeeding, "Public Policy, Economic Inequality, and Poverty: The United States in Comparative Perspective," *Social Science Quarterly* 86 (2005): 956–983.

5. Oscar Wilde, *The Soul of Man Under Socialism* (London: Penguin, 2001).

6. *The Three Ladies of London, 1583,* quoted in Lawrence James, *The Middle Class: A History*, 77.

7. Gustavo Gutiérrez, *Teologia de la liberacion: perspectivas* (Lima, Peru: Centro de Estudios y Publicaciones, 1971).

8. E. F. Schumacher, *Small Is Beautiful*, new edition (UK: Vintage, 2011).

9. P. K. Piff, M.W. Kraus, S. Côté, B. H. Cheng, and D. Keltner, "Having Less, Giving More: The Influence of Social Class on Prosocial Behaviour," *Journal of Personality and Social Psychology* (2010).

10. Benjamin Disraeli, *Sybil: or the Two Nations* (New York: Oxford Paperbacks; new edition, November 26, 1998).

11. Thomas Davenport and John Beck, *The Attention Economy: Understanding the New Currency of Business* (Boston: Harvard Business Review Press, 2001).

12. Quoted in Rajan, *Fault Lines*, p. 143.

13. Richard Sennett, *The Culture of the New Capitalism* (New Haven: Yale University Press, 2007), 6.

14. Max Weber, *The Protestant Ethic and the Spirit of Capitalism* (London: Penguin, 2002), 16.

15. Karl Marx, *Capital*, volume 1 (London: Penguin, 1991).

16. Robert Heilbroner, *The Nature and Logic of Capitalism* (New York: Norton, 1985), writes particularly well about the anxieties endemic to capitalism.

17. Max Weber, *Economy and Society* (Berkeley: University of California Press, 1956), 91.

18. E. Diener, C. Nickerson, R. E. Lucas, and E. Sandvik, "Dispositional Affect and Job Outcomes," *Social Indicators Research* 59 (2002): 229–259.

19. Philanthrocapitalism is an example of an idea that is accurate as a description of some important but exceptional cases and profoundly inaccurate as a generalization.

20. Alain Ehrenberg, *The Weariness of the Self: Diagnosing the History of Depression in the Contemporary Age* (Montreal: McGill-Queens University Press, 2008).

21. D. Kahneman and A. Deaton, "High Income Improves Evaluation of Life but not Emotional Well-being," *PNAS* 107 (8): 16:489–16:493.

22. *La fabbrica dell'infelicità. New economy e movimento del cognitariato* (Rome: Derive Approdi, 2001).

23. R. Easterlin and L. Angelescu, "Happiness and Growth the World Over: Time Series Evidence on the Happiness-Income Paradox," IZA Discussion Paper No. 4060, 2009.

24. Andrew Kohut, Global Views on Life Satisfaction, National Conditions and the Global Economy (Pew Global Attitudes Project, 2007); http://pewglobal.org/files/pdf/1025.pdf.

25. B. Stevenson and J. Wolfers, "Economic Growth and Subjective Well-being: Reassessing the Easterlin Paradox," Brookings Papers on Economic Activity, 2008, 1–87.

26. See www.gallup.com/poll/139604/worry-sadness-stress-increase-length-unemployment.aspx. This research also finds that the incidence of worrying is higher for those who have been unemployed longer, while the incidence of happiness is only slightly less for the long-term unemployed.

27. E. Diener, R. E. Lucas, and C. N. Scollon, "Beyond the Hedonic Treadmill: Revisions to the Adaptation Theory of Well-being," *American Psychologist* 61 (2006): 305–314.

28. N. Donovan and D. Halpern, *Life Satisfaction: The State of Knowledge and Implications for Government* (London: Cabinet Office, 2002).

29. See the speech by the Korean statistics commissioner, Insill Yi, pp. 1–2, drawing on an OECD 2005 report: http://www.oecd.org/dataoecd/56/29/44118771.pdf.

30. Egypt: The Arithmetic of Revolution, March 2011, Abu Dhabi Gallup.

31. This is the conclusion of J. J. Graafland and B. Compen, *Economic Freedom*

and Life Satisfaction: A Cross Country Analysis (paper published by Tilburg University, Center for Economic Research, 2012).

32. Tim Kasser, *The High Price of Materialism* (Cambridge, MA: MIT Press, 2003), 13.

33. Richard Ryan and Edward Deci, "Self-determination Theory and the Facilitation of Intrinsic Motivation, Social Development, and Well-being," *American Psychologist* 55 (2000): 68–78.

34. D. Kanner and R. G. Soule, "Globalization, Corporate Culture, and Freedom," in Tim Kasser and A. Kasser, *Psychology and Consumer Culture: The Struggle for a Good Life in a Materialistic World* (Washington, DC: American Psychological Association, 2003), 49–67.

35. Juliet B. Schor, *Born to Buy: The Commercialised Child and the New Consumer Culture* (New York: Scribner, 2004).

36. Research on adolescents also shows the corrosive effects of media culture. See Agnes Narin, Jo Ormond, and Paul Bottomley, *Watching, Wanting and Wellbeing: Exploring the Links: A Study of 9–13 Year Olds* (National Consumer Council, 2007).

37. Schor, *Born to Buy*; Moniek Buijzen and Patti M. Valkenburg, "The Effects of Television Advertising on Materialism, Parent-Child Conflict and Unhappiness: A Review of Research," *Applied Developmental Psychology* 24 (2003): 437–456; Moniek Buijzen and Patti M. Valkenburg, *The Unintended Effects of Television Advertising: A Parent-Child Survey*, Communication Research, 30 (SAGE Publications, 2003), 483–503.

38. G. Moore and R. Moschis, "The Impact of Family Communication on Adolescent Consumer Socialization," *Advances in Consumer Research* 11(1984): 314–319.

39. Women exposed to perfume advertisements with attractive, slim models become less satisfied with their own appearance; Marsha Richins, "Social Comparison and the Idealised Images of Advertising," *Journal of Consumer Research* 18 (1991).

40. Robert Frank, "Why Living in a Rich Society Makes Us Feel Poor" (*New York Times Magazine*, October 2000); (http://partners.nytimes.com/library/magazine/home/20001015mag-frank.html, 2000).

41. A recent study confirmed Mencken's definition. David Neumark and Andrew Postlewaite examined the behavior of a large sample of pairs of American sisters, one of whom did not have a job. Analyzing all the factors that might influence the sister to find a paid job, they found that relative income was the most powerful: a woman in their sample was 16–25 percent more likely to seek paid employment if her sister's husband earned more than her own. D. Neumark and A. Postlewaite, "Relative Income Concerns and the Rise in Married Women's Employment," *Journal of Public Economics*, Elsevier, vol. 70, no. 1 (October 1998)): 157–183.

42. The heart of the matter may be simpler than this. Lord Acton once wrote that all progress depends on dissatisfaction. Certainly a dynamic capitalist economy depends on dissatisfaction—to drive workers to work, and consumers to consume. Perhaps a dynamic society does too, and constantly navigates the balance between too little satisfaction and too much.

43. D. Lai, "Quantifying the Dynamics of the Chinese Labour Force: A Life Table Approach," *Social Indicators Research* 81 (2007): 171–180.

44. A section in my book, *The Art of Public Strategy*, explores what's known about financial and other motives for public officials, service providers, and volunteers (Oxford: Oxford University Press, 2009). I'm fascinated by the many experiments that have tried to bring clarity to these questions, such as controlled experiments to understand the interaction of motives and performance. For example, one study tested out giving payments, some small, some moderate, and some high, for participants who had to carry out tasks that required attention and imagination, fitting pieces of a metal puzzle into a plastic frame, remembering strings of numbers, and throwing balls at targets. Those promised and paid the most turned out to perform least well, the opposite of what might have been expected. Dan Pink, *Drive: The Surprising Truth about What Motivates Us* (Edinburgh: Canongate Books Ltd., 2010); D. Mobbs, "Choking on the Money: Reward-Based Performance Decrements Are Associated with Midbrain Activity," *Psychological Science* (2009): 955–962. http://www.fil.ion.ucl.ac.uk/~bseymour/papers/psychsci2009.pdf. The potentially detrimental influence of large incentives on performance has a basis in neuroscience too. A recently published paper suggested that large rewards cause basic reward pathways in the brainstem to become over-active and interfere with more high-level skill processing. David Marsden, *The Paradox of Performance Related Pay Systems: 'Why Do We Keep Adopting Them in the Face of Evidence that they Fail to Motivate?'* http://cep.lse.ac.uk/pubs/download/dp0945.pdf.

CHAPTER 6
ANTICAPITALIST UTOPIAS AND NEOTOPIAS

1. Gregory Claeys, *Cambridge Companion to Utopias* (Cambridge: Cambridge University Press, 2010), 13.

2. Moscow, Selected correspondence, 1846, p. 40.

CHAPTER 7
THE NATURE OF CHANGE

1. Letter from Marx to Pavel Vasilyevich Annenkov, 1846, in *Marx/Engels Collected Works*, volume 38 (New York: International Publishers, 1975), 95.

2. These are Ernest Gellner's words on Marx, from his introduction to *Notions of Nationalism*; E. Gellner, "Introduction," in *Notions of Nationalism*, ed. S. Periwal (Budapest: Central European University Press, 1995).

3. Blat literally means protection: everyone exchanged favors with everyone else in a shadow system ("to have no blat is the same as having no civil rights, the same

as being robbed of all your rights"). Quoted in G. Mak, *In Europe: Travels through the Twentieth Century* (UK: Harvill Secker, 2007), 450.

4. United Nations, *World Population Prospects: The 2008 Revision, Population Database*, New York: United Nations, 2009, available at http://esa.un.org/unpp/.

5. Mainly originating in developing countries where, parallel to what was observed in developed countries, fertility rates are assumed to decline as a result of growing prosperity as well as the education and emancipation of women.

6. For a time in the 2000s, it was thought that a high proportion of the U.S. productivity miracle of the late 1990s could be attributed to Walmart. This was the conclusion of a series of influential studies by Goldman Sachs. More careful subsequent research suggested that more of the change could be attributed to smaller retailers adopting similar methods, though there was no doubting the broader story of surging productivity in services. Jack Triplett and Barry Bosworth, *Productivity in the US Services Sector: New Sources of Growth* (Washington, DC: Brookings Institution Press, 2003).

7. A variant of this argument can be found in Tyler Cowen, *The Great Stagnation* (New York: Dutton Books, 2011), which argues that the "low hanging fruits" of modern industry have all been harvested.

8. John Maynard Keynes, "Possibilities for our Grandchildren," in *Essays in Persuasion* (New York: Norton, 1963). It was first published in London in 1930.

9. For a broader overview, see P. Barbosa and I. Castellanos, eds., *Ecology of Predator-Prey Interactions* (New York: Oxford University Press, 2004).

10. Daniel Bell, *The Cultural Contradictions of Capitalism* (New York: Basic Books, 1976).

11. According to the U.S. Department of Commerce, Bureau of Economic Analysis (BEA).

12. Quoted in Luc Boltanski and Eve Chiapello, *The New Spirit of Capitalism* (London: Verso, 2007).

13. Luc Boltanski's work on the new spirit of capitalism sets out in great detail how managerial language responded to the crises of the 1960s and 1970s with this new spirit. Luc Boltanski and Eve Chiapello, *The New Spirit of Capitalism* (London: Verso, 2007).

14. See Loren Baritz, *The Servants of Power: A History of the Use of Social Science in American Industry* (New York: Wiley, 1960).

15. James Utterback and W. J. Abernathy, "A Dynamic Model of Product and Process Innovation," *Omega* 3, no. 6 (1975): 636–656.

16. Karl R. Popper, *Conjectures and Refutations: The Growth of Scientific Knowledge* (London: Routledge, 1963), 341.

17. An interesting recent book which explores some of these dynamics is Michael Fairbanks and Stace Lindsay, *Plowing the Sea; Nurturing the Hidden Sources of Growth in the Developing World* (Boston: Harvard Business School, 1997).

18. See for example Anne S. Huff and James O. Huff, *When Firms Change Direction* (Oxford: Oxford University Press, 2000).

19. Joseph Schumpeter, *Capitalism, Socialism and Democracy* (London: Allen & Unwin, 1943).

20. Interesting comments on this phenomenon can be found in David Bohm, *On Dialogue* (London: Routledge, 2004).

21. Leon Festinger, *A Theory of Cognitive Dissonance* (Evanston: Row, Peterson and Co., 1957).

22. One symptom of this shift is the wave of innovations addressed not to productivity but rather to waste: examples include the "activist architect," Teddy Cruz, who uses "waste" materials from San Diego to build homes, health clinics, and other buildings in Tijuana, turning overlooked and unused spaces within a dense, urban neighborhood into a livable, workable environment; or the regeneration of Westergasfabriek by ReUse in Amsterdam, or the transformation of an old, disused elevated railway in New York into an urban park—the High Line.

23. I wrote about this in my essay "The Power of the Weak" in *New Times*, ed. M. Jacques and Stuart Hall (London: Lawrence and Wishart, 1989), which predicted an era of much more active networked power.

24. Donald Schon, *Beyond the Stable State* (New York: Norton, 1973).

25. H. Gardner, *Changing Minds: The Art and Science of Changing Our Own and Other People's Minds* (Boston: Harvard Business School Press, 2006).

26. T. J. Clark, *The Painting of Modern Life: Paris in the Art of Manet and His Followers* (New York: Knopf, 1984).

27. This happens at the very micro scale and at larger scales, and it's now become possible to model these erratic dynamics of change, showing how people of differing levels of suggestibility and conformity watch how others respond to change and choose their moments to go along, sometimes with the pioneers left stranded in a minority, and sometimes with surges as previously marginal views become mainstream.

28. The analysis here draws on the various analyses of contentious politics, and before them the "resource mobilization" theories of social movements, which tried to explain why even people who share a grievance don't usually act on it.

29. From an address given at Oglethorpe University.

30. David R. Marsh, Dirk G. Schroeder, Kirk A. Dearden, Jerry Sternin, and Monique Sternin, "The Power of Positive Deviance," *British Medical Journal* 329 (2004): 1177–1179.

31. Again and again, the driving force of revolutions has been the frustrated rising middle class losing patience with political and economic orders that give them no outlets.

32. Charles Tilly's work is the most comprehensive on the practical dynamics of change and transformation, and in particular the role of political and other entrepreneurs.

33. Peter Hall, *Cities in Civilisation* (New York: Pantheon, first ed., 1998).

34. I explored some of the characteristics of these creative places, the edge cities, in my book *Connexity* (Boston: Harvard Business Press, 1997), which drew on involvement in a network of creative cities during the 1990s. Mihaly Csikszentmihalyi,

Creativity: Flow and the Psychology of Discovery and Invention, (New York: Harper Perennial, 1997) provides a useful frame for understanding why creative places and groups thrive.

35. See the two pamphlets I co-authored with Jitinder Kohli for the Center for American Progress: "Capital Ideas" and "Scaling New Heights" for a survey of methods being used in governments to accelerate creativity. Both published by the Center for American Progress and the Young Foundation, 2010.

36. A good contemporary example is kaggle (www.kaggle.com), which offers prizes to computer programmers and statisticians to improve predictive models.

37. The "crowd-sourcing" was run by the Royal Navy's Board of Inventions and Research. See Jon Agar, *Science in the Twentieth Century and Beyond* (Cambridge, Polity Press, 2012), 95.

CHAPTER 8
CREATIVE AND PREDATORY TECHNOLOGY

1. Ray Kurzweil, *The Singularity Is Near: When Humans Transcend Biology* (New York: Viking, 2005).

2. But even military technologies can either concentrate power or disperse it. RPGs level the odds between highly sophisticated military machines and poor militia, whereas nuclear weapons tend by their nature to require the systems of big states to manage them.

3. This particular technology is provided by the French audience measurement firm Quividi, created in Paris, in 2006.

4. Their actions have been extensively documented on the Wikileaks website.

5. B-Å. Lundvall, ed., *National Innovation Systems: Towards a Theory of Innovation and Interactive Learning* (London: Pinter, 1992). This is the definitive account of the interwoven roles of states, science, and business in innovation.

6. Arnold Pacey, *Technology in World Civilisation* (London: Blackwell, 1990), 19.

7. Fred Block and Matthew Keller, *Where Do Innovations Come From? Transformations in the U.S. National Innovation System, 1970–2006* (Washington, DC: Information Technology and Innovation Foundation, 2008).

8. The UK Innovation Survey (2009) found that a large majority of innovative firms were involved in formal cooperation with others.

9. The interesting recent work of Benjamin Jones on the slowing of innovation includes: 'The Burden of Knowledge and the Death of 'Renaissance Man': Is Innovation Getting Harder, *NBER Working Papers* 11360, National Bureau of Economic Research, Inc. A more popular take on similar issues is Tyler Cowen's book, *The Great Stagnation.*

10. Benjamin Jones, "As Science Evolves . . ." http://www.kellogg.northwestern.edu/faculty/jones-ben/htm/As_Science_Evolves.pdf.

11. Eric Hobsbawm, *Age of Extremes: The Short Twentieth Century 1914–1991* (London: Abacus, 1999), 87.

12. See, for example, Edward Lewis, *Scientific Revolutions & Economic Depressions*, published online 1999. http://sciencejunk.org/.

13. The website www.Longwavegroup.com gathers together a wide range of useful materials on these theories.

14. This section draws in particular on the school of thought promoted by Christopher Freeman, Carlotta Perez, and Luc Soete in a pioneering series of books and articles on technological, economic, and social change in the 1980s and 1990s (much of this work took place at the Science Policy Research Unit at Sussex University in the UK; http://www.sussex.ac.uk/spru/).

15. Richard G. Lipsey, Kenneth I. Carlaw, and Clifford T. Bekar, *Economic Transformations, General Purpose Technologies and Long-Term Economic Growth* (Oxford: Oxford University Press, 2005).

16. N. Crafts and T. Leunig (2005), "The historical significance of transport for economic growth and productivity"; http://webarchive.nationalarchives.gov.uk/+/http://www.dft.gov.uk/about/strategy/transportstrategy/.

17. Nathan Rosenberg, *Inside the Black Box* (Cambridge, MA: Cambridge University Press, 1982); Richard Nelson and Sidney Winter, *An Evolutionary Theory of Economic Change* (Cambridge, MA: Belknap Press of Harvard University Press, 1985); Toby Huff, *The Rise of Early Modern Science* (Cambridge: Cambridge University Press, 1993).

18. W. Brian Arthur, *The Nature of Technology: What It Is and How It Evolves* (New York: Free Press, 2009), 85.

19. Moore's Law originally stated that the number of transistors that could be placed on an integrated circuit doubles every year (sometimes this is stated as two years or 18 months, and the law is also applied to processing powers). Metcalfe's Law states that the value of a communications network is proportionate to the square of the system's users (or connected devices).

20. Reinhart and Rogoff, *This Time Is Different*, provides the most compelling and comprehensive account of past crashes.

21. Carlota Perez, *Technological Revolutions and Financial Capital* (Cheltenham: Edward Elgar, 2002).

22. James Burnham, *The Managerial Revolution: What Is Happening in the World* (New York: John Day Co., 1941).

23. C. Freeman and C. Perez, "Structural Crisis of Adjustments, Business, Cycles and Investment Behaviour," in *Technical Change and Economic Theory*, ed. Dosi et al. (London: Printer Publishers, 1988), 60.

24. As in Europe, big business could see advantages in the socialization of risk: it ensured a more stable and efficient society, and tended to raise the relative costs more for small than for large firms.

25. Thomas Piketty and Emmanuel Saez, "How Progressive Is the U.S. Federal Tax System? A Historical and International Perspective," *Journal of Economic Perspectives* 21, no. 1 (Winter 2007): 3–24.

26. Now sustained by the Frascati Manual, the bible for R&D policy makers, which defines R&D as comprised of basic or fundamental research to acquire knowledge without an application in mind; applied research, where knowledge creation has specific practical aims; and experimental development, which draws on research to produce new products, processes, and systems. Frascati Manual: Proposed Standard Practice for Surveys on Research and Experimental Development, http://www.oecd.org/document/6/0,3343,en_2649_34451_33828550_1_1_1_1,00.html.

27. Joseph Schumpeter, *Capitalism, Socialism and Democracy* (London: Routledge: 1943), 132.

28. See, for example, Lundvall, *National Innovation Systems*; Tudor Rickards, *Stimulating Innovation: A Systems Approach* (London: Pinter, 1985); J. Gershuny, *Social Innovation and the Division of Labour* (Oxford: Oxford University Press, 1983); M. Njihoff, *The Political Economy of Innovation* (The Hague: Kingston, 1984).

29. Pacey, *Technology in World Civilisation*, vii.

30. This is the big message from Ralf Meisenzahl and Joel Mokyr's work on the industrial revolution, where tweakers and tinkerers like Richard Roberts in Manchester turned promising inventions like the spinning mule into powerfully effective ones.

31. Joel Mokyr, *The Lever of Riches: Technological Creativity and Economic Progress* (Oxford: Oxford University Press, 1990).

32. David Landes, *The Wealth and Poverty of Nations* (New York: Norton, 1998), 296.

33. OECD, "Global Value Chains," 2011.

34. A good recent example is Kevin Kelly, *What Technology Wants* (New York: Viking, 2010).

35. Maurice of Nassau devised detailed drill routines for his soldiers so that together they could function as a well-oiled machine; William Petty led the way in both the collection and analysis of statistics; and Lewis Paul and others observed the actions of women operating spinning wheels so as to replace them with machines.

36. John Gray, *The Immortalization Commission* (London: Allen Lane, 2011) is a fascinating account of earlier aspirations to extend life.

CHAPTER 9
THE RISE OF ECONOMIES BASED ON RELATIONSHIPS AND MAINTENANCE

1. I helped develop some of the world's first economic strategies focused on creative and cultural industries (I co-wrote the cultural industries strategy for London in 1985/6, and then worked with many cities around the world that wanted strategies for creative industries, from Singapore and Shanghai to Helsinki and Barcelona), as well as working on policy and regulation in telecommunications. My PhD, completed in 1990, was concerned primarily with the economics of networks and the emerging Internet. In each case I was a small part of the shift from an economy based on tangibles to one based on intangibles.

2. See Geoff Mulgan, *Communication and Control: Networks and the New Econo-mies of Communication* (Cambridge: Polity, 1991). I look at many inventions, from the telephone to the Minitel, which have been primarily used for social interaction, though their inventors, engineers, and promoters anticipated very different uses, such as education and entertainment. The same pattern has continued with SMS, social networks, Twitter, and mobile phones.

3. See "Sinking and Swimming: Understanding Britain's Unmet Needs," The Young Foundation (2009), for a detailed analysis of the changing pattern of material and psychological need in one developed country. The report shows that poverty of fuel, housing, clothes, and shoes has shrunk sharply in recent decades, but other kinds of poverty have become more prominent.

4. 7.8 percent of EU jobs growth came from services (out of a total of 8.1% growth in working hours between 1995 and 2005). See Charles Roxburgh and Jan Mischle, *European Growth and Renewal: The Path from Crisis to Recovery* (McKinsey Global Institute, 2011).

5. Healthcare Economist, "CBO Health Care Expenditure Forecasts; http://healthcare-economist.com/2009/08/26/cbo-health-care-expenditure-forecasts 2009.

6. It's been estimated, for example, that the purchasing power of the 60+ genera-tion in Germany amounts to nearly one-third of total private consumption and will grow to over 40 percent by 2050. Economic Policy Committee and European Com-mission, "The Impact of Ageing on Public Expenditure: Projections for the EU25 Member States on Pensions, Health Care, Long-term Care, Education and Unem-ployment Transfers (2004–2050), European Economy, Special Report, No. 1/2006 (HPCEC, 2006).

7. Rijkers Braun et al., Directorate-General for Research, Socio-economic Sciences and Humanities: Special Issue on Healthcare—Healthy Ageing and the Future of Public Healthcare Systems, EUR 24044 EN, November 2009, ISBN 978-92-79-13120-2, DOI 10.2777/47289, ISSN 1018-5593; http://ec.europa.eu/research/social-sciences/pdf/efmn-special-issue-on-healthcare_en.pdf.

8. The huge costs associated with acute care are also likely to fuel innovation in services that can prevent unnecessary costs. Once value can be measured and man-aged in relation to prevention, a stream of new business models become possible. For an overview of the emerging field of "Preventive Investing," see *Social Impact Invest-ment: The Challenge and Opportunity of Social Impact Bonds*, paper published by the Young Foundation, London, April 2011.

9. For one of many surveys, see J. Moncrief and I. Hirsch, "Efficacy of Anti-depressants in Adults," *British Medical Journal* 331 (2005): 155–157.

10. Another interesting example is the U.S. Elderplan, a small health manage-ment organization that encourages its more able members to care for others. The principle is that the young elderly build up credits and then cash them in when they are older and more in need, and it encourages its participants to take on duties within the network as well as benefiting from the support it provides. This idea has been discussed over many decades: Elderplan is a practical way of putting it into effect.

11. Jim Maxmin and Shoshanna Zuboff made parallel points when they wrote of the rise of a "support economy." James Maxmin and Shoshanna Zuboff, *The Support Economy: Why Corporations Are Failing Individuals and the Next Episode of Capitalism* (New York: Viking, 2002).

12. Gary Becker is one of the exceptions, along with a strong strand of feminist economics. But the vast majority of conventional economics, including the economics of work, simply ignores work that isn't paid.

13. Of course more use of collaborative consumption platforms would free up consumer spending for other purposes.

14. One commentator on the U.S. education industry (who, as a major figure in financial services, had warned of the looming crisis in sub-prime markets in the 2000s) described the risks of poor quality and exploitation of students, all supported by misconceived policies where "the government, the students, and the taxpayer bear all the risk and the for-profit industry reaps all the rewards"; http://www.nypost.com/p/news/opinion/opedcolumnists/subprime_goes_to_college_FeiheNJfGYtoSwmtl5etJP.

15. *The World Giving Index*, Charities Aid Foundation, London, 2009.

16. There are 7,000 cooperatives providing care, health, and employment services in Italy with 244,000 staff and 35,000 volunteers; 25,000 co-ops in Spain employ well over 300,000 people.

17. L. M. Salamon, M. Haddock, W. S. Sokolowski, and H. Tice, *Measuring Civil Society and Volunteering: Initial Findings from Implementation of the UN Handbook on Nonprofit Institutions* (John Hopkins University, Center for Civil Society Studies, 2007), Working Paper No. 23. The EU estimates that 11 million people work in the broadly defined social economy, and in the United States in the mid-2000s, charities alone employed nearly ten million paid workers and engaged just under five million full-time equivalent volunteer workers, equivalent to about 10 percent of the total workforce. L. M. Salamon and W. S. Sokolowski, *Employment in America's Charities: A Profile*, Nonprofit Employment Bulletin, 26 (Johns Hopkins Center for Civil Society Studies, 2006); http://www.ccss.jhu.edu/pdfs/NED_Bulletins/National/NED_Bulletin26_EmplyinAmericasCharities_2006.pdf.

18. The result was a series of privatizations, most of which ended disastrously with overreach and bankruptcy, followed by pressures for re-mutualization. Yet poorly run and governed mutual building societies turned out to be nearly as vulnerable to bankruptcy as greedy for-profits.

19. They've also introduced legislation to create new legal forms (such as the Community Interest Company in the UK and the L3C in the United States) that make it easier for civil society to take equity and investments.

20. See J. Defourny and M. Nyssens, Social Enterprise in Europe: Recent Trends and Developments, *Social Enterprise Journal* 4, no. 3 (2008), and J. Defourny and M. Nyssens, "Conceptions of Social Enterprise in Europe and the United States: Convergences and Divergences," paper presented at the Eighth ISTR International Conference and Second EMES-ISTR European Conference, Barcelona, July 9–12, 2008. See also Robin Murray, Geoff Mulgan, and Julie Caulier, *Social Venturing* (London: Young Foundation/NESTA 2009).

21. Charles Heckscher and Paul S. Adler, *The Firm as a Collaborative Community* (Oxford: Oxford University Press, 2006).

22. H. Chesbrough, *Innovation Intermediaries, Enabling Open Innovation* (Boston: Harvard Business School Press, 2006).

23. For the burgeoning literature on social innovation, see the many reports of NESTA and the Young Foundation, and also F. Westley, B. Zimmerman, and M. Patton, *Getting to Maybe: How the World Is Changed* (Toronto: Random House Canada, 2006).

24. FORA et al., *The New Nature of Innovation*—report for the OECD, 2009.

25. http://Nestainnovation.ning.com/.

26. E. Schonfeld, "Four Years After Founding, Kiva Hits $100 Million in Microloans," Techcrunch, 2009; http://www.techcrunch.com/2009/11/01/four-years-after-founding-kiva-hits-100-million-in-microloans//.

27. Another condition for growing new social models more effectively is the creation of more organized markets for outcomes, rewarding providers if they achieve demonstrable results, such as lower crime or unemployment. There is a good deal of experimentation under way with models of this kind, from payment by results, to Social Impact Bonds in the UK and Payment for Success Bonds in the United States. These models of "preventive investment" try to turn future savings to the state into a currency: so if a service can demonstrate that it will reduce hospital admissions, or prison numbers, or the number of teenagers going on welfare, it is rewarded with a share of the savings. See *Social Impact Investment: The Challenge and Opportunity of Social Impact Bonds*, paper published by the Young Foundation, London, April 2011.

28. See Geoff Mulgan and R. Murray, *The Open Book of Social Innovation* (London: Nesta/Young Foundation, 2010).

29. A recent public sector example of large-scale social innovation is Sundhed, the Danish eHealth portal, a collaboration of local and national government that brings together health information and online health services in one place. Patients can find health-related information and advice, online booking facilities, prescription ordering and renewal, online consultations with health professionals, and access to personal medical files. Doctors and nurses can get access to the patient appointment calendar, laboratory data, patient records, waiting list information from hospitals and so on. None of these elements is particularly revolutionary on its own, but when combined together they can transform the experience of healthcare. Evaluations show that roughly a third of users seeking information and advice on their health through Sundhed chose to delay or avoid a visit to their general practice physician, which led to a net saving of roughly 900,000 consultations with GPs every year. The introduction of electronic prescriptions led to annual savings of more than 12 million euros (compared to the 5 million euro cost of running the portal). Giving patients better access to health information and professionals simultaneously improved their ability to care for themselves and improved their satisfaction with the system. See https://www.sundhed.dk/service/english/about-the-ehealth-portal/background.

30. See the review of evidence on behavior change that I undertook for the UK

Department of Health in 2010. http://www.dh.gov.uk/en/Publicationsandstatistics/Publications/PublicationsPolicyAndGuidance/DH_111696.

31. Social policy still has a long way to go in matching the rigors of natural science, and offering falsifiable hypotheses to test, though there is a strong movement to promote greater rigor in measurement and testing. Yet the job of designing the things to be tested is much more like bricolage than deduction; a craft involving tools and judgment as well as data and research methods. A good overview from a generation ago is Jerry A. Hausman and David A. Wise, eds., *Social Experimentation* (Chicago: University of Chicago Press, 1985), and the National Bureau of Economic Research. For a more recent perspective, see *Using Evidence to Improve Social Policy and Practice, Perspectives on How Research and Evidence Can Influence Decision Making*, edited by Ruth Puttick with an introduction by Geoff Mulgan (London: NESTA, 2011).

32. L. Menand, *The Metaphysical Club: A Story of Ideas in America* (New York: Farrar, Straus and Giroux, 2001), xi–xii.

CHAPTER 10
CAPITALISM'S GENERATIVE IDEAS

1. For 135 countries with comprehensive data for indicators going back 40 years or more: per capita GDP doubled; life expectancy rose from 59 years in 1970 to 70 in 2010, school enrolment from 55 percent of all primary and secondary school-age children to 70 percent. The 2010 Report—*The Real Wealth of Nations: Pathways to Human Development* (New York: UNDP, 2010).

2. For a detailed discussion of the role of positional goods in the modern economy, see http://www.youngfoundation.org/our-work/research/themes/social-needs/positional-goods/positional-goods.

3. Fred Hirsch, *Social Limits to Growth* (London: Psychology Press, 1995).

4. Geoff Mulgan, *New Measures, New Policies: The Democracy of Numbers* (London: Young Foundation, 2009).

5. J. Stiglitz, A. Sen, and J. Fitoussi, Report by the Commission on the Measurement of Economic Performance and Social Progress (France, 2009).

6. Nicola Bacon, Marcia Brophy, Nina Mguni, Geoff Mulgan, and Anna Shandro, *The State of Happiness: Can Public Policy Shape People's Wellbeing and Resilience?* (London: Young Foundation, 2010).

7. By the 2030s, five billion of the world's eight billion people are likely to live in cities, two billion of them in the great urban slums of the Middle East, Africa, and Asia. U.S. Joint Forces Command, Center for Joint Futures: The Joint Operating Environment (JOE) 2008: http://www.jfcom.mil/newslink/storyarchive/2008/JOE2008.pdf.

8. Mill, *On Liberty* (London: Penguin Books, 1859).

9. Smith, *Theory of Moral Sentiments* (Cambridge: Cambridge University Press, 2002).

10. Norbert Elias, *The Civilising Process: Volume 1, The History of Manners* (Oxford: Blackwell, 1969).

11. R. Chartier, *On the Edge of the Cliff: History, Language and the Practices* (Baltimore: Johns Hopkins University Press, 1997).

12. E. Ikegami, *Bonds of Civility: Aesthetic Networks and the Political Origins of Japanese Culture* (Cambridge: Cambridge University Press, 2005).

13. The impact of migrants on entrepreneurship in the United States is documented in a study, "American Made: The Impact of Immigrant Entrepreneurs and Professionals on US Competitiveness," from the National Venture Capital Association.

14. Charles Sabel, *Learning by Monitoring* (Cambridge, MA: Harvard University Press, 2006).

15. See Ian Morris, *Why the West Rules for Now: The Patterns of History and What They Reveal About the Future* (New York: Farar, Straus, and Giroux, 2010), for a very helpful definition of social development.

16. The claims that a single global hive mind is appearing, a manifestation of Vladimir Vernadsky's noosphere, are intriguing, but sadly there is no evidence that the quantities of interaction made possible by the Internet translate into quality (despite the confident claims of many recent books). Crowds are as capable of stupidity as wisdom. But we are learning more about which types of crowd amplify stupidity and which dampen it, and collective intelligence is undoubtedly evolving fast, even if the capacities to sense, observe, aggregate, and process are doing better than the capacities to think or judge. See Geoff Mulgan et al., "Collective Intelligence," NESTA Draft Discussion Paper, 2011.

17. Boris Groysberg, *Chasing Stars: The Myth of Talent and the Portability of Performance* (Princeton: Princeton University Press, 2010).

18. The idea of the perfect community is a tool to think with, not a prescription; like most people I value privacy and boundaries, and find the idea of constant communication and awareness frightening. I also appreciate that boundaries and barriers to communication are vital to creativity: we need silence and space in order to think.

19. The idea of the Nash equilibrium has been used to analyze situations like war and arms races, how people with different preferences can cooperate (for example on standards), as well as traffic flows, and auctions.

20. Niklas Luhmann, *Love: A Sketch* (Cambridge: Polity, 2010) remains almost unique as a serious analysis of love in a modern society, and of why modernity has brought so much more attention to love.

21. Robert Ellickson, *The Household: Informal Order Around the Hearth* (Princeton: Princeton University Press, 2008), 105.

22. Stefana Broadbent is an anthropologist who leads the User Adoption Lab at Swisscom, Switzerland's largest telecoms operator. Her work suggests that typical users spend 80 percent of their time communicating with just four other people; that instead of work invading private life, private communications are invading the

workplace; and that migrants are the most advanced users of communications technology; http://www.economist.com/node/9249302?story_id=9249302/.

23. F. De Waal, *The Age of Empathy: Nature's Lessons for a Kinder Society* (New York: Crown, 2009).

24. Robert Ader, *Psychoneuroimmunology*, vol. 1 (New York: Academic Press, 2007).

25. 'Stayin' Alive: That's What Friends Are For (Provo, UT: Brigham Young University Press, 2010); http://news.byu.edu/archive10-jul-relationships.aspx.

26. G. Akerlof, *Animal Spirits: How Human Psychology Drives the Economy, and Why It Matters* (Princeton: Princeton University Press, 2009), 25.

27. Stefano Bartolini, Ennio Bilancini, and Francesco Sarracino, "Are Happiness and Social Capital Related in the Long Run? Some World-Wide Evidence," presented at the Symposium on Does Economic Growth Improve the Human Lot? Reassessing the Easterlin Paradox, IX ISQOLS Conference, July 19–23, Florence, 2009.

28. Bent Flyvbjerg, Nils Bruzelius, and Werner Rothengatter, *Megaprojects and Risk: An Anatomy of Ambition* (Cambridge: Cambridge University Press, 2003).

29. These also try to estimate what non-users might value, whether through "altruistic use" (knowing someone else might like it); option use" (having the opportunity to do something); "bequest use" (leaving something for the future); and "existence use" (satisfaction that things exist even if you don't enjoy them personally).

30. "Travel Cost Method" is one example that looks at the time and travel cost expenses that people incur to visit a site as a proxy for their valuation of that site. Because travel and time costs increase with distance, it's possible to construct a "marginal willingness to pay" curve for a particular site.

31. The following books provide a good overview: C. J. Barrow, *Social Impact Assessment: An Introduction* (London: Arnold, 2000); H. Becker and F. Vanclay, *The International Handbook of SIA* (Cheltenham: Edward Elgar, 2003); H. A. Becker, *Social Impact Assessment: Method and Experience in Europe, North America and the Developing World* (London: UCL Press, 1997); Scholten, Nicholls, Olsen, and Galimidi, *SROI A Guide to Social Return on Investment* (Amstelveen, The Netherlands: Lenthe Publishers, 2006).

32. France is often portrayed as hostile to entrepreneurship. But according to the most reliable international survey, it has a higher proportion of people interested in starting a business in the next three years than the United States, and a higher proportion who own and manage a newly created business. See the Global Entrepreneurship Monitor—Global Report 2007.

33. Israel Kirzner, *Competition and Entrepreneurship* (Chicago: University of Chicago Press, 1973).

34. Ludwig von Mises, *Human Action: A Treatise on Economics* (San Francisco: Fox & Wilkes, 1949), 252–253.

35. Joseph Schumpeter, *The Theory of Economic Development: An Inquiry into Profits, Capital, Credit, Interest and the Business Cycle* (New Brunswick, NJ: Transaction Publishers, 1934).

36. I first set out a variant of this argument in Geoff Mulgan and Charles Landry, *The Other Invisible Hand: Remaking Charity for the 21st Century* (London: Demos, 1995).

37. Georg Simmel, *The View of Life: Four Metaphysical Essays with Journal Aphorisms*, translated by A. Y. Andrews and Donald J. Levine; With an Introduction by Donald N. Levine and Daniel Silver (Chicago: University of Chicago Press, 2010).

38. J. Kao, *The Entrepreneurial Organisation* (Englewood Cliffs, NJ: Prentice Hall, 1991), and *Jamming: The Art and Discipline of Business Creativity* (Harper Business, 1997) are both particularly good accounts of the creative dimension of innovation.

39. The positive and negative affect scale (PANAS) was developed by Watson, Clark, and Tellegen in recognition of the fact that measuring happiness or misery on a single scale does not capture the complex relationship between the different emotions. D. Watson, L. A. Clark, and A. Tellegen, "Development and Validation of Brief Measures of Positive and Negative Affect: The PANAS Scale," *Journal of Personality and Social Psychology* 54 (1988): 1063–1070.

40. Daniel Kahneman, Peter P. Wakker, and Rakesh Sarin, "Back to Bentham? Explorations of Experienced Utility," *Quarterly Journal of Economics* 112, no. 2 (1997): 375–405.

41. http://www.vtpi.org/tca/tca0502.pdf.

42. For a fuller analysis of discount rates, the roles of "exponential" and "hyperbolic" rates, and why their level tends to reflect social structures and the strength of social bonds, see the chapter on value in my book, The Art of Public Strategy.

CHAPTER 11
NEW ACCOMMODATIONS

1. http://news.bbc.co.uk/onthisday/hi/dates/stories/december/1/newsid_4696000/4696207.stm.

2. http://www.nzhistory.net.nz/death-of-michael-joseph-savage.

3. Dani Rodrik, *One Economics, Many Recipes: Globalization, Institutions, and Economic Growth* (Princeton: Princeton University Press, 2007).

4. The legislation of a better society is, Rousseau wrote, "an enterprise for above human powers" which requires to implement it "an authority which is nothing." *The Social Contract* (London: Penguin, 1968). Our ideal revolutionary leader is one who is willing to dissolve him- or herself. The same may be true in business: the ideal creator of a new technological era doesn't try to turn his or her success into an enduring new monopoly.

5. Roberto Unger, *The Self Awakened: Pragmatism Unbound* (Cambridge: Harvard University Press, 2007).

6. One great advantage of the United States is its high spending on higher education—3.3 percent of GDP compared to 1.3 percent in the EU; but another advantage, arguably more important, is its better use of human capital.

7. Geoff Mulgan and Mary Abdo, "Innovation in Higher Education," in *Blue Skies: New Thinking about the Future of Higher Education*, ed. L. Coffat (London: Pearson Centre for Policy and Learning, 2011).

8. See A. B. Markman and K. L. Wood, eds., *Tools for Innovation* (Oxford: Oxford University Press, 2009).

9. This is part of the logic of the Studio School model now being implemented in a network of new schools in the UK. See www.studioschooltrust.org.

10. "Fixing the future" was the slogan used for a campaign I helped initiate with the late Diogo Vasconcelos, to encourage governments to respond to the crisis of 2009 with investment in innovation rather than bailing out failed industries.

11. In a series of essays in the 1940s, Hayek criticized the ways in which intellectuals privileged the kinds of knowledge they were most familiar with—systematic inquiry and science—as opposed to the less systematic knowledge of the everyday. Friedrich A. Hayek, "The Use of Knowledge in Society," *American Economic Review* 35, no. 4 (1945): 519–530.

12. There is extensive econometric data on the correlations between R&D expenditure and growth; but there is very little agreement on whether the R part of this, research, really does cause economic growth, and whether its effects are primarily felt through human capital rather than through the value of knowledge.

13. A few universities have done very well: in the mid-2000s, the income flowing to the most successful U.S. universities was: $193 million to University of California; $157 million to New York University; $61 million to Stanford; $60 million to Wake Forest; $56 million to Minnesota; and $43 million to MIT. But for most the sums are far lower. Japan's most successful university, by contrast, managed license income of only $1.4 million.

14. See Geoff Mulgan and Tom Steinberg, *Wide Open: The Potential of Open Source Solutions* (London: Young Foundation/Demos, 2006).

15. See for example Michael Kremer, "Patent Buyouts: A Mechanism for Encouraging Innovation," *Quarterly Journal of Economics* 113, no. 4 (1998): 1137–1167.

16. See "Using Evidence to Improve Social Policy and Practice, Perspectives on How Research and Evidence Can Influence Decision Making," edited by Ruth Puttick with an introduction by Geoff Mulgan (London: NESTA, 2011).

17. I suggested one way of doing this in *Wide Open: The Potential of Open Source Solutions*, co-authored with Tom Steinberg (London: Young Foundation/Demos, 2005).

18. For more information on statistical production techniques, see Edward W. Deming, *Out of the Crisis: Quality, Productivity and Competitive Position* (Cambridge, MA: MIT Press, 1986); or Edward W. Deming, *The New Economics for Industry, Government, Education*, 2nd ed. (Cambridge, MA: MIT Press, 2000).

19. According to the *Economist*, only 17 percent of businesses surveyed use more than 75 percent of the data they collect. McKinsey estimates that a better use of big data in the U.S. health sector could generate $300 billion annually.

20. See for example the Mydex project in the UK (www.mydex.org).

21. Examples include London's data store provided by the city government and others such as Sunlight Labs and Social Innovation Camps. These become even more effective when they can gain access to the internal data, for example, to see where there are recurrent problems and requests.

22. My guess is that most will end up with hybrid ownership and governance structures, neither fully within the public sector nor wholly outside it.

23. Rajan's comment can be found in his *Fault Lines: How Hidden Fractures Still Threaten the World Economy* (Princeton: Princeton University Press, 2010).

24. Contrary to some claims, Community Reinvestment Act requirements had little to do with the sub-prime explosion: most of the uneconomic mortgages provided by the banks that went bankrupt were not covered by CRA legislation.

25. Crowdcube and Kickstarter have raised $180 million; £150 million has been raised for peer to peer lending in the UK by Zopa and others.

26. The Banco Etica in Italy, for example, is based on radical principles: access to finance, in all its forms, is a human right; ethically oriented finance is aware of noneconomic consequences of economic actions; efficiency and soberness are components of ethical responsibility; profit produced by the ownership and exchange of money must come from activities oriented toward common well-being and shall have to be equally distributed among all subjects that contribute to its realization; maximum transparency of all operations is one of the main conditions of all ethical finance activities; the active involvement of shareholders and savers in the company's decision-making process must be encouraged; each organization that accepts and adheres to the principles of ethical finance undertakes to inspire its entire activity to such principles.

27. Adam Smith, *The Wealth of Nations* (London: Penguin, 2003), 660.

28. Recent books from mainstream economists are investigating these issues, which a decade or two were mainly discussed in the green movement. Examples include Diane Coyle, *The Economics of Enough* (Princeton: Princeton University Press, 2010).

29. These and related ideas were described in the book I commissioned in 1996 on *Guaranteed Electronic Markets* by Nick Wingham Rowan (published by Demos), though it took another decade before a flood of new websites started to put the ideas into practice on a larger scale.

30. These come at a cost—higher charges for consumers. The question is whether in the long term the added productivity gains outweigh these costs. They may also benefit other countries—as Germany's feed-in tariff benefited Chinese producers.

31. See "Fostering Innovation for Green Growth," OECD, 2010.

32. See D. T. Mortensen and C. A. Pissarides, "Job Creation and Job

Destruction in the Theory of Unemployment," *Review of Economic Studies* 61, no. 3 (1994): 397.

33. A good example is a simple system to enable sole traders to employ one other person—setting up a bank account in their own bank that deals with all issues of taxation and compliance.

34. Brian Sutton-Smith, *The Ambiguity of Play* (Cambridge: Harvard University Press, 1997).

35. Aaron Antonovsky, *Unraveling the Mystery of Health: How People Manage Stress and Stay Well* (San Francisco: Jossey-Bass, 1987).

36. Rick H. Hoyle and Erin K. Bradfield, *Measurement and Modelling of Self-Regulation: Is Standardization a Reasonable Goal?* Duke University, Manuscript prepared for the National Research Council Workshop on Advancing Social Science Theory: The Importance of Common Metrics, Washington, DC, February 25–26, 2010.

37. Robert Kanigel, *Apprentice to Genius* (Baltimore: John Hopkins University Press), 1993.

38. Lynn Smith-Lovin and Miller McPherson, "Social Isolation in America: Changes in Core Discussion Networks over Two Decades," *American Sociological Review* 71, no. 3 (2006): 353–375. Those who were only one friend away from being socially isolated rose from 25% in 1985 to 44% in 2004.

39. Just as the economy is becoming more relational, so is the state, with greater attention to subjective measures, and the fine-grained detail of how the state relates to individuals and how it supports other organizations to attend to relationships. This represents a fundamental shift in the role of the state, but it's one that has only just begun and can be hard to see amidst the pressures brought to bear on public spending. I've set out in much more detail the implications of this for public policy in a series of papers titled "The Relational State," published by the Young Foundation (with a new version forthcoming in 2013), and drawing on work with a number of governments around the world including Singapore, the UK, Australia, and Hong Kong.

40. Kathryn M. Connor and Jonathan R. T. Davidson, "Development of a New Resilience Scale: The Connor-Davidson Resilience Scale," *Depression and Anxiety* 18, no. 2 (2003): 76–82.

41. M. Rutter, "Resilience in the Face of Adversity. Protective Factors and Resistance to Psychiatric Disorder," *British Journal of Psychiatry* 147 (1985): 598–611.

42. This approach is set out in *Sinking and Swimming*, published by the Young Foundation in 2009, a detailed quantitative and qualitative analysis of changing public needs.

43. D. Skuse, S. Reilly, and D. Wolke. "Psychosocial Adversity and Growth during Infancy," *European Journal of Clinical Nutrition* 48 (1994): Suppl 1: S113–S130.

44. B. Ballas and D. Dorling, "Measuring the Impact of Major Life Events upon Happiness," *International Journal of Epidemiology* 36 (2007): 1244.

45. An overview of much recent research on the links between optimism and dispositions on the one hand, and health outcomes on the other, can be found in Michele M. Tugade, Barbara L. Fredrickson, and Lisa Feldman Barrett, "Psychological Resilience and Positive Emotional Granularity: Examining the Benefits of Positive Emotions on Coping and Health," *Journal of Personality* 72, no. 6 (2004): 1161–1190.

46. M. Waysman, J. Schwarzwald, and Z. Solomon, "Hardiness: An Examination of Its Relationship with Positive and Negative Long-term Changes Following Trauma," *Journal of Traumatic Stress* 14 (2001): 531–548.

47. S. Kidd and G. Shahar, "Resilience in Homeless Youth: The Key Role of Self-Esteem," *American Journal of Orthopsychiatry* 78, no. 2 (2008): 163–172.

48. C. E. Cutrona and V. Cole, "Optimizing Support in the Natural Network," in *Social Support Measurement and Intervention: A Guide for Health and Social Scientists*, ed. S. Cohen, L. G. Underwood, and B. H. Gottlieb (Oxford: Oxford University Press, 2000), 278–308.

49. Cited in "Tomorrows' Owners, Stewardship of Tomorrows Company," London Tomorrows Company, 2008.

50. Avner Offer, *The Challenge of Affluence: Self-control and Well-being in the United States and Britain since 1950* (Oxford: Oxford University Press, 2006).

51. Germany has more than twenty such currencies. One example is the Chiemgauer, which circulates in Prien am Chiemsee in Bavaria. It is sold for an equivalent amount of euros through local charities which receive a 3 percent commission, and it is accepted as payment in 600 local businesses. In 2008, there were 370,000 Chiemgauer in circulation with an annual turnover of Ch3 million. In the UK, similar initiatives have been started by Transition Towns, a group of community-led organizations that focus on energy and climate change issues. There is the Totnes pound in Devon, the Lewes pound in Sussex, the Brixton pound in London, and the Stroud pound in Gloucestershire. Like the German currencies, the Brixton pound is designed to support local businesses and encourage local trade and production. One Brixton pound is equivalent to one pound sterling. People can swap their pounds sterling for Brixton pounds at issuing points and then use them in local shops. Local business can then decide to give customers special offers for using the money. Spice is another model that embeds the time bank within a local school or housing association. See Geoff Mulgan, *Twin Economies* (London: Demos, 1996), for an overview of the field at that point and proposals for how these could be grown in scale.

52. Bitcoin's advantages are that it's irreversible, wholly anonymous, and entirely free from control by banks or governments. These advantages, however, also make it particularly attractive to criminal organizations and particularly vulnerable to the problems of volatility faced by any currency without a primary manager.

53. Edgar Kahn, one of the most prominent advocates of time credits in recent years, believes that this equality of time valuations is an essential feature of progressive time banks, and marks them out as a new, different, and progressive economy.

54. Viviana Zelizer gives an interesting example of this from a small firm where having the option to give time in this way helped pull the workforce together. See Viviana Zelizer, *Economic Lives* (Princeton: Princeton University Press, 2011), 237.

55. Looking at "indicators of innovation and entrepreneurship including new company start-ups, take up of e-commerce, investment in R&D and the annual rate of GDP growth . . . no association between any of these indicators of economic vitality and the degree of equality or inequality of incomes in a country can be identified." Peter Saunders, *Beware False Prophets* (London: Policy Exchange, 2010), 61. This assessment draws on the OECD's study, Measuring Entrepreneurship, Paris, 2009.

56. See Autumn Stanley, *Mothers and Daughters of Invention* (New Brunswick, NJ: Rutgers University Press, 1995).

57. The questions that are being put to respondents by the UK Office of National Statistics are:

> Overall, how satisfied are you with your life nowadays?
> Overall, how happy did you feel yesterday?
> Overall, how anxious did you feel yesterday?

58. For some of the relevant literature on the rapidly evolving field of methods for measuring societal progress, see the following: M. Nussbaum and A. Sen, eds., *The Quality of Life* (Oxford: Clarendon Press); G. Esping-Anderson, "Social Indicator and Welfare Monitoring: Social Policy and Development Programme," United Nations Research Institute Development, 2000; R. Veenhoven, "Quality-of-life and Happiness: Not Quite the Same," in *Health and Quality-of-Life*, ed. G. DeGirolamo et al. (Rome: Il Pensierro Scientifico, 1998).

59. http://thjodfundur2009.is/english/.

60. Iceland's revived moral consensus allowed for hard-headed moves on macroeconomics to stabilize the currency, and to reduce the debt, which within two years had persuaded the IMF that Iceland was a miraculous turnaround, a model for others to follow. The society remains divided, however, on some fundamental questions—its road back to health will not be easy.

CHAPTER 12
OUTGROWING CAPITALISM

1. James P. Hawley, "Antonio Gramsci's Marxism: Class, State and Work," *Social Problems* 27, no. 5, Sociology of Political Knowledge Issue: Theoretical Inquiries, Critiques and Explications (June 1980), pp. 584–600, published by University of California Press.

2. In *The Rookie*, 1990.

3. Greek poet C. P. Cavafy said that the best way to approach a problem is at a tangent.

Acknowledgments
· · · · · · · · · · · · · · · ·

THIS BOOK evolved out of many conversations: with critics of capitalism as well as enthusiasts, players as well as observers. Some were immersed in big firms and global markets, others were campaigning against them, and many were somewhere in between. They ranged from social entrepreneurs such as Muhammad Yunus to innovators like Dee Hock (the visionary founder of Visa), Rosabeth Moss Kanter, Sam Pitroda, and the late Diogo Vasconcelos (my closest collaborator in helping to grow a global social innovation movement). They included regulators such as Adair Turner (head of the UK's Financial Services Authority), as well as several politicians who had to confront the recent crisis head on (including Prime Ministers Kevin Rudd, Gordon Brown, David Cameron, and George Papandreou, and the European Commission's Jose Manuel Barroso). I learned a lot from conversations about capitalism with some of my intellectual heroes, including the late Charles Tilly and Daniel Bell (who both guided me to a more coherent view of how change happens), Manuel Castells (whose analyses of the interconnections between finance, communications, and politics have been immensely helpful), Carlota Perez (whose influence will be apparent at many points in the book), Richard Sennett (who has been a collaborator on many things and has developed a brilliant grasp of the cultures of the modern workplace), Bruno Latour (for showing the relevance of the pragmatist tradition, and a radically different way of thinking about science), and Roberto Mangabeira Unger (who in many guises has been a constant reminder of the plasticity of the world). Will

Hutton and Martin Wolf, coming from different political standpoints, have both shown just how penetrating the very best journalism can be.

David Goodhart, the then-editor of *Prospect Magazine*, gave me a chance to air some of these ideas in print at an early stage, while Bruno Guissani and Chris Anderson allowed me to share them at TED. Many others around the world gave me chances to discuss the ideas, from SITRA in Finland to Tsinghua University in China and the LSE in London. Carmel O'Sullivan ably helped with some of the background research on chapter 11. Al Bertrand at Princeton University Press has been a firm but constantly supportive editor, and I had very useful comments from Will Davies and Rushanara Ali among others. My family (Rowena, Ruby, and Fintan) and colleagues tolerated me being diverted on rather too many occasions: their support has been greatly appreciated; few of us could write without a circle of care and tolerance around us. Any errors of fact or interpretation are of course all mine.

Index

......

predation and, 75–76, 128, 148. *See also* ecosystems; green economy

nature: capitalism and, comparison of, 100–101; human (*see* human nature)

negative externalities, 201–2

Nesta, 192

Netherlands, the, 231, 239

Neumark, David, 301n.41

New York: Brooklyn, Member to Member Elderplan, 269; the High Line, 304n.22; Ithaca HOURS, 269

New Zealand, 159, 232

Nietzsche, Friedrich, 27, 72

Nordhaus, William, 53, 58

North, Douglass, 55

North Karelia Project, 195–96

Norwegian Government Pension Fund, 249

Obama, Barack, 24

OECD. *See* Organization for Economic Cooperation and Development

Offer, Avner, 94

Olson, Mancur, 64, 297n.33

Olympics, "brand exclusion zone" in the London, 71

Omidyar, Pierre, 206

open innovation, 59

optimism: of capitalism, 23, 92; cultural contradictions and, 126–27

Oresme, Nicolas, 37

Organization for Economic Cooperation and Development (OECD): education and economic growth, linkage of, 54; mortality and spending on health, inverse correlation of, 178; Wikiprogress, 195

Orwell, George, 127

Owen, Robert, 111–12

ownership, virtues of widespread, 246

Pacey, Arnold, 149

Pareto, Vilfredo, 83

Paris Great Exhibition of 1900, 108–9

Park, Won-Soon, 192

Patients Like Me, 180

Paul, Lewis, 307n.35

Pauli, Wolfgang, 114

Peer2Peer University, 238

Peirce, Charles, 44, 197

Perez, Carlota, 156–61, 306n.14

perfect equilibrium, 208

performance, crises of, 135–36

permaculture, 113

Perrow, Charles, 18

Peters, Tom, 126

Petty, William, 307n.35

philanthrocapitalism, 93, 300n.19

Piff, Paul, 86–87

Pirate Party, 113

Plato, 106

Plautus (Titus Maccius Plautus), 62

play, 260–61

Polanyi, Karl, 33, 69–70

Popper, Karl, 129

population growth rates and generational relations, 119–20

positional goods, 202

positive and negative affect scale (PANAS), 314n.39

positive externalities, 200

Postlewaite, Andrew, 301n.41

power laws, 83, 155

Powers, Richard, 58

pragmatism, 197

Pratham, 195

predation: of capitalism, 3–4, 8–9, 62–72; cycles of, 127–28, 156–60; defense of by predators, 131; economic theory on, 63–66; the financial crisis of 2008 and, 27; future opportunities for, 76–77; the golden rule and, 66–67; ideology, victims' acceptance of, 132; the means of destruction and, 72–76; nonprofits provide some assurance against, 187–88; rent-seeking, 64–66. *See also* critics of capitalism

preventive investment, 310n.27

Prince, Chuck, 89

production, shift to new models of, 254–57

productivity: of capitalism, 8; as divine will, 62; economic growth, efforts to explain, 53–62 (*see also* economic growth); of life beyond work, 225–26; as moral dimension of capitalism, 39–42

product life cycles, 127

property rights: investment incentives and economic growth, contribution to, 58–59; new accommodations needed regarding, 242–43

public choice theory, 64

Rajan, Raghuram, 246

Rand, Ayn, 72

Rand Corporation, 187

Rawls, John, 105

R&D. *See* research & development